GREAT DAY...
TODAY!

Tyler,
I hope and pray this book
encourages you.

Keep the Faith,
Bill Krumer
Galatians 6:9

GREAT DAY...
TODAY!

A TRUE STORY *of* FAITH, FAMILY, *and* FOOTBALL

BILL KRAMER

with Brent Batten

O'LEARY
PUBLISHING
The Influencer's Press

NAPLES, FL

Published in the United States by
O'Leary Publishing
www.olearypublishing.com

The views, information, or opinions expressed in this book are solely those of the authors involved and do not necessarily represent those of O'Leary Publishing, LLC.

The author has made every effort possible to ensure the accuracy of the information presented in this book. However, the information herein is sold without warranty, either expressed or implied. Neither the author, publisher, nor any dealer or distributor of this book will be held liable for any damages caused either directly or indirectly by the instructions or information contained in this book. You are encouraged to seek professional advice before taking any action mentioned herein.

ISBN (print): 978-1-952491-17-7
ISBN (ebook): 978-1-952491-18-4
Library of Congress Control Number: 2021910862

Proofreading by S.R. Boris Boland
Book Design by Jessica Angerstein

Printed in the United States of America

Dedication

This book is for my four daughters, and their children and grandchildren. I want you to know what God did for our family.

I don't want you to think that God is some genie in a bottle that you pray to, and POOF — He makes your team win, or makes bad things go away. I want you to know that God loves us and sent His son Jesus, who was all man and all God, to live among men. Although Jesus was the only man to never sin, the men He lived with killed him. God allowed it, and Christ surrendered Himself for us. In doing this, the debt for our sins is paid if we will only accept this truth. Accepting this truth restores our relationship with a perfect and holy God, and allows us direct access to Him.

Again, this direct access does **not** make God a genie in a bottle; the Bible is clear that in this life we will have tribulation. What our relationship with God **does** give us is what every human on the planet craves: love and peace. The Bible calls this "peace that passes all understanding." I have experienced this unexplainable peace too many times to count, and it is a thing that cannot be understood until it is experienced. My hope and prayer is that all my girls and their spouses and children, and all of the family who come after me, will experience the peace and love that comes from accepting Jesus Christ as their Lord and Savior.

Trust in the Lord with all your heart and lean not to your own understanding. In all your ways acknowledge him and he shall direct your paths.

— Proverbs 3:5-6

Let us not grow weary in doing good, for in due time we shall reap if we faint not.

— Galatians 6:9

Brent Batten is a gifted writer and a friend. Brent is also exceedingly patient, as this book has taken nearly 12 years to write. I am grateful for Brent pushing me to finish. He reminded me often that I don't have to be a professional writer to tell my story. Brent also spoke to several people who have a part in this story and added their perspective. You'll notice the gray box behind Brent's work to bring those interviews into the story.

BEGINNINGS

My earliest memories are of my mom, my four older sisters, and me in a two-bedroom place in south Tucson, Arizona. We had very little but each other. Mom worked a lot. We learned to care for each other and to be grateful.

I played organized football for the first time at the beginning of my sixth-grade year. I played for the Raiders of the Pop Warner League in Yuma, Arizona. We wore silver and black. My coaches worked construction by day and would come to practice in their work clothes – occasionally with beer pretty strong on their breath. When you are in a huddle, you get a lot of different smells. I was one of the smallest guys on the team and rode my bike several miles to and from practice. I played wide receiver and nose guard, and I was in heaven.

My seventh-grade year, I played for a guy named Paul Brown. He wasn't THE Paul Brown, but he was to me. Coincidentally, our team was the Browns. I wanted to be a running back. Even though I was small, Coach Brown gave me a chance. When it was time to give out uniforms, Coach Brown had the boxes sitting on the open tailgate of his pickup truck. An assistant coach with a roster would call each boy's name, and then Coach Brown would look through the jerseys and say the jersey number loud enough for all of us to hear. This was a big deal, as nearly everyone had a favorite number in mind. I distinctly remember my name called and Coach Brown saying, "Are you kidding? That kid has more moves than O.J. Simpson – 32!" This was 1975, and that was a very good thing. It was the first time I remember an adult male I wasn't related to saying something positive about me.

This book tells the story of my life from 1998-2001.

CHAPTER 01

1998

By any logical standard, I shouldn't have been the football coach at Naples High School. In January of 1998, I had just finished my third year as head coach at Miami-Dade County's American High School. Our team had gone 9-3, including the school's first playoff win in 16 years. I was making good money — enough to allow my wife, Sue, to be a stay-at-home mom to our three young daughters. We had recently moved from a home in the school's tough, urban environment to an 11-acre spread owned by Sue's parents, Duke and Angel Sistrunk. Granny Angel was an incredible cook who loved to feed her family, babysit, and even help with the laundry without being asked.

I had replaced Charlie Yanda, a legend in Miami. Charlie had earned his degree from the University of Miami while playing both football and baseball. He was old-school tough. Charlie did not mince words; everyone who played for him or worked with him knew exactly where he stood. I had nothing but love and respect for Charlie, and still do, but I had to be me. I have an entirely different style and plan than he did, and I knew I did not have a chance of success if I was not authentic.

I loved the coaches I was working with; they were like brothers to me. But the truth is, I was burdened to do more than we were doing and do it in a different way than we had been doing it. Another truth is that old habits are hard to break, especially bad habits. I wanted to get our focus off the scoreboard and put it on our relationships and on creating a culture of excellence in every aspect of our program.

Football can be an incredible tool for molding young men. There are lifelong habits of commitment, dedication, and teamwork to be learned. There are cycles of illiteracy, illegitimacy, poverty, and abuse that can be broken. Education can be gained. Destructive behavior and habits can end. I was working hard to transform the program around the belief that coaching is ministry when the phone rang.

Embarking on his fifth search for a new coach in 10 years as Naples High School athletic director, Ernie Modugno had set up a booth at a statewide coaches' convention in search of the right man. Naples, in spite of success in just about every other sport, had managed just one winning football campaign during Modugno's tenure. That wasn't enough. "Football is the premier sport in Florida," Modugno said. "Winning affects your school climate. It affects your athletic budget. We weren't winning. We weren't making any money. I was spending all my time trying to raise money. It was an economic decision, more than anything, to try to find the best coach we could."

At the convention Modugno talked to a scout who ran a recruiting service. He suggested Modugno give a fellow named Bill Kramer a call. "He said, 'I've got the perfect guy for you. He's the rising star in Florida football,' " Modugno recalls. The scout didn't have the contact information on Kramer, but he handed him a card and offered to get it, if Modugno was interested. Back in Naples, while narrowing down the list of applicants, Modugno came across the card. "I don't know why I made the call, but I did." He got the number and made another call, to Kramer.

"I said, I'm Ernie Modugno, the athletic director at Naples High School, and I'd like to talk to you about being our next football coach." There was a pause. Then Modugno heard, "I'm listening."

"We were on the phone for an hour," said Modugno. "I hung up the phone and called (NHS Principal) Gary Brown. I said, 'Gary, I've found our guy.'"

My first impression of Ernie Modugno was that this guy was really smart but knew very little about running a football program. He cold-called me to interest me in the vacant coaching job at Naples High School, and by the end of the conversation I had agreed to come for an interview. I told him I wasn't really interested in the job for myself; I wanted to get the lay of the land and then see if any of the guys I knew might be interested in it.

As the conversation wore on, my wife Sue settled onto the couch behind me where she could eavesdrop more easily. She was holding our third little girl, Kelly, who had been born two months earlier. Our two oldest girls — Katie, age 5, and Courtney, age 3 — were outside playing on the playground that I had built for them. The playground was a labor of love and was over the top. I had built it in the ultimate sandbox. It held three dump truck loads of premium sugar sand; the same kind that was used at the best golf courses south Florida could offer. After the call, I turned to Sue and said, "Well, I'm interviewing for a job on Monday, but I'm not taking it."

In the hectic two days leading up to the interview (I didn't have a resume ready or any knowledge of Naples High football), I reached out to college coaches I had known for years. Their consensus was that Naples High football was "ugly."

My only experience with Naples was when Sue and I had brought the girls to a three-day weekend at the Naples Beach Hotel. It was the first weekend in August, and the last family time before football started in 1997. As chance would have it, on our way out of town we drove right by the Naples High campus. We admired the on-campus football stadium, as those did not exist in Miami-Dade public schools. Both of us distinctly remember Sue asking, tongue in cheek, "I wonder if they need a football coach?"

While I'm not a spiritual guru, my faith is very important to me, and a verse that I had come across recently kept sticking in my head. It is from II Chronicles 16:9 and reads, *For the eyes of the Lord run to and fro throughout the whole Earth, to show himself strong on behalf of those whose heart is loyal toward him.* In the back of my mind, I considered the possibility that I would have a chance to hire a staff of men who wanted to do what God wanted them to do and wanted to use football as a tool for that. This is not to say I sought perfect men, because we're all flawed. But it is to say that we would have a common frame of reference, a very high standard, and a method of reconciliation when we screwed up — which we inevitably do.

CHAPTER
02

Ernie Modugno stands just over 6 feet tall, with blond hair, piercing blue eyes, and immaculate attire. I knew from our phone conversation that he was born in Germany, and when I first saw him he reminded me of the high-ranking military officers in all the old World War II movies I used to watch. He has the same disciplined, almost formal, air about him; he could be in shorts and a T-shirt, and somehow he'd look dignified. Gary Brown is a short, thin man with white hair. If I were casting a movie, Gary Brown would play everyone's favorite grandfather. He had a ready smile, and was so relaxed and humble that he immediately put me at ease.

I was shocked at the lack of facilities. The weight room was a joke. Video equipment? Ask the librarian, maybe she'll loan you a VCR. The salary they were offering was a third less than what I was making. And by the way, I'd be required to teach a full day, as opposed to the two classes I was leading every day at American High.

Health insurance for my wife and three young girls, including a new baby? That would not start until the first of January… 1999. In the meantime, I could feel free to go out and buy some on my own.

Still, I had a sense of possibility for Naples High football. The program's shortcomings were obvious, but there were positive signs as well. When I asked for something, Ernie and Gary answered the same way: "We can get you that." Later, I found out that in some cases, they were making promises that were only *theoretically* possible.

"I never out-and-out lied to Bill," Modugno says now. "There was a lot of smoke and mirrors, though," he admits. "I really wanted him. I knew what a big catch he would be for Naples High School." Modugno realized early on that his coaching candidate was a man of faith. He also understood that in a public school setting, there were bound to be questions, accusations even, that the coach was pushing religion to his young charges. He quickly dismissed those concerns.

"He's a devout Christian. I'm an agnostic atheist; someone who can't understand why Bill feels the way he does about God. I also understand how important it is for young people to have guidance," he said. Some of the first to worry about Bill's faith were the ones using foul language and anger to motivate football players. "Typical football coaches, if you will," said Modugno.

"Bill's not trying to convert people. He's trying to give them guidance. He's really, truly trying to make them better sons, better fathers, better human beings. He's made me a better athletic director, a better human being. When I think how fortunate we are to have Bill Kramer as a role model..."

My one-hour interview wound up lasting several hours, and before I left, I was offered the job. To my surprise, I didn't say no. I told them I did not want to take a pay cut. I wasn't asking for a raise, but it certainly made zero sense to take a pay cut. I told them I was willing to negotiate with the superintendent if that would help, as it is common throughout the country for head football coaches to negotiate with superintendents, school boards, and booster clubs. Gary and Ernie asked me to give them a little time to see if they could find a way to match my salary. I agreed to pray on it with Sue, and we all agreed that we would tell no one about the meeting.

Later that same week, Ernie called and asked if I could bring Sue over to see the school. He told me he had talked to some members of the football booster club, and it might be beneficial if I met with them. There was a Best Western very close to the school, and he would make arrangements for us to stay there if we agreed to come. I talked with Susie, and we agreed. The following Friday morning we loaded up the girls in the minivan and were off to Naples High. Sue and I were amazed that everyone we met was so nice. The campus was clean and pretty, and as we walked the campus during lunch, the kids we met were all polite and friendly.

While Sue stayed back at the hotel and got the girls to bed, I went to the Collier Athletic Club to have dinner with the booster club. The Collier Athletic Club was a fancy place modeled after the Downtown Athletic Club in New York City. It was hard not to be impressed. There were a half-dozen couples at the meeting, and all of them seemed very enthusiastic to get me to Naples and to help with the program in whatever way they could. I told our story and did all I could to impress on them that it just did not make sense for me to take a job with less pay, at a smaller school, with worse facilities, and without health care for those four beautiful girls back at the hotel. We ended the meeting the same way that the last meeting with Gary and Ernie ended. If they could meet my salary, I would consider making the move.

Over the next few weeks Gary or Ernie would call me to let me know that there was no movement on the salary issue. I would tell them I wasn't coming, and they would ask for a little more time. Each time I said OK, and that Sue and I would continue to pray. I also accepted Ernie's prompting and visited the school a couple more times. I saw positives like the potential in the school's stadium. Put a good product in it, and it could generate excitement and revenue for the school. Then there were the kids who had stuck with the program. On one of my visits to Naples, I asked to meet with the players. The message from these guys was very clear. They said it in different ways, but a young quarterback named Rob Richter summed it up when he said, "We'll do anything; we're tired of being embarrassed."

Clearly, I had a better professional and domestic situation at American High. Better money, family and friends nearby, plus I had 20 of 22 starters returning from the previous year's 9-3 team; the future looked very bright.

In Collier County, we had no friends or family, a higher cost of living with less pay, none of the tools necessary for a successful football program, and no safety net.

Through a series of phone calls and meetings, there was ongoing persistence on their part and continual resistance on mine. But the idea of a football staff made up of men who wanted to do what God wanted them to do, and who wanted to use football as a tool to grow great husbands and fathers and community leaders, wouldn't leave me alone. Sue and I prayed about it. "Lord, if you don't want us there, please slam the door. Make it go away." After the third or fourth week of the back and forth, we finally got the call and were told that they were just not able to come up with any more money. Susie and I both decided that was the door slamming, and that was that.

About a week after the hard "no," I met with Guy Shashaty, a good friend of mine who was our offensive captain during my freshman year playing football at Liberty University. Guy was a former teacher and coach who was thriving as a financial advisor in Miami. Guy was all-in on the idea of using football as a tool and hiring a staff of like-minded guys that God would call to work with us.

Guy asked, point-blank: "If it weren't for the money, would you have told Naples yes?"

"Yes," I admitted.

"Then you've got to go," he said. "Remember, it's all God's, anyway."

I promptly replied, "Shut up, Guy. It's easy for you rich guys to talk about how it's all God's; I can't even look at a house in the neighborhood you just bought in."

Not long after Guy left that day, Sue approached me with a simple and direct question, "Do you feel at peace about telling them no?" The mini-vacation in Naples stuck in her mind, as did the campus visit. She remembered the pretty high school and the on-campus stadium. The people, the city, seemed nice. She was a mother with young children. She realized there were positives, and she knew that if God was calling us, we had to put feet to our faith.

And then her question: "Do you feel at peace about telling them no?"

I had been married long enough to know not to answer this wrong. It was kind of like the question, "Do I look fat in this?" So when Sue asked me if I felt peace about saying no, I answered her question like any smart husband: "Do you?"

Neither of us knew it until that moment, but we'd both arrived at the same conclusion via different routes. We hugged and prayed; Sue cried, and I got choked up. After we composed ourselves, I grabbed a phone to track down Gary Brown. Come to find out, Gary was taking advantage of a President's Day three-day weekend and was holed up somewhere without a phone. When we finally did connect, I told him God was calling us to Naples, and that we were taking the job. On the other end, Gary Brown was ecstatic.

In the end, the decision went far beyond plusses and minuses listed side-by-side on a piece of paper. I couldn't weigh it out on a balance sheet. Analytically speaking, it didn't make sense. I have told my girls and my players many times that there is truly only one really safe place to be… and that's right where God wants you to be, doing whatever it is He wants you to do. Naples is where God wanted our family to be, and using football as a tool to love and grow young men is what He wanted us to do.

CHAPTER

03

You would think that taking a job in an unfamiliar town, at a smaller school with shabbier facilities and fewer wins, for less pay, would be indisputable proof that I was taking the job for reasons other than prestige, money, or wins. Not so. The hardest thing about taking the job at Naples was leaving my job in Miami. I'd been at American High School for 11 years, the last three years as head football coach. I believed I had established a sense of family among the players, some of whom were desperately in need of exactly that.

When I called the players together to tell them I was leaving, I found out I was right. We were a family, and I was the member choosing to walk out. I'm not sure how to summarize the players' reaction. Betrayal? That's too strong. Abandonment? That's a strong word, too. But at the very least, there was profound disappointment. I tried to make them understand that Sue and I knew that God wanted us to go to Naples. A few understood, but the rationale mostly fell flat among the ranks of the players who had made the commitment to our program. "You're going there? At least take a better job," the slighted players grumbled.

> Graduating senior guard Ben Jackson recalls the meeting. "It was a sad state in the locker room. When you've got something great going, you hate to see it go. They (the younger players) had felt they were going to the promised land with Coach Kramer." As a senior who was leaving American anyway, Jackson accepted the transition more philosophically than the younger players. "A man's got to make a man's decision."

Among peers on the staff at American, the attitude was more forgiving than that of the players. "If you can get out of Dade County, get out now," they confided.

I have fond memories of American High. I worked for a legendary coach in Charlie Yanda, one of the winningest and most colorful coaches Miami has ever seen. Charlie was one of a kind. He could conjure profanity and vulgarity together in a manner both comical and totally intimidating. And Charlie loved his players. Charlie Yanda was also a man of integrity. Integrity comes from the Latin root integritat, which is where we get the word integer, and it has more to do with the state of being complete or whole than anything else. Charlie was the same guy on or off the field.

There are two events that stick out in my mind from my first year coaching at American High School. Both had a profound impact on me. One of them came the first time Charlie asked me to do something meaningful during a game. That fall of 1987, I coached the junior varsity offensive line and was a spotter in the box on varsity game nights. Midway through the season, we were in the locker room at halftime of a tight game. Charlie asked me to go out and check the clock and tell him how much time was left before halftime ended. I bolted from the locker room, realizing that this was a field promotion.

The field at Milander Stadium was maybe 20 yards from the locker room, so soon I was standing by the fence peering up at the scoreboard which clearly showed 2 minutes and change left in the intermission. I hustled back and let Charlie know, and he quickly called the group up and let go with one of the most forceful tirades I had heard in my life. He used up nearly all of the two minutes, and when he was finished, every man in the locker room was voicing his battle cry, banging his helmet, and fighting to get through the doors to the football field.

Unfortunately, as we burst through the fence on the field, it was obvious that something was wrong. The band was still playing. It must've been comical to watch our guys in front try to stop and turn back as the guys in back trampled them. What had looked like 2 minutes to me was actually 8 minutes. There were several burned-out lights on the scoreboard clock, and now there were really just under six minutes left in the break.

So Coach Yanda called the guys up near the gate, and we mostly just stood around and watched the band play. We also mostly stood around and listened to Charlie cuss me out. He would scream at me until he had no breath, was purple, and I actually feared he might pass out. Then he would glance at the clock and see time left, take a big deep breath, and cuss me out some more.

I was embarrassed; not because the players were listening, or because of the language he was using. He was not hurting my self-esteem. I was embarrassed because I'd been at that game for a half and didn't realize the scoreboard was screwed up. I had become complacent, and deserved all the chewing that my rear end was getting. And as for Charlie losing his mind? We didn't panic when fish swam or birds flew; why would we panic over Charlie using colorful language to paint an unforgettable picture for me?

The other event I remember from that first year came when we were coming home after playing Miami Beach High early in the season. You could count on it every week. Charlie would sit in the front right seat of the offensive team bus. After each game, as we pulled out of the parking lot, he would give his "Windows halfway!" command, which mystified me. Why would Coach care where the windows were set? It was hot and humid in Miami, and we would get more air if the windows were all the way down.

We were soon on the Julia Tuttle Causeway, which connects Miami Beach with the mainland, and about to merge onto I-95, when the volume from the back of the bus rose significantly. I was sitting directly behind the bus driver, and Charlie sat in his usual spot — front seat, passenger side. I stood up to see out the windows on the passenger side and made out a couple of old Caddys with ragtops and what we used to call trues and voes, for tires and wheels. These were decked-out rides. They had their windows down, and the fellas inside were fussing at our guys through our half-opened windows. I saw hands raised out their windows and heard what sounded like firecrackers going off. While everyone else on the bus seemed to be blending in with the floorboards, I was standing and trying to get a better view of what was going on. My cognitive dissonance came to an abrupt end as Charlie yanked down on the V of my shirt and screamed, "Get down, you dumb sonofabitch, they're shooting at us!"

The windows command suddenly made sense. Putting the windows halfway up puts an extra steel bar in the middle of the top opening and the bottom panes of glass in the event that the locals start throwing rocks – or start shooting. No one was injured that night, although the police did dig bullets out of the bus when we got back to school. It didn't even make the local news.

I learned a lot about coaching from Charlie Yanda. Countless times, in my head, I would replay the audio of Charlie speaking. I finally decided to start writing down the lessons he had taught me. That led to a document I created and posted in my office titled "Yanda's Seven Cardinal Rules." I had been at Naples High four years when Charlie finally retired from the Miami-Dade school system. I wrote Charlie the following letter thanking him for what he had instilled in me:

December 20, 2001

Dear Charlie,

I read in the Miami Herald that you are retiring. I want you to know how much I appreciate all that you have done for me. You gave me my first assistant coaching job and my first head coaching job. You probably don't even realize many of the pearls of wisdom that I took from you. I teach them to my coaches today. Here are Yanda's Seven Cardinal Rules:

7. Don't punish the coaches. Coaches work hard. Don't punish the coaches when disciplining players.

6. The fastest way for a coach to get fired is mismanagement of money. Do it right and keep records.

5. Football is a game of emotion and aggression. You must bring both or you will get beat like the sorry dog you are... and no one will feel sorry for you.

4. It's not live hand grenades, relax and have fun.

3. Football better be a top priority; it isn't everything, but it better be a top priority.

2. You gotta go to work every day.

1. Blocking, tackling, and running the football . . . fundamentals, fundamentals, fundamentals. No scheme or game plan matters without fundamentals.

Thank you Charlie,

Bill

CHAPTER 04

I was going to Naples, but the peculiarities of the school calendar prevented a clean break. By now it was February. There were still three months left in the school year. As department chair for health and physical education at American High, I couldn't just walk away. Plus, I had a crop of seniors headed to college. I needed to do all I could to make sure their academics stayed up to par and they completed the steps required of them. I had been at American High 11 years and had a bunch of personal and sick days built up. My principal allowed me to work three days a week, then use personal and sick days to take off Thursdays and Fridays. That's when I'd come to Naples, stay in the Best Western a stone's throw from the school, and do the thousand things it takes to start a successful football program — basically from scratch.

My top priority was meeting and building relationships with the current players. When the lunch bell rang each day, I would hustle around the cafeteria and campus, introducing myself to students. I asked every guy I ran into if they had an interest in football. Most of the conversations went something like this:

"You like football?"

"Yeah, I like watching it and I used to play."

"How come you don't play for Naples High?"

"Cuz they suck."

"Not anymore," I would say, "We're going to be great!"

That was the gist of most conversations. Thankfully, most of the responses were polite, and many left the door open at least a crack.

After engaging the players, my next priority was finding the group of coaches that I was certain God was lining up to help me use football as a tool at Naples High School. The coaches at American High were great guys, and a few were like brothers to me. But none of them were compelled to go like I was. I didn't fault any of them for not wanting to move, and they didn't fault me for making the move.

The first guy who crossed my path was not on my American High staff, but he was coaching in Miami. He was the defensive line coach and strength coach at Miami Central High School. Our first meeting was an accident. Had Miami Central High Head Football Coach Roger Coffey been where he was supposed to be, Sam Dollar and I might never have met. But when I went to cross-town rival Central in the fall of 1997 during the pre-game ritual of the video tape exchange, I couldn't find Coffey. I searched the building and eventually found Sam in the weight room. It wasn't tough; Sam Dollar stuck out like a sore thumb. He was the only white guy on the Miami Central football staff. And when I say white, I mean blonde hair, blue-eyed, Oklahoma-country-boy white. To say he was an anomaly in Miami's inner city is putting it mildly.

I was immediately struck with how engaged his students were and how orderly the weight room was. The weight room was in a building separate from the main school building. Outside his weight room, there were literally crack vials among the trash on the ground; but inside his weight room, all was well with the world. My initial thought was that this guy would be great at American High. We chatted as Dollar helped me with the tape exchange. Dollar recalls little of that first meeting, other than us reaching a common belief that free weights are better than machines. I soon would have an indelible impression of Coach Dollar after his defense held my previously-unbeaten American team to 7 points in Central's win over us a week later.

The week after my very first interview in Naples, Dollar and I had our second meeting, at the American Football Coaches Association national convention. The convention happened to be in Dallas that year. Dollar was sleeping on the floor of some coaching buddies' hotel room and foraging for food. Like many coaches at the convention each year, he was looking for the next better job and looking to learn as much as he could to improve himself as a coach. I mentioned to Sam that I was seriously considering taking the job at Naples. "Yeah? Where's that?" Dollar asked. "On the other side of the state," I told him. I asked if he had a resume. As it happens, he did. In fact, he had about 100 in the backpack he was carrying.

A month later, my interest in Sam Dollar was picking up. Dollar and I began working out together, and he agreed to ride over to Naples on one of the several trips I made as I was getting the lay of the land in Naples. The two hours over and two hours back gave us a chance to really talk.

Sam Dollar had been raised in a Christian home and played football at Evangel University, a private Christian school in Springfield, Missouri. The idea that football could be about more than winning appealed to him. He appreciated the time at Central, but he was ready to get back to an environment with, as he put it, "Guys that want to do what God wants them to do, and who understand what that means." We shared beliefs about football; but more importantly, about life as well.

Once Sam and I knew he was on board, I was able to convince Mr. Brown to hire Sam as a substitute teacher at Naples High. He'd teach his assigned classes during the day, and work on football stuff at lunch and after school. He designed a weight room, based on the promise that funding to equip it would someday be available. He passed out brochures, hoping to generate interest in spring football, which loomed just ahead. Prospective players were given study guides to familiarize them with terminology.

"They had very limited knowledge of the game," Dollar recalls. Gradually, interest began to grow. The students said, "All right, spring football. This might be something to at least check out." Looking back, Dollar says what struck him most about those early practices was not what was there, but what was not there.

"The intensity of hitting. The desire to come out and hit somebody with the force it takes to be successful on the football field.

There was a lot of soft hitting. It was like a bunch of cotton balls running into each other." Dollar went out of his way to applaud the occasional solid hit. "They didn't know how to do it right," Dollar said.

As spring practice approached, Dollar noticed a Naples High baseball player who had "defensive tackle" written all over him. He began talking to the young man, junior Zach Sutter, with an eye toward luring him and his leadership ability onto the football field. On the last day to pick up equipment for spring football, May 1, Dollar sought out the recalcitrant Sutter at school.

"Come on. Let's get you a helmet. Let's get you some shoulder pads. If you don't do it today, you can't play. Just come out. Give us a chance. You won't regret it," Dollar said Sutter agreed. Zach was a good guy; not very vocal, but popular with all of the student body. Kids took notice that he was playing football.

"He loved it. He stayed with it. It was that type of thing with a bunch of guys. Just give us a chance," Dollar said.

Through all of this, I was diligent in my prayer life and my Bible study. One of my daily topics of prayer was asking God to send me the guys he wanted and to give me the wisdom to know who that was. I was determined that we would hire the right guys, or no one. We needed men and their families who understood that this would not just be another coaching gig; this would be a lifestyle and mission. The scoreboard would never define us; rather, we would be characterized by our relationships with our Creator, our families, our players, and each other.

Ernie Modugno had given me a stack of resumes. After he advertised in national magazines and on various websites, there had been a lot of interest. Evidently, there were a lot of people trying to get to Naples, Florida, and be the head football coach. As I went through the resumes, I found one from a coach named Paul Horne. Paul had been a head coach at a small school in Virginia and was currently teaching and coaching in Georgia. He had played every position on the offensive line, including tight end, while earning his bachelor's degree at William & Mary. Paul's wife, Shannon, was a West Point grad and was currently on active duty at Fort Stewart in Georgia.

I can't remember verbatim Paul's mission statement at the top of his resume, but he talked about his relationship with God and how it would help him communicate with, and respond to, the needs of the young people he worked with. I thought it was bold for someone to have written that. It would be a deal-breaker with many possible employers. In my case, it made me pick up the phone. A few minutes into my first phone call with Paul Horne, I felt a rare connection. We spent hours on the phone together over the next several weeks, and we both felt strongly that he should come to Naples.

The rub was that he was going to have to sell his house in a market that wasn't moving, and had not been moving in some time. The other biggie was that the Army would have to allow his wife Shannon an early-out or a different job, either of which would allow them the flexibility to move. That happening in a timely manner seemed next to impossible, as Shannon was a West Point grad and in the middle of her post-grad commitment. As if life isn't complicated enough, Shannon was pregnant with their first child. The short version is that after much prayer, it happened. Paul took a bath on his house, but that was a sacrifice he was willing to make to come to Naples. Shannon would be given an Army Reserve job which would allow her to fulfill her commitment.

Paul Horne is an impressive physical specimen. He is 6 feet, 3 inches, and about 250 pounds without an ounce of fat. As the players would say, he was "roped up." Paul was a couple of generations removed from Russian immigrants, and the "big Russian bear" moniker fit perfectly. His brown hair and dark tan contrasted with his bright blue eyes, giving Paul a presence. If this guy speaks, players and coaches alike are going to listen.

"I didn't know where Naples, Florida, was," Horne admits, when Kramer first contacted him. "I had to find it on a map," he said. But he quickly learned where Kramer was, in a football sense. "Bill and I spoke; it must have been close to four hours. We talked about play calling, tradition, what makes a program. We even talked about helmet design. It was a very high-level football conversation. I hung up the phone and said, 'I like this guy.' "

Not long after that Paul got another phone call, this one from a candidate who had beat him out for the head coaching position at Mt. Hebron, in Howard, Maryland. He was wondering if Horne would be interested in an assistant's job. The new coach began the conversation with, "Dude . . . "

"I remember thinking, 'Did he just say "dude" to me?' " "His first word to a prospective coach was dude," Horne said. The decision to move to an unfamiliar area, away from established

friends and a family support system, wasn't an easy one. Horne talked it over with his wife.

"We prayed on it. I came out and said, 'I think we need to move to Naples.' Despite the uncertainties, I had this peace about moving to Naples."

As an offensive-minded coach, I determined very early in my career that as the head coach, the first person that should be hired is your defensive coordinator. The next person should be a secondary coach for the defensive backs. If you don't have a good person in that job, you get caught with your pants down in a hurry on a Friday night. So I was a little out of order, spending so much time and energy with Paul as our offensive coordinator and line coach before I had a secondary coach. Little did I know that problem was going to be the first of countless problems that Paul Horne would solve for me.

Within days of Paul's commitment to come to Naples, I got a call from him. He was fired up about a remotely-possible solution to our need for a secondary coach. A friend he was on the phone with asked Paul if he'd talked to former William & Mary football teammate Jamie Lemmond lately. Paul told her he had lost touch with Jamie for the last couple of years. The friend told Paul that she had recently spoken with Jamie, who had gone from coaching college football into full-time Christian youth ministry and was now looking to get back into coaching. It just so happened that Jamie played defensive back at William & Mary and was a secondary coach.

It wasn't long until I was on the phone with Jamie.

I knew in moments that this was a godsend. One of the questions I've asked guys when interviewing is, "Do you want to be a head coach?" If they said yes I wanted to be intentional about growing them towards that. When I asked Jamie, he said, "Yes, I want to be your head FCA coach." FCA (Fellowship of Christian Athletes) is an organization that allows students, whether they're athletes or not, an opportunity to hang out together as a school club and encourage each other to do the right thing. In this case, doing the right thing is basically keeping the commitments you've made to your faith and your future, and loving the folks around you. Lots of guys have told me they want to be a head football coach — but "head FCA coach" was a first. The job pays zero dollars and requires a lot of time and energy, if done right.

I explained to Jamie that I couldn't guarantee him a teaching job. He was a social studies teacher, and the only certain social studies job was already committed to Paul Horne. I told Jamie the principal guaranteed that he could be a substitute, a job that would pay him about $60 a day on the days that he'd be needed. Beyond that, the coaching stipend would net him about $1,200. Jamie told me he would be praying about it. He was in the middle of running a summer youth camp, and would not be able to move anywhere for several weeks. He also told me that he had been offered a coaching job at Lehigh University; the Lehigh job came with a car and a credit card.

Before he hung up, Jamie asked for the address where I was staying. I gave him Duke and Angel's Ft. Lauderdale address, as we still had nowhere to live in Naples. I figured that Jamie wanted the address to send me a "thanks but no thanks" letter. Instead, I found out about Jamie's answer to prayer a few weeks later, when a couple boxes addressed to Jamie Lemmond — in care of Bill Kramer — arrived at Duke and Angel's house.

When I got hold of Jamie on the phone, he said that he was certain that God wanted him in Naples. Jamie had already called Kevin Higgins, the head coach at Lehigh, and told him. I talked to Kevin several months later, and he was thrilled for Jamie and for us. Most of all, he was thrilled that Jamie was right where God wanted him, doing exactly what God had called him to do.

Jamie was about 6 feet tall, with thinning blonde hair. He had this slightly crazy look in his eye that gave me the sense that "this is the guy who is liable to do anything at any time." It turned out that the crazy look in his eye is from a childhood accident, which caused one of his pupils to have an extra bump in it that extends into his iris. Jamie had the accident your mom warned you about — a neighbor boy shot him in the eye with a BB gun. I soon came to find out, the BB gun story aside, that Jamie *is*, in fact, the guy who is liable to do anything at any time.

Sam, Paul, and Jamie motivated me. These guys were stepping out on faith because they believed in God, and because they believed in me. None of this was convenient, but we individually and collectively knew that God was calling us to be difference-makers in Naples.

CHAPTER

05

I also made sure to interview any of the coaches from the previous Naples High staff who wanted to stay. One said point-blank that Naples' woes had nothing to do with players, or lack thereof, and also had nothing to do with other schools recruiting Naples High's best athletes. Nor did it have to do with a lack of commitment from the administration.

What P.J. Moriarty told me was that, no matter what I heard, the truth was that the coaches were not investing enough positive energy in the players. P.J., who had played at Naples and was working for the school as the groundskeeper, believed the right staff with the right attitude could succeed where others had failed. P.J. Moriarity would be a terrific wide receivers coach and the only member of the previous staff we retained.

Ron Byington was the head coach of the local Pop Warner team. They had experienced tremendous success, including a national championship. There were many in town who thought Ron should be the next head football coach at Naples High School. He was a corporal with the Collier County Sheriff's Office, and one intimidating dude. He was about 5 foot 10 and shaved his head bald. His arms were gigantic and his chest was even bigger. The first time we met, I remember thinking, *this guy must bench 500 pounds*. I was almost right. If you're a bad guy, he is your worst nightmare. Ronnie is as smart as he is strong.

Ron is also one of the kindest men I've ever met. Right after we had accepted the job at Naples High, we were standing just inside the entrance to the Naples High administration building. Ron saw Sue standing with those three little girls, and immediately reached into his pocket, pulled out a key to his house, and gave it to me. He gave me directions and instructed me that anytime either of us would like to stay there, even for just a few hours, his house was our house. Having a quiet clean space is especially important to a nursing mom; Sue and I were amazed and grateful.

Of all the churchgoing folks I've met in my life, I wonder how many of them would have made the same offer. Ronnie was interested in the head football job at Naples High School and could have easily seen me as a rival. Instead, he saw the humanity in the situation before the rivalry. He's been a great role model for me. He was an even better Youth Relations Deputy and defensive line coach for Naples High.

George Bond was a 30-year veteran of teaching and coaching. When I met him our first spring, he was the department head for social studies, and taught advanced placement courses with an intensity and sense of urgency that is legendary. George, like Paul Horne and Jamie Lemmond, was a graduate of the College of William & Mary. He began his teaching and coaching career in Virginia and was actually on the T.C. Williams High School staff during the time that is depicted in the award-winning movie *Remember the Titans*. George is extremely bright and hard-working. He had risen through the ranks at Naples High, serving at different times as athletic director and dean of students.

I sought out George and asked him to interview, based on what I had been told about him. He told me firmly and politely that he had no interest in coaching anything other than the hurdlers on the track team. He hadn't coached football in years, because when he was brought to Naples as a young teacher and coach by then-Head Coach Dick Pugh, there had been a real and sustained commitment to football done the right way at Naples High. Coach Bond said that not long after Coach Pugh left, Naples football had slipped into such a state of mediocrity that he simply could not be a part of it.

I knew in my heart that George Bond was rare and extremely valuable. He had more local knowledge than anyone I had met. He was a fierce competitor. He was detail-oriented to the nth degree, and he really wanted to do what God wanted him to do. After several meetings and several more prayers, George Bond accepted the position of head junior varsity coach. Our first year, we only had a varsity and a JV team, as we just didn't have enough bodies to field a freshman team as well. George was the perfect mentor to all of those newbies.

Ryan Krzykowski was a local product who had gone to a rival school and won the Winged Foot Award his senior year. The Winged Foot is the highest honor that any athlete in Collier County can win. Modeled after the Heisman Trophy, the award is for exceptional athletes from any sport who are also exceptional academically. Ryan attended Yale, where he played football and graduated with a degree in economics. Soon after graduating from college and after prayerful consideration, Ryan realized that God was calling him to teach and coach at the high school level. He spent our first spring as a substitute teacher and was hired to teach math at Naples High our first fall.

When I interviewed Ryan, he was obviously very smart; he also obviously knew very little about football. The best part was that he didn't try to fake it. He knew what he had been taught to play his position, but he had not been a student of the game. As complicated as we sometimes make football, I was confident there was nothing in our system that Ryan could not learn quickly. Ryan was the JV offensive coordinator and worked with the young quarterbacks, running backs, and wide receivers. We had a local sports legend and Yale grad working with our youngest players. When I say it out loud, I am still amazed.

Dan McDonald and Tony Ortiz were both from Ron Byington's staff with the local Pop Warner team. Both were terrific young coaches, full of passion for the kids and football. Both of them were enthusiastic about being a coach in the mold that we were talking about. Whatever they lacked in football acumen was made up for in the quality of their character. Dan and Tony were guys who would do whatever was needed whenever it was needed. They are both such good guys that I often worried that others would take advantage of them.

Dan McDonald was a sheriff's deputy and worked with Paul Horne coaching the offensive line; Tony Ortiz was an Exceptional Student Education aide at Naples High and coached the JV offensive line. Our final coach was Courtney Schultz, who worked with the JV defensive backs. He was a couple years removed from his college graduation and taught social studies at Naples High. He expressed an interest in coaching with us, not because he had a great football IQ, but because he was really motivated by the idea that we would use football as a tool to help young men become great husbands, fathers, sons, and brothers.

I know I was fortunate and blessed to have found that many quality men so quickly, but my good fortune and blessings were by no means exhausted. The pieces just kept falling into place – except for one memorable day, when the pieces just fell.

CHAPTER

06

Toward the end of July, Sam Dollar's imaginary weight room became a reality. The weightlifting equipment that we had ordered on a hope and a prayer rolled up on a big Yellow Freight flatbed, all ready for us to unload and assemble. I had given my word and my IOU to a local architect who had two children graduate from Naples High. His wife was an assistant in the attendance and discipline office, and they both were wonderful people who loved NHS. He wrote a check to cover the cost of the weight room equipment so that we could get it ordered, with the understanding that we would raise the money to pay him back.

While it might not be classified as a miracle, we did raise the money, and it was pretty miraculous to me when those power racks and power clean platforms were set up in the weight room.

Until then, we had been teaching how to power clean and squat with broomsticks. It does not breed a lot of confidence when you look around the weight room and see guys strength-training with broomsticks. It also does not breed a lot of strength.

It was important that we had all of the coaches on the same page. Every football program has its own method and terminology. I had to make sure that all of our coaches spoke the same language and did things the Naples way. I do not have meetings unless they are absolutely necessary. That summer, as our troops finally all arrived, we needed to meet pretty regularly. I soon discovered that it is extremely important that all of our coaches are not just on the same page, but on the exact same sentence on the same page.

We didn't have a coaches' office, so we met in the principal's conference room. One evening, a lady interrupted our meeting. She walked in speaking only Spanish, and my rudimentary understanding of Spanish prevented me from understanding her. I asked Coach Ortiz if he would please ask the lady if he could help and see what she needed. Tony got up from his chair, walked toward the woman, and asked her how he could help her . . . in perfect English. She just looked bewildered. I had assumed that, because Ortiz was his surname and he'd told me that he recently returned from visiting family in Puerto Rico, perhaps he had some grasp of the Spanish language. He did not. It was an abrupt and — in the view of the assembled coaches — hilarious reminder of what happens when you assume.

Beyond staff development, we needed facilities development. When I was shown the facility on my initial interview, I told Ernie Modugno that Naples High was like a shiny apple that is rotten on the inside. To the casual observer it looks wonderful, but anyone who sinks in their teeth would soon find it disgusting. One of the selling points Ernie had emphasized was that facilities improvement was a priority. In fact, he told me more than once that they had plans for an athletic facility with a field house that were drawn up by the same architect who had built the NFL Hall of Fame in Canton, Ohio. I have asked countless times to see the plans; they have yet to show up.

Not only did we not have a coaching office, but the small locker room was nearly 40 years old. The lockers were rusted, bent, and broken. The door latches did not work; they were irreparable, as replacement parts were no longer in production. Between the locker room and weight room were several small storage rooms and a small janitor's closet with a mop sink. I asked Gary Brown and Ernie Modugno if any of those rooms were expendable, and if it would be possible to remodel a bit to create an office for the coaches. If we knocked down all the interior walls and left the block exterior, the room would be a whopping 18 feet by 10 feet. I was hoping to use the existing plumbing for a bathroom. That thought never would have occurred to me, except that I was in the middle of a remodel at my new house just down the road . . . more on that later.

Gary and Ernie gave their approval with the caveats that we would have a plan. We would have an engineer look at the existing structure; and we would, first of all, do no harm. We contacted a local engineer, and he came and looked at it, gratis. He assured everyone that the interior walls did not bear any weight, and we could grab sledgehammers and start banging away.

We did just that. We worked before and after lifting sessions for nearly a week, with coaches pounding walls, chiseling old concrete from the floor, and hauling rubble. It was hard to believe that a space that size would have so much rubble. Late in the week, we were nearly finished. As I made a Burger King run, Coach McDonald stayed with three of our players and finished the last bit of the demo so that we could start building a bona fide, itty-bitty coaches' office. Coach Byington was also there, cleaning up the weight room after the last lifting session of the day, and helping with the demo as needed.

I drove up, fries still warm, and parked right in front of the covered breezeway that led to the locker room and soon-to-be-office. As I opened my car door, I heard a loud BOOM. I looked up to see bodies flying out the door in a giant plume of smoke, as if they had been shot into the breezeway.

My first words were, "We're all fired. We haven't coached a game yet, and we're all fired." I peered through what I realized was dust, not smoke, and stared in at a scene from a disaster movie. The ceiling had caved in. There were loose wires sparking and arcing, throwing strange shadows on the walls.

If I lived a long three-wood from the school, Gary Brown lived a smooth pitching wedge away. After making sure everyone was OK, I jumped in my car and drove to Gary's house. I explained our problem and asked him to look at it.

Our consensus on the short drive to school was that our engineer had blown a call, and that we were fortunate no one was hurt. Gary said the first thing to do was to get the power off, and the second thing would be to see if he could get someone there to help us clean up. It was just after sunset on a summer Friday night. The odds of both happening seemed as dim as the darkening sky. Two phone calls later, we had an electrician coming, and we had found an ally who would haul the rubble away by Monday morning — if our coaches would pile it in the corner of the parking lot.

The cloud of dust had a silver lining, and it was this: Ernie Modugno decided we were a danger to ourselves as construction workers. He called a local builder friend, explained the situation, and asked him to come take a look. Ernie's pal offered to finish it up for us. Our room was so small, and our demolition so complete, that he could have a crew finish it out in no time. Three weeks later, we had a football office, complete with a tiny coaches' shower, two telephones, and whiteboards. In 1998, with the 21st century looming on the horizon, Naples High football was entering the 20th century.

As we worked hard to upgrade the facility, my mind often went to the meeting with the booster club at the fancy Naples Athletic Club. Those folks had pledged support and to provide "extras," and now I was in need of some extras. We needed to create a weight room, acquire video cameras and editing equipment, and at the very least, get T-shirts and shorts for our football players. A couple months in, I realized that I still had no contact with any booster club members. Since taking the job, I had asked Ernie several times in passing if he could forward me the numbers of the folks that we had met with. I figured that Ernie was as busy as I was, and that he had not gotten around to forwarding me that contact information. A serendipitous trip to our Publix market remedied that.

I bumped into one of the guys who had attended that Collier Athletic Club meeting. Buddy Shultheis was a Naples alum who had played offensive line for the University of Florida, starting every game for three years. When I saw him in Publix that day, I almost sprinted to him. Finally! I could connect with someone from the football booster club.

Our conversation was awkward from the start. He seemed reticent, and while I didn't want to press, I absolutely had to get a booster club going. Eventually, Buddy agreed to have lunch with me, and he told me he would bring another alum with him to a meeting at a TGI Friday's near campus.

As soon as we settled in, I felt an awkwardness that I could not identify. Buddy had Don Eytel with him; Don had played at Naples High and was currently working for a local hospital system. Neither of these guys seemed fired up to help Naples football, and I just did not get it. At one point in our conversation, I finally just got down to it. What was going on? Everyone at the meeting at the Collier Athletic Club had seemed so supportive, but since I had accepted the job . . . nothing, nada, zilch.

Buddy and Don had a hard time making eye contact as they explained to me that there really wasn't an active football booster club. They said their dads had been active members when they had played at Naples High. Everyone at that Collier Athletic Club meeting was basically faking it.

I was incensed. It was all I could do to contain myself. Two things calmed me: first, I remembered that we were on mission; second, I knew I needed to move forward, period. Before we left that meeting, Buddy Schultheis had committed to being the president and Don Eytel had committed to being the treasurer of the newly-named Naples Touchdown Club.

Things were moving forward on all fronts; not as I had envisioned, but moving forward nonetheless. It is a good lesson to remember. It may be hard. It may seem fruitless. But we won't move forward and make progress unless we simply keep trying each day to make at least some small gain beyond the day before.

CHAPTER

07

Naples High School sits an easy bicycle ride from one of the prettiest coastlines in America. The white sand beach stretches seven miles from north to south. It is lined with mansions to rival those of any exclusive enclave in America. There are high-rise condos where millionaires live stacked on top of each other, and landscaped parks where those not quite fortunate enough to live right on the beach can easily mingle with those who do.

Sue and I were determined to buy a place in the Naples High School zone. We wanted to see our players and their families while at the grocery store or gas station, and they needed to see us. It was also really important for our girls to go to school with future Golden Eagles. Both of us also knew that with the hours I would be working, I had to live close if I wanted to be the husband and father that God expected me to be.

We discovered Naples at about the same time as the rest of the world, and property values were skyrocketing. Once I accepted the job and was doing my weekend commute, Susie began to make occasional trips with me to do house hunting. While I was at the school doing my new job stuff, she would load up 4-month-old Kelly, 3-year-old Courtney, and 5-year-old Katie, and drive around the neighborhoods in the Naples zone looking for homes for sale.

Anything we could afford was small and beyond fixer-upper status. We were praying about it daily. I reminded myself that God created the universe and everything in it in six days, and then chilled out on the seventh, so He wasn't panicking even though I felt like it. Sue was Sue. She kept smiling, encouraging, and doing whatever it took to get the job done. As a young mom of three little girls, part of Sue's daily prayer was that God would put us in a house with good neighbors. Still, it was looking more like our goal of living near the school was beyond our grasp. Then God stepped in.

Joe and Peggy Sadelfeld both taught at Naples High. Joe taught Latin and health, and Peggy taught home economics. They both grew up in Ohio and had graduated from Ohio State, where Joe lettered in both basketball and baseball. We met the Sadelfelds on one of our first visits to the school and liked them instantly. Joe and Peg lived near the school, something teachers could do in the days before the Naples real estate boom. Talk about a godsend, Peg and Joe Sadelfeld are two of the sweetest people God ever created, and in short order, they became part of our family.

Peg and Joe were not the only close friends we had. It just so happened that Pat and Jill Manley lived about five doors down from the Sadelfelds. Jill happened to be the assistant to our athletic director, Ernie Modugno. Pat was the principal of a nearby middle school. Like the Sadelfelds, the Manleys took our family in almost immediately. In fact, the Manleys took us into their home, literally. At the conclusion of the school year, Jill and Pat were heading out of town on vacation and asked us if we would house-sit for them for a week or so. I am betting that they really did not need house-sitters at all, but that they felt bad for both the new coach, who was by that time living at the Best Western, and for his commuter wife and children.

Pat Manley had a sister in town, Mary Cunningham. It was no coincidence that Mary and her husband Larry asked us to house-sit when they left town that summer too. Gary and Sandy Brown also happened to need someone to stay at their house that summer. Looking back, I really don't know if I could have hung in there emotionally when things got tough in the late summer of '98 if I had not had these real family times while we were house-sitting. It is amazing to me how God used those sweet people to sustain me and our family. There is a great lesson for all of us who claim to believe in God and believe that He wants us to love those around us. We have to put feet to our faith. I am eternally grateful that the Sadelfelds, Manleys, Browns, and Cunninghams were not too busy, too financially strapped, or too self-centered to get out of their own comfort or convenience zone and help our young family.

Another bonus for us was that all of these folks had deep roots in education and all of them are really smart. The Sadelfelds were teachers. Both of the Manleys were in education on the administrative end. Larry Cunningham had been a local principal before he retired, and Mary Cunningham had been a teacher. They understood. They had a realistic idea of what it would take to climb the mountain we were attempting to overcome. Mary and Larry had four adult children, and I was fortunate to meet Bubba Cunningham and his wife Tina. Bubba was an assistant athletic director at Notre Dame, and I liked him from the moment I met him. As proof that the nut doesn't fall too far from the tree, Bubba offered for me to bring Sue and the girls up to stay with him and his family so we could go to a Notre Dame football game. A great idea, I thought, but the idea of me going out of town to any football game during the season seemed pretty farfetched.

Joe and Peg Sadelfeld knew we were having no luck finding a home in the Naples school zone. Peggy told us about a Mrs. Drake who lived across the street from her. Mrs. Drake and her husband had built the house in 1971 when they retired to Naples from Everglades City, where Mr. Drake had been the mayor. After her husband died, Mrs. Drake wanted to sell the house, but was unable to due to some legal complication. Peggy suggested it might be worth my while to look into it.

Some would say it would be a cold day in hell before a one-income family on a teacher's salary could afford a house in Naples proper. As I got out of my car and walked to the front door, the thing that struck me about the little house was the roof. It looked like it was covered in heavy snow. I found out later the snow on the roof was actually a foam insulation, which had been sprayed on, then painted white. The snow wasn't real, but Mrs. Drake was.

She was the prototypical little grandma; or perhaps I should say aunt, since the neighborhood called her "Aunt Bea."

I explained our situation to Mrs. Drake, and asked if she might be interested in selling. She said she was, but after her husband's death, she had sold the lot adjacent to the rear of the house. Somehow, the legal description of her new property boundary was in dispute, and she could not sell it until it was resolved. She had been told that settling the dispute would be complicated and expensive, and she had neither the money nor the inclination to mess with it. Would she sell in the event that we could get it settled? Yes, she said she would, if it cost her nothing.

A couple days later, Gary Brown asked me how the house hunt was going. I told him about the situation with Mrs. Drake's house. In his understated way, he said, "I may be able to help."

As fate — or God's plan — would have it, his son-in-law, Kevin Coleman, was a top land attorney in Florida. Kevin's wife, Barb, was an English teacher and alumna of Naples High. Barb and Kevin Coleman have more than their fair share of good looks and intelligence. They also give more than their share of kindness and generosity. By the end of the day, Gary Brown had contacted Kevin, and Kevin had contacted me. He offered to help me with whatever legal work needed to be done to clear up the title and make the house sellable.

The legal battle over the 9-foot piece of land in question produced a file 8 inches thick, Coleman recalls. "What he thought he owned, he really didn't own. If a normal closing is a five, this was an eight-and-a-half or a nine. It was a bear, that's for sure," Coleman said.

47

Coleman did the work for free. "Naples football had kind of languished a little bit," he said. Helping the new coach was his way of helping out, and ensuring domestic tranquility.

By the first week in July, after the most convoluted land dispute that one of the best land attorneys in Florida had ever dealt with, we closed on the little house on the corner, across the street from Peg and Joe Sadelfeld, the best neighbors in the world. I'm reluctant to classify this as a miracle, but bear in mind that I walked up to a house in the perfect location; a house without a "For Sale" sign in the yard and no listing with a broker. I then asked the kind lady in it if she would like to sell, and was told it just wasn't possible due to an unfathomable legal quandary that should have taken a very long time and a lot of money — neither of which I could afford. Somehow, I was moved into that house in time for football season. Whether it was a miracle or not, I thank God all the time for our home and for the folks who made it possible.

CHAPTER 08

Mrs. Drake kept an immaculate house. Other than the snow globe roof, it had barely changed at all from the day the Drakes moved there in 1971. I soon recognized that avocado green must have been terribly popular in 1971.

The house had avocado linoleum, avocado shag carpet, avocado appliances, and even avocado wallpaper. The Brady Bunch would have thought it was really cool. The galley kitchen was just about wide enough for one butt to fit in it at a time. Two butts were definitely out of the question. There was also the perfect amount of cabinet space for Mr. and Mrs. Drake, but not for a family of five. Sue and I both knew we had work to do; the place needed remodeling. I was just the man to do it; our financial situation dictated so. I don't want to say that it was a big job, but I soon had my own parking spot at Home Depot.

Thankfully, Gary Brown introduced me to the coolest Canadian south of the border, Joe Joy. The name fits. His salt-and-pepper hair and mustache framed perpetually smiling eyes, and his can-do demeanor was a salve whenever I was overwhelmed. Joe could answer any technical question I had about construction. Without his expertise, I would have been absolutely lost.

Some of my coaches also pitched in. They would work with the kids in the weight room or on the field, and then swing by and paint a wall or build a cabinet or help get the old floor up. You name it, my coaches were willing and able. I'm guessing that a couple of them got more than they expected when they asked if I needed any help.

I had been away from the girls except for occasional weekend visits since the first of May, the first day of spring football. Here it was, the end of July, and I still didn't have the house ready for them. Sue had driven over on most weekends, but I soon discovered that I am an emotional weakling. I am miserable away from my wife and children. We talked on the phone. I mailed them children's books, with tape recordings of me reading the books to them. "At the tone, please turn the page," I said, the tone being me shaking my keys.

With two weeks to go before the start of our first season, I found myself at the nadir of my professional and personal life. I was taking a break from trying to get the world's most secure linoleum up from the concrete when there was a knock at the door. I stayed on my paint bucket seat and hollered, "Come in," eagerly anticipating the countertop guy. I had a hard time seeing who it was, because I had just put in eye drops for what the doctor at the clinic had described as bi-orbital cellulitis. For good measure, the doctor had also diagnosed me with strep throat.

"I am so glad to see you. I really need those countertops so I can get my sinks in and the water running," I said.

"Sure you do. By the way, do you have permits for this job?" the gentleman replied.

"Permits? I'm just swapping stuff out myself; I don't need any permits."

"Well" he said, "I am an inspector from the City of Naples and I guarantee you, you need permits."

He went on to tell me I was going to be "red-flagged" — that's inspector-speak for "all work on this house will stop," until I had permits. He was good enough to give me the name of the person at Naples City Hall I needed to see and describe the seemingly insurmountable steps I needed to take to get my permits.

When he left, I sat back on my paint bucket in stunned disbelief, trying to process what was going on. It wasn't five minutes before there was another knock at the door. This time it was Ernie Modugno.

"How you doing?" he asked. The hard swallow that followed had more to do with the lump in my throat than the strep in my throat. I said, "I may have bitten off more than I can chew." Assuming I meant some particular part of the house, Ernie asked, "What part?" With all the self-pity I could muster, I said, "Coming here."

After he left, I went into what was to be my bedroom, with its concrete floors, primer on the walls, and the lone bulb hanging from the ceiling by exposed wires. I was mad at Ernie for calling me, mad at myself for answering, and mostly mad at God for not making this road I was on smooth and easy. I missed my wife. I missed my kids. I hadn't had a paycheck in two months, and to top it all off, I had maxed out my Home Depot card.

I lay on the bed and tried to pray. My prayer turned to fussing, then finally to tears; and unfortunately, tears are all too rare for me. I asked God what the deal was, and why would He call me here if it was only to crash and burn. I then sensed the God who loves me providing an answer.

I realized that the Creator of the universe was not going to give me more than I could handle, and if I would quit trying to control the situation and just let him be God, I just might be pleasantly surprised. Again, the verse from 2 Chronicles came to my mind: "The eyes of the Lord run to and fro throughout the whole earth looking for those that love Him so that He can prove Himself mighty on their behalf." God will prove Himself mighty, if we just let Him.

I composed myself, washed my face, and went downtown. I sat outside the office of the man the inspector told me to see. It was just after lunch. The receptionist said he was in, but had meetings all day. I said that I would wait until he was free, and that if he had any cancellations or just a moment to spare, I would take very little of his time. I checked back with her every 30 minutes, to no avail.

As I sat there watching her work, I could see she was getting annoyed with me. Just before 5 p.m., the building began to empty. I sat praying silently that somehow, I would get to see this guy today. I happened to overhear someone say "Bill," and figured that this was the same Bill that the inspector had mentioned. I hopped up. Beyond the now-angry receptionist, just down the hall, I saw two guys saying their goodbyes. Over the angry lady's protest, I asked the guy who looked more in charge if he was Bill Overstreet. He said he was.

I asked for five minutes of his time, and he reluctantly agreed. As I passed through the swinging gate to his office, the look on the receptionist's face was lethal. I sat down in his office and as quickly as I could, I explained what had transpired that morning. He asked me what brought me to town. When I told him I was the new football coach at Naples High, he said to no one in particular, "Looks like our new football coach has got himself into a pickle." He assured me that since I was doing the work myself, and that as long as what I had done was up to code, the permit process might go forward pretty quickly. The first order of business was to see the plans that I had, and to make sure I showed every single thing I was doing. All I had was my chicken scratch on a legal pad, but after cleaning it up a bit, Bill said it would do.

He walked out to the receptionist, instructing her to set me up with an inspection the next morning. Barring anything unforeseen, she should permit me at the regular rate, and he would waive any fines. The receptionist almost came unglued. Here she was at work, half an hour past quitting time, and this yahoo with the legal pad plans was going to be treated like he had a brain, which he obviously didn't. Bill chuckled away all her concerns and assured her it would be all right. I can say for certain that if looks could kill, I would have died in the City of Naples Building Permits Office that day.

CHAPTER

09

I was up early the next morning, and the inspector was too. By 7:30, he was poking and prodding and checking everything out. As he checked items off his list, I felt a sense of relief.

Then he asked me about the doors that led out of the side of the house to a little patio. I had replaced the original sliding doors with new French doors that met Dade County's hurricane codes, the toughest codes in the country. I explained to him that the original doors jumped off the track regularly, and the rubber seals around them were worn out. Having lived through Hurricane Andrew in Miami in 1992, I figured that replacing the sliding doors was a priority. I showed him all the paperwork on the doors.

He told me that the City of Naples did not have the engineering plans from the manufacturer, and while they very well may be wonderful doors and safer than what I had, I would be red-flagged until those doors came out and were replaced with approved doors.

But these were on sale, I explained.

The guy at Home Depot should have told me that they weren't OK, the inspector replied. Had I installed them a half-mile away outside the city limits, they would be OK, he added, but only city-approved doors were to be used within Naples city limits.

Knowing that my Home Depot card was maxed, and knowing that they were not going to let me return those used doors, I asked the inspector about getting them approved. "Head downtown," was his best advice. I jumped in the car and headed back to City Hall. It struck me that the same receptionist might be there again, and this time I might need her help. It also struck me that I might not get her help.

Lo and behold, there she was. As I explained my situation, I couldn't help but notice the delight she took in explaining to me how lengthy the process of getting exterior doors approved was. It would require raised-seal plans from the engineer who designed them, and certified results of all the stress tests conducted to verify that they actually operate as designed. I thanked her and fought the negative thoughts in my head. The documentation that came with the doors gave the phone numbers for the company — there was a number in Germany, a number in Spain, and a number in Miami. I sat on my cot on my concrete floor under my bare light bulb, and figured the least I could do was call the Miami line.

The voice answering was nice enough as I gave her the Reader's Digest version of my predicament, but we just weren't connecting. She was answering other calls, and someone else was talking to her at her desk. Knowing me, I was probably talking way too fast. After a few minutes she said, "OK, who is this again?"

I told her my name, and she asked, "Bill Kramer . . . did you ever teach at American High?" When I told her I was the same person, she went nuts. "Mr. Kramer, this is Yolanda, remember me? I was in your second-period health class my sophomore year." I asked her last name, and when I heard it, I did recognize her. We talked about all the folks we knew in common.

I gave her an expanded version of my situation, and when I finished, she said, "Mr. Kramer, you are not going to believe this, but . . . " I interrupted her to say, "Yoli, I want you to know, I am no spiritual guru and not into hocus pocus, but whatever you are about to tell me, God has His hand in it." She told me that may be true, because the owner of the company was in the Miami office at that moment. She offered to get him on the phone with me.

After being on hold for a two-minute eternity, a man's voice picked up. He made it clear that he really liked Yoli, and that he was giving me about 60 seconds as a favor to her. I relayed my predicament to him as clearly and concisely as I could, and when I was finished, he said, "Well, Coach Kramer, you're not going to believe this, but . . ." I gave him the same "I'm no spiritual guru" disclaimer as I had given to Yoli, and told him that whatever he was about to say might just be a God thing. His reply was, "You know, Coach, you just may be right."

Standing right next to him, he informed me, was the engineer who designed those doors. The man lived in Germany and hadn't been in Miami for a year. But he was there that day, and would be happy to help me. I ticked off the list of everything I needed for the city, and the owner assured me that before noon the next day, I would have all the documentation and raised-seals I needed. Before I hung up, I thanked him profusely. After I hung up, I thanked God profusely.

The courier arrived before 9 a.m. He had several impressive cardboard tubes and a fancy folder. He handed them to me and was gone in a blink. I now wonder if I should have tipped him. I was so surprised and so grateful that it never even crossed my mind.

I changed clothes and headed to Naples City Hall. I was determined to be nice to the lady behind the desk, even though my inner jerk wanted to stride in like the conquering hero. It just so happened she was at the counter. She stared in disbelief as we pulled the different documents from the tubes and the folder. Among the documents was a cover letter signed by the owner and the engineer, with their personal numbers and instructions to call immediately should anything further be required.

Here I was, less than 48 hours removed from being red-flagged, and it appeared as though I was about to be granted full-go on my house. The receptionist went from extremely skeptical to reluctantly impressed, which was a quantum leap. Bill Overstreet admitted he had never seen anything like it. Maybe, he allowed, Naples would win some football games.

In short order, I was headed home with all of the permits and inspection schedules I would need. A miracle? Perhaps not. But then again, I'm not sure I want to be the recipient of a miracle.

To receive a miracle, you have to need a miracle, and that seems like a pretty scary position to be in.

The little house with the white roof.

CHAPTER

10

The coaches came into the season fired up and really focused on what our process with the players and with each other would be. I truly believed that if our process was great, our outcome would be great. If we could stay focused on the day-to-day process, then all the changed lives and wins would take care of themselves.

Each year we went on a coaches' retreat, and each year we had a different theme. We spent a few days immersed in what we could do to grow and improve ourselves as men and as coaches, and we made sure when we left the retreat that we were on the same page. I spent a good bit of time preparing for the retreats and praying about what our focus as coaches should be for each year.

The first year's theme was plain to me from the outset. Our first task was to love our players. The scriptures that our coaches focused on were I Corinthians 13 and Ephesians 5:25. The characteristics of love are explained in I Corinthians 13, and Ephesians 5:25 is a command telling husbands to love their wives.

When we looked deeper into it, we realized the fact that we have to be told to love our wives is significant. After all, wives aren't told to love their husbands. In fact, they are told to respect or honor their husbands. But it all makes sense. Some years ago, *Time* magazine came out with an article describing the differences between men and women, based on scientific research. It is research used in the advertising industry every day.

Men and women are wired differently. Women tend to be much more emotionally-centered and motivated, and men tend to be much more ego-centered and visually motivated. Men tend to need to have their ego stroked more often than women. That is why God commands the wife to respect or honor her husband. Women tend to need to have their emotional needs met more often than men. That is why God gives husbands the "love your wives" command. It should also be noted that we are commanded to do these things because, very often, they go against our nature.

Our coaches' takeaway from the weekend was that love is a choice we must make every day. We were going to choose to love our wives and kids, love each other, and love our players every day.

CHAPTER

After the coaches' retreat, before the first day of school, the coaches and I experienced another first. The first day of football practice.

We met it with a tremendous amount of enthusiasm and apprehension. While we had been running and lifting weights (light weights) all summer, we had not done any real football. In Florida, the state dictates that the first three days of training are conditioning only. Players may not wear full pads, and there is no contact allowed. South Florida in August is nothing but tropical heat and humidity, but you would not know it by the way our players and coaches bounced around the field. At the beginning of the year, everyone is undefeated, and we were acting like it.

Because of the limited nature of the first three days, we did way more talking and walking through plays than we would have if we were in full pads. At the end of practice, we had a series of timed sprints. In my system, the players knew exactly how many there would be, and the time limit for each position. I used to get discouraged when I played football and the coach would tell us to get on the line, and we ran until he was tired. There are many versions of this open-ended conditioning. I just couldn't coach that way.

I wanted to know exactly what was required of me and to measure myself against the standard. Being vague gives the impression that the coach is winging it, and/or just doesn't like his players. I had done my best to make the times doable by all the players at each position. The rule was if everyone makes their time, practice would be over. If anyone failed to make their time, then that sprint didn't count; we would add five seconds and try again. If anyone missed that one, we would add five seconds and try again, and so on, until eventually we could all crawl across the line.

Because of limited space on the Naples High campus, we practiced on the baseball outfield. The configuration of the baseball field dictated that we couldn't sprint in a straight line for more than about 70 yards. In this case, we were sprinting 60 yards, and we were doing just fine until the very last sprint. Well, actually we were plugging along until the very last sprint.

I kept hearing grumbling from our biggest and best player. He was a returning senior lineman, and he was the real deal. He was huge, with great feet, rapidly improving strength, and terrific agility. I was told he was a standout in wrestling and track, and we all felt like he could be our only legitimate Division I recruit in that senior class.

I could hear him muttering under his breath as we lined up for the first sprint, and it only got louder and more defiant as we ran. Coaches kept yelling out encouragement to our players, asking them to encourage one another as they ran. But our D-1 guy saw it otherwise. As we approached our last sprint, I was running through my mind the conversation we would have in private after practice. I didn't feel like I had a strong enough relationship with him to call him out in front of his pals. I was counting down on the last sprint, and he was bringing up the rear until he got within about 10 yards of the finish line, when he shut it down completely. By the time I got to, ". . . three, two, one, time!" he was 2 yards from being finished. I knew he was testing the boundaries, and that how I handled this would be important. So I hollered at everybody to get back on the line; we had one more, because everyone had not made their time. Mr. D-1 said loud enough for everyone to hear, "This is bull****!"

I nearly exploded, but hollered out much louder, "Come on, you can do this! Your teammates and coaches are counting on you. Let's go!"

I explained that we would add five seconds, and that everyone could make it this time. The rest of the crew was not happy about more running. Most had given their very best, and were counting on being done on that last sprint. Most had also sprinted the last one as fast as they possibly could and were feeling the effects. We lined up and went again. I was in good enough shape at the time to stride with them, and I did so pleading with our big boy to give great effort and be done. Again we had the same result. As I counted down, again he slowed down just enough to miss his time, and again I added five seconds. We all lined up to do it again. I was starting to get fired up, and yelled to our best athlete that he was being incredibly selfish, making his teammates run extra.

After adding 10 more seconds, the time to make was so easy that a steady jog would bring an end to the day, and once again everyone made their time except Mr. D-1. He managed to just miss again. At that point, I was seething. He said nothing as I lined them up for the third extra sprint. We now had an additional 15 seconds. When it was all over, he had just missed his time again. As he walked across the finish line, he looked up to the sky and yelled out, "This is bull****!"

I completely lost my cool. I shouted at him that the only bull**** around here was his attitude, and that he was setting a horrible example for his team. I told him I could not F-ing believe he thought he was that much better than his teammates, and as of that moment his football career at Naples High was over. As he threw his helmet to the ground, I told him to go ahead and take off all of the sh** that he was wearing that belonged to us, and leave. He tossed his helmet down and hollered back, "This is all F-ing bull****!" I told him I agreed with him. He was exactly right, it was, "all F-ing bull****."

As soon as the 10-second exchange was over, I felt sick to my stomach. Not because I had just fired probably the best athlete on the team, but because of the manner in which I had done it.

I had quit my job and moved my family across the state. I had committed with and to a cadre of good men to rearrange our lives, all in order to establish a new way of molding and motivating young men — not just to be good football players, but good people. Here it was, the first day of practice, and I had failed my first test.

After the team finished the last sprint, we huddled together, as we did after every practice. I was conflicted. I wanted to apologize for the language, but I realized I could not put that toothpaste back in the tube. My biggest fear was that I would apologize and then the lid would come off again down the road. What then? Another apology?

After a quick silent prayer, I decided all I could do was deal with the moment. I apologized to the team for my language, and I explained to them that I should have responded differently. As we headed in, several senior players came to me and told me they weren't bothered at all by the language, but they were bothered by losing their friend. They told me they thought we had to have him if we wanted any chance to win. I explained to them that my decision was made, and it was final. We would be better as a team without him. Before I got all the way to the locker room, several younger players told me not to worry about the language. They were glad I had dealt with the situation the way I did.

My gut still hurt, and the thought of my language stayed near the front of my mind for some time after that. In our coaches' meetings, we had made a priority out of not using foul language and had all committed to avoiding it. The only foul language I had heard on our field was my tirade on the very first day.

It was not many days before our dismissed player's mom drove up. I happened to be leaving the office, and I could see him in the passenger seat as she got out of the car. She told me that she thought I should let him back on the team. She explained that, the year before, he hurt his knee and the coaches didn't make him run when it hurt. She said there were even some weeks when he couldn't practice, but he never missed a game. I explained to her that the doctor had cleared her son, and either he didn't want to run with his team or was physically unable to. In either case, if he couldn't or wouldn't, he was in no position to play football.

Mom could have gone to the athletic director or the principal with her complaints, but she didn't. I'm guessing that the boy didn't want to play all that much. I've heard more than one top coach warn against spending 90 percent of your energy on the 10 percent of players who won't get with the program. You let the 90 percent of the players suffer if you do. This seemed like one of those cases.

While that first-day failure sticks in my mind in vivid detail, much of that time remains sketchy in my memory. We definitely had a running theme of working hard to help our players keep the commitment they made to play football. While we didn't have a lot of rules, our attendance policy was very straightforward. Being late or having one unexcused absence would result in the player getting "O-P-P" and not starting the next game.

O-P-P is shorthand for opportunity, and it meant an opportunity to get right with the team after an infraction. It could take the form of running, a combination of running and push-ups, or an exercise we called the "scalded dog," which involved moving on two hands and one foot. We liked to think that it was something most players preferred to avoid. After two unexcused absences, it was O-P-P and sitting out the next game. Three unexcused meant the player would no longer play football that season.

In order to maintain the integrity of the program, we had to make sure that AWOL players came to practice. That way, all they had was the O-P-P for being late, and the three-strikes-and-you're-out policy didn't kick in. On more than one occasion, I asked Ron Byington to find the missing kids. Ronnie was a terrific sheriff's deputy and knew the kids, knew all their hangouts, and knew how to get them back to school. On a few occasions, I would halt practice and go with Ron until a player was located. I always asked parents to support us in bringing their sons back to practice. Most of them did.

A few days after firing our one big-time prospect, another of our best players, a corner named Al Green, was missing from morning practice. I got on the phone and talked to his mom, Ella. She fully supported us coming and getting Al out of bed and using whatever means we chose to get him to practice. Ron knew the lay of the land like the back of his hand, and knew exactly where Al lived. When we got there, Al was in his bed lying under a sheet with a pillow over his head. His mom and step-dad Richard, who was also a sheriff's deputy, explained that they had tried everything to get him up to go to practice. I tried to be diplomatic as I asked Al to get up. "Come on, Al. Let's go, brother."

"I'm not going; I quit."

"You can't quit, Al; we're a family. You made a commitment, and now you have to stay part of the family. Think about it like the mafia."

"I ain't going. I don't want to play anymore. I ain't in no family. I quit." He kept the pillow over his face as he spoke, but it was really easy to hear that his mind was made up.

"Al, here's the deal. I love you too much to let you quit and so does your mom. She gave us permission to do whatever we have to do to get you to practice, so go ahead and get up and grab some shorts and a shirt, because the whole team is waiting on you right now. If you don't get up, Coach Byington and I are going to drag your tail out of here."

Al turned to the wall and said emphatically, "I ain't going. Leave me alone!"

At that point, I turned to Ronnie and said, "You get his legs." And quick as a blink, Ronnie had his ankles and was dragging him off the bed. I caught Al under the armpits, and we began to haul him out. This was no easy task; Al was strong and motivated, and began to kick and buck.

Thankfully, Ronnie Byington is really strong, and he was not having any of it. I can still see Al grabbing on the door jambs, hollering about how he was quitting and how he didn't want to play, and that we weren't allowed to grab him and we better leave him alone. By the time he got to practice, the team was done stretching, and Al was calm enough to join them. Thank goodness for moms like Ella. She is, more and more these days, a rare breed.

Parents who let their kids quit a sport when they're sore, discouraged, or "just don't like it anymore" are doing their children an incredible disservice. At the very least, the individual should finish the season once it has started and then reevaluate their desire at the end. I remind my players repeatedly that the only true test of commitment is time, and that the only way to measure a person's commitment is to see if they stick when they don't feel like it. If we feel like doing something, then it requires no commitment; no self-discipline. We can only measure our commitment when things don't go our way, and we are really uncomfortable, dissatisfied, discouraged, and want to quit. What kind of an attitude do we have then? How is our effort?

CHAPTER 12

I had been working in and around Naples High School for four months. But working at a school out of session is very different than working at the same school when it is in session. As the first day of my first school year at Naples High approached, I had no idea what kind of reception I would get. I knew the transition would be tough, if for no other reason than in the Miami-Dade County Public School system where I came from, head football coaches — by contract — could not teach more than two classes. Many coaches taught none, but were given an administrative duty. In my case, I taught two, one being a weight training class for our football team. The notion is that, among academic support for players, college recruiting, fundraising, dealing with the myriad vendors, and media obligations, not to mention actual game planning and practice planning, being a head football coach is a full-time job in itself.

When I visited at conventions and clinics with coaches from all around the country, they were amazed that coaches in Florida had to teach any classes at all. In Collier County, I was required to teach a full class load, as were all coaches and assistant coaches. Originally, Mr. Brown assumed I would teach physical education and mainly run the weight room. I felt strongly that the defensive coordinator, Sam Dollar, should have that job, since it didn't require nearly the time prepping and grading as most of the teacher positions in the school. Dollar had certifications in PE and math. I felt like if he was going to find a way to stop the folks we would play, he would need a position that was not cumbersome after hours. Plus, I had seen the way he handled himself in the weight room. I also figured that if other high schools or colleges tried to lure him away, as they often did, I would have an attractive teaching position to offer his successor.

I was fortunate to have a number of certifications. My bachelor's degree is in both health and physical education, and I have a master's degree in computer science education and another one in guidance and counseling. After discussing it with Gary, we decided the counseling position would offer me the most flexible time.

Wrong again.

My frame of reference was that Charlie Yanda had been the department head for guidance at American High School. After his lunch duty in the cafeteria each day, he would head straight to the football office, where he spent the rest of the day. My counseling position turned out to be very different from that, and seemed to be ever-expanding. When Gary Brown initially told me I would be coming as a counselor, he said I would be the counselor for students who had English as a second language. Before long, my boss in the guidance office told me I would also coordinate all college recruiter visits with the seniors. Soon after that, I was told I was in charge of the local scholarship program. At that point, I started wondering about this "flexible time" thing.

By the week before school started, I was told I was now the testing coordinator for the school and would be responsible for all standardized testing. That included the High School Competency Test, which was being phased out; the Florida Comprehensive Assessment Test, which was being phased in; and the Stanford Achievement Test. Interestingly, I was not offered either the ACT or SAT. It was not until years later that I discovered those two come with a nice stipend for the person who coordinates them.

As if all that weren't enough, I was given the task of creating and distributing the monthly senior newsletter; and finally, the piece de resistance — a new category of student was created for me . . . "tweeners." Because I would obviously have so much time on my hands, my fellow counselors decided it was a good idea to assign, as my counselee, any student who was not on the proper grade level. This is typically not your self-starting, rule-following adolescent. If a student for any reason had failed a class, and was not on his or her proper grade level, I was their man. I look back now at these sweet colleagues, many of whom are good friends now, and I can't help but wonder, "What were you thinking?"

To compound things, the administration moved me into the exact office that the former head coach had occupied, and he was moved to a smaller office down the hall. The former coach was

Bob Bradford. Bob was a nice guy. Every person I ever met who knew Bob would say the same thing: "Bob is a nice guy."

The folks he had worked with felt extremely loyal to him, so by contrast I was the bad guy walking in the door. Add to this the fact that I am a "Type A" person who is nearly always in a hurry, who tends to walk fast and talk fast, and it is understandable that Bradford's pals were skeptical. Another reason for skepticism: I was the fifth head coach in the last 10 years at Naples High. The only winning season in the past 14 years was achieved with a Bob Bradford-coached team. So even though I had nothing to do with his firing, and hadn't ever actually applied for the job, I was definitely the villain.

Bob wasn't the only other former Naples High head football coach working at Naples High; there were two others. Bobby Bentley and Bill Broxson were both terrific guys too. Besides those three, there was also a previous defensive coordinator for Naples High who was in the building. He was a Naples alum, had played at the University of Michigan, and had been a graduate assistant coach at Michigan while he completed his master's degree. Talk about a pedigree. He had applied for and been denied the head coach job that I was just given, and he was not happy about it.

I knew that we were coming into a hostile environment. I repeatedly told the coaches we would eventually win folks over with our work ethic and our integrity, but there was no telling how long that would take. While most of the negativity was in the form of gossip in the break room and comments during department or faculty meetings, it soon became apparent to me I would have to adapt to a whole new level of disdain when I met the secretary for the guidance counselors.

She really, really liked Bob Bradford, and she really, really did not like me. I always had real respect for her, because while the other Negative Nellies would smile to my face and then hammer me behind my back, this gal never smiled to my face and made it infinitely clear that the sooner I left, the better off we would all be. I don't know if her job description included picking up the counselors' mail and distributing it, or if she just did it out of the goodness of her heart. In my case, she ran out of goodness. She would deliver the mail to every counselor but me. Not a big deal, but at the very least she was an authentic human being.

She also seemed to really enjoy scheduling appointments for me with parents and then not telling me. When the parents walked in, she would often say, "Mr. Kramer, I told you about this appointment," within earshot of the parents and whomever happened to be in my office at the time. The worst part for me was, she was an expert. She knew everything there was to know about running that guidance department, and she could have coached me up and saved me loads of time. As I prayed each day, I asked God to help me not get angry and lose my cool with her. The moment I did, I would confirm everything that she already thought about me. I also knew that I needed her help, and that she did not need a thing from me. I decided to try to win her over with kindness. She drank tea throughout the day, and at the time, my father-in-law Duke had honeybee hives at the house we had just moved from. This gave me the opportunity to bring her fresh honey for her tea. I found some small comfort in the irony.

The night before the first day of school, I was at the school working late. I wanted my desk completely clear before the deluge that is typical of opening day. Counselors had been working for a week, registering new students and fixing schedules, and while that was a busy time, it was nothing compared to the start of school.

I left the office close to midnight, as ready as I could be. Upon my return early the next morning, I logged on to my computer and waited for the troops to arrive. Before long, I had a student and parents in front of me along with a translator, and I thought things were going along quite nicely until I tried to print the schedule for the student. It was then that I noticed my printer was missing.

Whoever took that printer knew how to hinder a counselor on opening day. I wound up hand-writing the schedule and then heading past my next counselee, directly to the principal's office. I explained to Mr. Brown that I had been in late the night before and returned early that morning, and somehow in the interim my printer had gone missing. Mr. Brown called someone who would know about these things and then informed me that we didn't have an extra printer. There was nothing he could do. He assured me that he would resolve the issue as quickly as possible.

It was my first day, and I was not familiar with teacher names, room numbers, or subjects taught. It only occurs to me now as I write this that in the long run, not having a printer probably helped me. Writing helps retention. As Carl the *Caddyshack* groundskeeper might say, "I had that goin' for me, which was nice."

CHAPTER

13

As we lined up to kick off the 1998 season, our goal was improvement. We would videotape practice and games, grade the video, then go over the grades and the video each day with our players. Our focus was on improving day to day and week to week. We felt like we were getting every bit of effort from our players, but the reality was that we were small and slow. At least we were really weak, too.

I remember asking Coach Dollar if our guys were taking weak pills. Regardless, I was determined to control what I could control — my effort and my attitude. We were in, all the way in, and I was not about to look back now. The coaches and I agreed that if we could put the best athletes on defense, run the ball and eat the clock on offense, and then play great special teams, we would have a chance to be competitive . . . or at least not get completely dominated.

In Florida, high school teams are allowed to play a preseason classic, basically an exhibition game, the week before the season starts. We were playing a team from Lee County to our north, and we were heavy underdogs. In the second quarter, our quarterback, Rob Richter, ran straight up the field for a nice gain and was tackled. There was nothing extraordinary at all about the hit, which made what happened next all the more surprising. He went to the huddle, called the next play, got under center, and started his cadence. Suddenly, he stood up and called timeout. I was bewildered. I had a standing rule that no one calls a timeout without checking with me . . . not a player or a coach, no one. As he walked to the sideline, I was pretty fired up; it was all I could do to speak calmly. I asked, "What's up, Robbie?"

Cool as a cucumber, he looked at me and said, "Coach, I just broke my collarbone." I was stunned. "What? Are you sure? How do you know you broke it?"

Rob replied evenly, "I felt it pop on that last tackle, but I wasn't sure. When I clapped my hands to break the huddle I could feel it moving around in there. I thought I could still go, but when I got under center, I thought I might fumble the snap."

I was sick. Rob was one of the best football players on our team; a born leader and a committed kid. His backup was out with an ankle sprain, so I was forced to play our JV quarterback. It took some work to stay positive as Rob went directly to the emergency room to get X-rays.

After halftime, as we walked through the gate that led to the field, Rob's father, Garrett, walked up and gave me the news.

Rob's diagnosis was correct; he had broken his collarbone. As I looked past Garrett towards the bleachers, I could see Rob talking to a group of people, wearing a sling on his arm. The pit in my stomach grew.

"I am sick," I said. "First, because of all the work that Rob has done to get ready for the season; and second, because I have to look at one of our best players standing there in a sling."

"Well," Garrett replied, "I understand the first part, Coach, but I gotta say you are wrong on the second part. Rob has a broken collarbone, and right now that makes him one of your worst players. You are going to have to go coach-up one of the guys that really is one of your best players." Garrett had earned a Bronze Star and a Combat Infantryman Badge in Vietnam. He knew something about leadership, and he taught me a tremendous lesson that night.

As we prepared for our regular season opener against newly-opened Gulf Coast High School, I realized that if we were going to win a game, this might be our best chance. They were a first-year school, and like us, they were a brand-new staff with brand-new kids and brand-new systems. By halftime, the score was 34-0 in our favor.

I was told later that parking for the game was a nightmare; it seems a bunch of folks who didn't normally come to the football games were coming to see what the new coaches were all about. The thinking was, since we were playing a first-year school, perhaps we had a chance. Evidently the thinking also was that all the fans could show up right at game time, which made for a disaster in our small parking lot. Consequently, a majority of the fans were late into the stadium. Many of them told me later that as they came into the stadium, they assumed the home and visitor scores were reversed. They could not believe that Naples High could put up that many points on anyone.

While the coaches and I were happy to start with a 40-0 win, we knew that we were fortunate. Our opponents, like us, weren't very good, and our two-platoon system gave us a great advantage when it came to making adjustments during the game. If a player is always on the field, it is difficult to communicate scheme changes with him. Our coaches sat our players down between every series and talked over what we were seeing and how it compared to our game plan. If we needed to make changes, we could.

Week 2 found us overmatched athletically, but Cape Coral High, like nearly every team we played that year, played their six or seven best guys on both offense and defense. Our staff convinced first themselves and then our players that if we could hang with Cape for the first half, we could beat them in the second. At halftime the score was 0-0, and we had turned the ball over five times. Our defense was playing lights out. What came to be known as the Dollar defense was in the birthing process, building the foundation for what was soon to be a force in Florida high school football. As the second half started, we could see Cape begin to fatigue. Our offense did a better job protecting the football, and we managed to put 21 points on the board. The final score was 21-0, Naples. We had already doubled the win total from the previous year, scored more points than had been scored in 10 games the previous year, and had not given up a point. Our success made the kids in the stands holding the "Fire Kramer" signs more palatable to me.

Week 3 found us on the road for the first time, playing Riverdale, an opponent who by all rights should have beaten us soundly. Thanks to Sam and Paul and their ability to make game-time adjustments, we were ahead at halftime 7-0. A touchdown in the third and another in the fourth quarter put us up 21-0, and after the first three weeks we were undefeated and had not been scored on.

The fans, parents, and players thought that Vince Lombardi, Paul Brown, and Bear Bryant had been reincarnated and put on our staff. Our campus was buzzing, and I would go to church late and leave early to avoid the well-wishers who wanted to chat.

The coaches and I were much more realistic about what was happening. We knew we were hoodwinking our opponents. They just weren't prepared for what we were doing. We also knew the smoke and mirrors we were using would be figured out soon. After three consecutive shutouts and 82 points in three games, our opponents would stop taking us for granted.

Week 4 was a whirlwind – literally. By Monday evening, every news channel was leading with the story of an organized storm coming through the Atlantic that looked like it was headed for Naples. The storm was supposed to hit sometime late Thursday or Friday. Before I knew it, the game for that week had been moved up to Wednesday.

Every man on our staff believed that our one possible advantage was preparation. With a game on Wednesday, we would basically be able to teach our guys where to line up versus their base formations — nothing more. This game was going to come down to pure athleticism, not our forte.

We lost a close contest to Cypress Lake High School in a nearly empty stadium on a Wednesday night. The weekend storm was just that, never materializing into a hurricane. Nearly every other local school wound up playing that Friday night; in retrospect, I should have fought tooth and nail to do the same.

The Thursday of Week 5 found our JV playing Barron Collier at their place. To my way of thinking, too much was made of this. I hadn't yet caught on to the passion of the Naples-Barron rivalry, even though the clues had been there since before my first day on the job. As soon as I arrived in Naples, I started hearing the question, "When are we going to beat Barron Collier?"

It got so bad that when meeting fans or alumni, I asked that they not mention Barron Collier. This didn't sit well with most, and was outright offensive to some. I told people that in my 11 years coaching football in Miami, I had never even heard of Barron Collier. This alienated both the Barron fans, who thought their team was the best thing since sliced bread; and Naples fans, who deep down thought Barron was the best thing since sliced bread, and that beating them would make us the new best thing since sliced bread.

My view was simple. We needed to build the Naples program into one that everybody could be proud of. I couldn't blame any player or parent for wanting to be a part of another program. The general lack of support for Naples High football was demoralizing at best. If all the Naples folks could have taken the time and energy they spent fussing about other programs and invested it in the Naples program, we wouldn't have needed to worry about other programs.

The much-anticipated JV game that Thursday night was not close. We didn't have enough players to field both freshman and JV football teams, so we were lining up a mostly freshman team against a Barron Collier program that had a wealth of talent on varsity and could afford to have good young players on the JV squad. I met Paul Horne on our sidelines midway through the first quarter, and our guys were already on the short end of the stick. Our boys played hard, but were simply overmatched. Paul and I weren't worried so much about the score, but we wanted to see the dynamics between the coaches and the coaches, the coaches and the players, and the players and the players. We liked what we saw, and felt like it was just a matter of productive time before we were going to be good.

With around a minute left in the game, we left. Paul and I both wanted to avoid the parents in our stands who wanted to gripe about how Barron Collier was running up the score. That was also the reason we watched from the sidelines, outside the coaches' box, away from the coaches and team, instead of from the stands.

The focus of the Barron-haters was just wrong. All we can control is what we can control. We cannot worry about the other guys. I found my car, and as I headed home, I passed an ambulance going in the opposite direction, lights flashing and siren blaring. I remember wondering what that ambulance was about, and being glad we didn't have anybody needing one in that game.

I was wrong again.

CHAPTER

14

I had not been home long when the phone rang. George Bond was on the other end. I heard the strain in his voice as he told me that Rusty Larabell was being transported to Naples Community Hospital. I really didn't get it at first. I left the game right at the conclusion, and as I left, I could see everyone lining up to shake hands, as is the custom. How on earth could Rusty be hurt at that point? I just couldn't wrap my mind around what George was saying. He said that Rusty had become unconscious after the game. 911 had been called. The ambulance was originally taking him to North Naples Hospital, close to the Barron Collier campus, for observation. Somewhere en route, the ambulance made a U-turn and high-tailed it to Naples Community Hospital, the parent hospital of the North Naples facility — farther away, but better equipped to deal with serious cases.

That's all they could tell him.

I told Sue what was up. I had already said prayers with her and the girls as they went to bed, and I headed out the door.

This was not my first go-round with running to the hospital to check on an athlete. My first year as a head coach in Miami, I had two players transported to the emergency room at Miami's Jackson Memorial Hospital in the same game.

On the last play of the first half against Miami Springs High School, Isaiah "Big Ike" Walker, our 6'4", 300-pound, all-state defensive lineman, caused a fumble, picked it up, and ran it toward the end zone. His jaunt began at about midfield with our Miami Springs opponents in hot pursuit, frantically trying to keep him from scoring. Big Ike had no idea that anyone was near him, and as he approached the goal line, he put his arms out like an airplane with the ball in one hand. Just then, a 5'8" wide receiver who might have weighed 160 pounds jumped on his back and bull-dogged him to the ground. Somehow, Ike's cleat caught in the turf, and his leg appeared to have disconnected at the knee. It just kind of swung in a weird circle as he fell to the turf. He was taken to the hospital as a precaution, for what they thought was a routine knee injury. But the doctors discovered that Ike had sustained a catastrophic leg injury; every ligament and the vascular supply had been torn at the knee. Ike underwent hours of surgery to save his leg. Fortunately, the surgery was successful.

I immediately implemented a rule that anyone who scores a touchdown must run through the back of the end zone and then hand the ball to the official.

CHAPTER 14

In the third quarter of that same game, our weak-side line-backer, Travis Crawford, was hit right under the chin on a crackback block by a wide receiver; it may have even been the same Mr. Hustle who tackled Ike. Regardless, I remember kneeling next to Travis and holding his hand as he lay on the field, unable to move his legs. They drove an ambulance onto the field, and as they loaded him to take him to Jackson Memorial's emergency room, my only thought was to get that game over as quickly as possible so I could check on my guys at the hospital. Ike's leg injury was serious enough to end his football career, while Travis wound up walking out of the hospital the next morning; he would only miss one game.

CHAPTER

15

As I drove to Naples Community Hospital, I ran the game back in my head and tried to remember any big hit or play that might have hurt Rusty badly enough to put him in this situation. I also prayed as I drove, and asked God to make Rusty all right.

I went through the emergency room doors and found a mostly empty waiting area. The nurse behind the sliding glass window told me that Rusty had been taken to the intensive care unit. I felt sick to my stomach. The situation was beginning to sink in. I prayed silently as I walked, again asking God to make Rusty be all right, and asking Him to give the doctors and nurses wisdom as they worked with Rusty. The first person I saw in the ICU waiting room was George Bond. He was clearly upset, but got straight to the point. There was something wrong with Rusty's head. The doctors were assessing and determining a course of action. He told me that Rusty's big brother Ben was in the ICU with them.

He also told me what he knew about what happened after I left Barron Collier. George had gathered with the team and was talking to them after the game, as he did after every game. He noticed Rusty sitting on the bench, with Ben standing in front of him. George knew something was not right. He sent the team to the bus, and as he made his way to see what was going on, he could hear Ben telling Rusty to stay awake. Coach Bond saw that Rusty was not responding, and immediately began trying to find a trainer and a cell phone to call 911. Unlike in a varsity game, an ambulance isn't typically posted at a JV contest.

As Rusty slid into unconsciousness, Coach Bond instructed one of the assistant coaches to manage the usual end-of-game stuff, accounting for equipment and getting players and coaches on the bus and back to the school. That would allow Coach Bond to follow the ambulance to North Collier Hospital, where Rusty was to have been taken for observation. The ambulance's sudden diversion to the main hospital campus threw him for a loop.

Some of that night runs together in my mind, but I distinctly remember as we stood in the ICU waiting room, Coach Bond was saying that he couldn't believe we were "going through this again." What I didn't find out until later that week is that on Nov. 21, 1975, in the final minutes of the last game of the Naples High season – a game that just happened to be Naples' homecoming game against a talented Key West team – defensive end Pete Staver tackled a Key West player, emerged from the pile, took a few steps, and then collapsed in the end zone.

George Bond was there that night, too, only a few years removed from his college graduation. He was part of the vigil for Pete Staver, and remembered when Pete was taken off life support three days later. Having been through the pain and sorrow of such an experience once, I can only imagine what George Bond was going through as he relived it more than 20 years later. I knew our football field was named after a player who had died, but I had never known the details until Rusty was in the hospital.

Once I learned all I could from George, I headed toward the foreboding double doors at the end of the waiting room. On the other side of those doors leading into the ICU, I came directly to the nurses' station. The area was a big square, with the nurses posted in the center and rooms with movable glass walls around the perimeter.

I made every effort to avoid looking through any of those glass walls. I did not want to see anything that was behind them. I had just begun to explain who I was to the lady behind the desk when Ben walked up from my left. His eyes were red and swollen, and his voice cracked as he called my name. I instinctively hugged him as I asked what was going on.

Ben was one of the first guys I met when I moved to Naples. He had played defensive back at Missouri Valley College and was interested in coaching with us. Since he was in the middle of starting a new business, Benjie wasn't able to commit to coaching full time. Instead, he was around as often as his schedule allowed, helping out wherever he could, including being on the sidelines that night.

Ben loved the notion of using football as a life-shaping tool, and was definitely a guy who wanted to do what God wanted him to do. Rusty was following in his big brother's footsteps as a football player and as a young man. Like Ben, he was kind, disciplined, and hard-working. Rusty would stay after workouts to help clean up and was always a source of encouragement to his teammates and coaches. We coaches recognized that even though he was only a sophomore, Rusty was a guy who would be a building block for our program.

With tears in his eyes and a catch in his throat, Ben told me that at the end of the game, as both teams were lining up to shake hands, Rusty had come to him and told him that his head hurt. Ben handed him a nearby water bottle and asked him if he wanted some water. As Rusty began to drink, he sank to the ground and had some sort of seizure. EMS was called, and Rusty was taken to the hospital. It had not taken long for the doctors to tell Ben that Rusty had swelling on his brain and needed surgery immediately to reduce that swelling.

Ben said all we could do was wait. I asked him if we could pray. We ducked around the corner and opened our hearts to God. We admitted our fears and begged God to make Rusty be all right.

I called Ernie Modugno, woke him up, and told him what had happened. Ernie was at the hospital in very short order.

Ben and I then went out to the ICU waiting room, where we met George, and the three of us began to dissect every detail of the game, trying to figure out how this might have happened to Rusty. None of us remembered him taking or delivering any significant blows. He had not once mentioned anything to anyone about discomfort of any kind during the game, in which he had played defensive back and returned kicks. In spite of the JV loss that night, he had been one of the best players on the field.

When the doctor came out, he told us the surgery went as well as it could, and that all we could do was wait. He said Rusty was being put into a chemically induced coma; the next 24 to 72 hours were extremely important. He explained that they had no idea what the cause was, and once Rusty stabilized, they would have to perform some more tests to see what else would need to be done.

None of us would be allowed to see Rusty for at least a few hours. The doctor encouraged us all to go home and rest, as it was now early Friday morning. Benjie made it clear he would not be leaving and insisted that the rest of us go home. I stayed with Benjie a bit longer, but he finally convinced me to go home and get a few hours of rest. I wasn't sure if I could sleep, but I knew I had a full day of work ahead of me. At the very least, I needed to shower and get in a shirt and tie for work. As I slid into bed next to Susie, she asked me if Rusty was OK. I told her it didn't look good. The last thing I remember is us holding hands and praying together as I slipped off to sleep.

CHAPTER

16

By the time I got to school the next morning, it had already been decided that night's varsity game against Barron Collier would be postponed. I soon found my days following a pattern: I would get up, go to work as early as I could, and attend to my email before the first school bell rang. I would get as much of my to-do list done as I could before 11 a.m., and then go to the hospital for an hour or so. By 11, the doctors would have had time to digest everything that had happened overnight and would be able to give me any new information or prognosis. The hospital being just a couple miles from the school, I would be back on campus by noon. At the conclusion of school lunch, I had to hustle to get the rest of my to-do list done, knowing that football practice was looming at 2:30. Practice ended at 5 p.m. each day, and I would run home, grab a quick bite, shower, and head back to the hospital. I would stay late and head home in the wee hours to get a little sleep.

Rusty was in and out of surgery a couple of times that week as doctors tried to relieve the pressure on his brain. They reiterated that the first 72 hours were critical, and that Rusty would either begin to get better at that point, or he would not. They also told us that talking was good for him, as familiar voices would help his brain to process.

Ben and Polly, Rusty's older sister, were incredibly faithful, sitting and talking to him hour after hour.

I could barely bring myself to walk into Rusty's room. I did go in, held his hand, and talked to him, but for very short periods of time. I would steal glimpses of Rusty as he lay there — tubes in his head and nose and mouth and both arms. The swollen face I glimpsed was not the boy I knew; I could hardly bear to look at Rusty like that.

I was embarrassed at my own frailty in not being able to spend more than a few minutes with Rusty. I felt hopeless and powerless and afraid, all at the same time. In one of my weakest moments late one night, I remember leaving Rusty's room and walking alone into an empty hallway. I was trying to pray and felt bone-dry inside. I heard a noise, turned, and Gary Brown was standing there. With choked breath and clenched teeth, barely able to suppress the sobs I could feel welling up inside of me, I said, "Gary, I did not sign up for this. I just don't think I can do this. I don't think I can do this anymore." Looking back, I am embarrassed by my self-pity and self-centeredness.

CHAPTER 16

Gary Brown looked me in the eye. "Bill," he said, "We are going to play a football game again next Friday night. It would be a lot better if you were still the coach." I don't remember responding or if we talked further, but those words stuck to my insides.

Later that long night, I was in that same hallway and began to pray silently; I didn't feel like I was connected at all. Most of that was because I had just realized my own mistake of making the situation about me. I had to fight through feelings of self-pity that were trying to overwhelm me.

All at once, God spoke to me. Some may call it a moment of clarity, others a gestalt moment or an epiphany, but I know that in that moment, God impressed on me that He brought me and these coaches to Naples for moments like this. Who better to stand firm in their faith and simply love and minister to those around them than a group of men who are doing their level best to be obedient to God? From the first day in Naples, I had told anyone who asked that we were not in Naples just to build a football program; any of us could have done that anywhere. The reason we gave from the moment we agreed to come to Naples High was that we wanted to be where God wanted us; that place was Naples.

Everything – the unlikely interview process, the soul-searching over whether to take the job, the miracle of finding a house and making it livable, the coaching staff that God had called together – had brought me to this point.

God did not bring me to Naples High School to quit.

CHAPTER 17

One of the duties I inherited at Naples High was the job of reading the announcements over the PA system each morning. It gave me a good chance to update everybody on campus with what was going on. The first morning after Rusty went to the hospital, I was thinking that even though it was Friday and our usual Fellowship of Christian Athletes meeting day was Wednesdays, we should have an emergency FCA meeting. Ahead of reading the announcements, I checked with Jamie Lemmond and he also thought an FCA meeting was a good idea. I let the school know.

My idea behind the Friday FCA meeting was simple. In times of crisis in the United States, our president, regardless of political party, appears on TV and asks the country to pray. I figured if it's good enough for the president and the country, it's good enough for us.

Jamie thought it would be best if the kids could just get together in small groups and pray for Rusty, his family, and the doctors. Jamie Lemmond was incredibly talented and energetic. He knew every group game and icebreaker invented by man. Best of all, Jamie was a great example to all of someone who loved God and loved kids.

That first special FCA day that we met in the auxiliary gym, there were the usual 100 or so FCA members. As the days went on, the numbers increased, and within a week there were hundreds in the gym each day. I would begin with a Rusty update, and then invite questions. I would ask if any kids had anything they wanted to say. It was amazing to watch kids come forward and challenge their peers to live a life of significance. In various ways and with different personal stories, kids would get in front of their peers and explain that God loved them and wanted to have an intimate relationship with each of them.

These kids were real, vulnerable, and transparent. The effect was remarkable. Hundreds and hundreds of kids came to the gym each day to pray for Rusty. Numerous students — some I knew and some I didn't — came up to me and told me of the commitment they made to God. The tone and tenor of our school was changing. This is not to say that Naples High wasn't already a terrific place; it was. But imagine a significant number of students in any school wanting to be all that God wants them to be, and then those students making whatever subtle or dramatic changes were necessary for that. It was a breathtaking experience.

The first Friday at the hospital, I had the privilege of meeting the Rev. Michael Harper, the director of pastoral services for Naples Community Hospital. He was kind and compassionate, and available for anyone. There were a lot of people hurting. Along with Rusty's family, our coaches and their wives were constant figures around the ICU, as were many of the Naples High students. I don't remember the exact timing, but sometime during that first day or two, the idea was brought up that we should have a prayer vigil for Rusty.

Rev. Harper was willing to arrange it, and we decided to plan one for Sunday night. I'm not sure how word got out. This was before many high school kids had cell phones and before social networking. The word did get out, and we had several hundred folks show up. Many local pastors and youth pastors were there, and several of them asked if we were meeting with the kids at school. I told them about the FCA club meeting we had on Friday, and invited whoever wanted to attend to come to the gym Monday at lunch. Many of them did show up, and as we met each day that week, more and more came. In fact, during that time a youth pastors' network was created in town, and as far as I know, they still meet on a regular basis.

Another daily meeting had been happening all year and continued during that tragic time. Because of time and schedules, the only time George Bond could get together with his junior varsity football team and assistant coaches was after school, immediately before practice. George would do this each day, reinforcing the values we were teaching as the foundation to build our fledgling football program. At the first parent meeting and every meeting thereafter, we said that our priorities were our faith, our family, and our future – including how we prepare academically, socially, and athletically. George Bond was and is a master teacher. His advanced placement courses were legendary for their rigor, and for his preparation and ability to communicate the material.

He put those skills to work with his young team at that difficult time. George took time each day to care for and love his young team. As Rusty lay in that ICU ward, George was able to use those meetings to relay the most recent information on Rusty and answer whatever questions the boys had about their friend and teammate.

The boys surprised us all when they went out and beat a much bigger and more talented team the Thursday after the Barron Collier game. As they met in Coach Bond's room the Friday after that big win, he made an offer. If anyone wanted to swing by his house the next day, they were free to jump in the pool and eat the hot dogs he would be happy to grill. I'm guessing that George's wife, Ricki, had to run to the store for more food, since every boy on the team came over and stayed for hours. George said it was a healing time for all of them. It was also the first time he had heard any laughter in more than a week.

CHAPTER 18

Each day brought something new. The media were everywhere: at school, at practice, outside the hospital. Rusty's mom, Dee, was understandably distraught, and as the days of no sleep and little or no food added up, I began to really worry about her as well. Rusty had a younger brother, Josh, who was a year behind him in school. By all accounts, Josh idolized Rusty, and all of us kept close watch on him as the horrible drama unfolded. Early on, Dee asked me to be the spokesperson for the family, and I agreed. I had no idea what I was agreeing to.

The media were insatiable. It became difficult to field the same questions over and over. It was one thing to answer the same question from different folks. The part that bothered me was when a person from the media would ask me the same questions repeatedly; asking directly, rephrasing, or from a different angle.

They asked if Rusty would get better. I didn't know.

They wanted to know what happened during the game to cause this. I didn't know.

My answers didn't change. It seemed as though those folks either thought I was lying to them about something, or they were trying to get me to misspeak. Regardless, while I was very uncomfortable with it, I realized they were just doing their job the best way they knew how.

I had a habit of whooping and hollering while the guys were stretching each day at the beginning of practice. I would always holler out, "GREAT DAY TODAY!! WHOOO BABY!! IT'S A GREAT! . . . DAY! . . . TODAY!" I did that to set the tone each day. I believed that I needed to help the guys realize that the only things we can ever really control are our own attitude and our own effort. The whooping and hollering became increasingly difficult for me during that 1998 season. I struggled to stick to my core values.

When we talk about core values, we must get feelings out of the way. I would tell the guys, "If you don't feel it, fake it." By that, I meant there will be plenty of times you don't feel like being a good student; or later, a good husband or a good father. In those instances, we need to fake it if we don't feel it. We know what our core values are, and we must stay committed to them especially when we don't feel like it. There is no discipline involved in doing what is best for you and your future when you feel like it; that's easy. The real discipline comes when you don't feel like it. Real discipline is when a kid does his homework while a pal tugs on him to go to the mall. Real discipline is when a dad on a business trip remains faithful to his wife, even though his marriage is struggling and he has an attractive opportunity to cheat. Those are the times that you might not feel it, but you must fake it to stay committed to your core values.

So, each day during that ordeal as we went to practice, I would holler out, "GREAT DAY TODAY!" I didn't feel it, and neither did the rest of the coaches or the kids; nevertheless, I was determined to stay true to my core.

As the days went on, Rusty's condition did not improve. We all continued to pray for a miracle, but by Tuesday and Wednesday the doctors began to ask some hard questions. It was determined that if God did not provide a miracle, Rusty's organs would be harvested and given to young people who desperately needed their own miracle. Rusty's family spent time together, talking and crying and praying, trying to figure out a timeline in the event that Rusty did not improve. By Saturday, we knew Rusty had had no brain activity for some time. The only things keeping his heart beating or his lungs breathing were those machines.

Sometime Saturday afternoon, Ben told me we would be saying goodbye to Rusty the next morning; then, the machines would be turned off. Rusty's organs would be harvested and given to kids his age whose lives might be spared or dramatically improved through Rusty's gift.

I went into his room for the last time that Sunday morning and said goodbye. I remember telling him I loved him and that we would make him proud of us. I was determined to run a program where our vertical and our horizontal relationships were more important than the scoreboard. It was nothing but sadness and gloom, and it makes my chest tight just thinking about it today. After my goodbye, I could not bear being around there and I left the hospital.

On Sunday morning, October 11, 1998, at 11 a.m., 10 days after falling unconscious on the sidelines of the Barron Collier football field, Rusty Larabell was taken off of life support.

CHAPTER

19

At that time I had only been to one funeral in my life, that of my Grandpa. As a kid, I spent summers with Grandpa and my Uncle Rick, who lived in the same trailer park. They were consistent examples of how men should behave, and a sharp contrast to my stepdad, whose abuse was all that was consistent in the chaos he created.

Grandpa died during the last semester of my senior year in college. I was student-teaching in Roanoke, Virginia, but got permission to leave for a few days and attend the funeral in Arizona. When we met with the church folk and the funeral director before the funeral, the only thing I asked was that I not see Grandpa dead. I didn't need the verification. I could take Grandma's word for it. I wanted to remember him alive. I wanted my memory to be of Grandpa and me throwing worms at the rainbow trout in the water in the White Mountains of Arizona. My job was to escort Grandma down the aisle to her seat. I asked that the casket not be open until I was done, so I could get to the back and avoid seeing Grandpa.

I walked Grandma down the aisle, put her in the seat next to my mom, and then headed to the back as they opened the casket. What I didn't realize was that they would somehow sit him up in the casket at a slight angle, so that everyone could see the body from their seats. What I saw in that split-second glance was not my Grandpa, and I wish that I didn't have that snapshot in my head.

Rusty's family asked if I would speak at his funeral. I agreed; thankfully, they did not want an open casket. I could not imagine talking with Rusty's body propped up right in front of me.

The funeral was held at First Baptist Church Naples. The casket was just below the pulpit at the front of the stage. The seats that were usually on the stage for the pastor, music leader, and others leading the services were gone. Flowers and wreaths were set on and about the stage, and there were easels with pictures of Rusty.

It hit me hard that right where Rusty's body lay in that polished wooden casket was where newlyweds took their vows and babies were dedicated. The connection between all of life and an inevitable death was made irrevocably clear to me in that moment.

Rusty's family had asked for both Jamie Lemmond and me to speak. That put both of us in the front row, looking right at the coffin and the transformed stage. The church was standing room only. I don't know how many people fit in that building, but

I would guess that somewhere between 1,000 and 1,500 people were there.

Jamie went first, and was right on the edge of being out of control. His message was that God loves us and was sharing our pain in losing Rusty. Jamie became distraught as he spoke; his tone was raw and visceral, and difficult for me to listen to. This was a side of fun-loving Jamie that I did not know existed. By the end of his talk, Jamie had calmed down, and actually seemed at peace. In hindsight, I think that speech was a cathartic experience for him.

When Jamie finished, he had no seat. Someone had squeezed into the pew we were in, and now there was no space for him to come back to his seat next to me. He had no choice but to sit on the steps that led up to the stage and pulpit. As I rose and made my way to the pulpit, my breath caught in my throat. It was a dramatic change in perspective as I looked down on the casket and out at the crowd.

I talked about Rusty and how he was an example to all of us. I said that Rusty was and is a building block for our program, and through Rusty's death many lives had been changed for the better, as kids and adults alike considered their relationship with God. I challenged everyone there to make Rusty's death a starting point for them to value what is truly valuable: our vertical relationship — the one with our Creator; and horizontal relationships — those with our family, friends, and community. These relationships should be top priority in our lives, I said. I didn't speak longer than 10 minutes, and when I finished, I sat on the stage-steps next to Jamie. Somebody had taken my seat too.

The final speaker was Forrest Head, the youth pastor for First Baptist. Pastor Head told the crowd that Rusty had accepted Jesus Christ as his personal Lord and Savior at a contemporary Christian concert several years before. He said it was the family's wish that everyone there had a chance to do the same.

Pastor Head explained that every person has done wrong; has sinned. He said that when the Bible says all have sinned and come short of the glory of God, it means **all** of us, and our sin separates us from a perfect God.

He explained that the Bible tells us God loves us so much that while we are sinners, God sent his only son, Jesus Christ, to pay the price that our sin requires. As harsh as it sounds, the Bible is clear that the wages of sin are death, and this death is a spiritual and physical death.

Pastor Head explained that the good news is: Jesus willingly died for us so that we could have a restored relationship with our Creator. All we have to do is accept this free gift, and believe that Jesus Christ is who He says He is, and that He did what He said He would do. Then, we can be saved and have an authentic, healthy relationship with God.

At the end of his talk, Pastor Head said we were going to sing a song chosen by Rusty's family. He said that if anyone wanted to make a decision for Christ or to talk more about it, they could walk to the front during the song. A pastor would pray with them, go through the Scripture with them, and help them find the answer to any question they had.

I sat there next to Jamie with my head bowed. I tried to pray and keep at bay the swirling thoughts and fatigue, which had hit me as soon as I finished speaking. As the song went on, I had the distinct impression someone was watching me. I think everyone has felt this at some time. I tried to dismiss the feeling, but couldn't, and decided to sneak a peek at the audience.

A pair of eyes in the middle of the auditorium met mine. I quickly glanced away, bowed my head, and determined to focus on praying, as the pastor had asked. But still I could not shake the feeling. He was older than I was, 50-something, with dark brown hair, a medium build, and dark eyes that were locked on me.

I tapped Jamie on the leg and caught his sideways glance. "Jamie," I whispered, "Check out that dude in the middle. I think he's staring at me." Jamie peeked from behind his hands which were folded in front of his face, leaned slightly towards me and said, "Yep, that guy is definitely staring at you."

"Probably not good," I said. "Stay by me when this is done, just in case." At that point, the singer was on the last verse of the song. The service was just about over. No one had come forward, and then the guy staring at me started moving, making his way to the aisle.

I poked Jamie and said, "Jamie, he's coming up here, and he's still staring at me."

"Just talk to him," Jamie said. "I'll be right here."

"I'm not talking to him," I said. "What am I supposed to say?"

"Just talk to him," Jamie repeated, without looking up.

"C'mon Jamie, you were the youth minister. You talk to him. I have no idea what to say. You know how to do this."

Jamie's response was no help, as he whispered, "He ain't lookin at me."

The guy was getting closer, and I had no idea what to do. So I pulled out the last resort. As the saying goes, the head coach has the biggest whistle. Slightly louder than before, I said, "Jamie, I'm the head coach, and I'm telling you to go talk to this guy."

"You ain't my head coach in here." Jamie's response was immediate and confident.

By now, the guy was a few paces from me. He had made his way past the pastor who had tried to help him, and was standing directly in front of me. I got up, took his hand, and to this day I remember what he said. "Hi Coach, my name is Tom. I have a lot of money and new cars and a house by the beach, and I'm empty inside. I need Jesus."

That was not what I had expected. I asked Tom if we could pray together. Before our heads were even bowed, I saw another person start down the aisle, and then another and then another. In a matter of moments, it was a deluge of folks coming to the front to begin or renew their relationship with God.

"Look at that," I told Tom. "The song was over and we were all headed home. But you listened to God and came up here, and look what you did! Your obedience inspired others."

And boy, did it! Before long, there were not enough counselors for all of the people coming forward. Pastor Head grabbed the microphone and started asking people to separate according to groups. There were middle schoolers who came forward, high schoolers, and adults. There were even whole families who had walked into the building separately, and who were now coming forward intact. I had never seen anything like it in my life.

I have many times remembered the impact Tom had on those around him when he laid down his pride and fear, and responded to God's prompting. Tom's example of putting feet to his faith motivated hundreds of people to move forward and make positive changes in their lives – which for many will last an eternity. Each of us has this ability if we will realize it.

Rusty Larabell

CHAPTER

20

The next several weeks of football games were numb affairs. Our coaches were very diligent in both caring for our players — taking whatever time was needed with whomever to be a sounding board and mentor — and preparing each week to win a football game. While we may have succeeded at the former task, we failed at the latter. We finished with seven straight losses that 1998 season, but our team did hang tough together. As the season progressed, so did our play on the field. We were actually playing much better in our last two games — both close losses — than we did in our first three shutout victories.

There was an interesting phenomenon surrounding our program and school. The student body was enthusiastically supporting our football team and treating our players like champions, even though we were accumulating loss after loss.

For example: each year at Naples High, the seniors create a senior T-shirt. The shirt always has a slogan or theme, and is often required for entrance to various senior-only events. The class of 1999 followed the lead of late-night talk show host David Letterman. The front of the shirt said, "Top Ten Things About Being A Naples High Senior," and the back of the shirt gave the Top Ten list. Interestingly, somewhere in that Top Ten, it said:

We finally have a winning football team.

That was a really cool thing for me; here were a bunch of kids loving on a bunch of other kids in a way that was really counter to our pop culture. If someone had told me before the season that we could go 3-7 and then be celebrated on a T-shirt as being winners, I would have told them they were out of their mind.

Thanksgiving was a melancholy time for me. When Sue and I made the commitment to come to Naples, we had geared ourselves up for a difficult first year. I really had no idea it would be as mentally, physically, emotionally, and spiritually taxing as it was. It had to be tough on Sue too, but she never, ever complained — not once. Whenever I came home, no matter how late, she was pleasant, smiling, and encouraging. And there was always something really good to eat.

The best description of Sue Kramer I have ever heard is when a friend told me that being around Sue is healing. Being around Sue Kramer *is* healing. Besides taking care of me, Sue was also keeping our family financially afloat by being extremely frugal;

being a great mom to a 1-year-old, a preschooler, and a kinder-gartener; and doing everything that needed to be done around the house.

In those days, house phones on land lines were still the norm. Susie was adept at handling whatever calls came in — college coaches recruiting our guys, vendors, parents, boosters, or coaches' wives. Sue Kramer handled all of it.

The hours I was working had become ridiculous. I was working seven days a week and spent every day during the Thanksgiving and Christmas breaks trying to catch up on the guidance counselor stuff that seemed to grow daily.

And of course, football is never-ending. When we talk about college recruiting at Naples High, we are talking about us contact-ing colleges and giving them as much information as we can. We were trying to convince college coaches to recruit our guys and eventually offer them college scholarships. The recruiting piece was overwhelming; it literally never stopped. It could have easily filled a 40-hour work week, every week of the year.

The end of the season also brought our post-season foot-ball banquet. Every sport at Naples High has an end-of-the-year awards celebration of some kind, and I wanted the football cel-ebration to treat our players and parents like the champions they were becoming.

At American High the previous year, we had the banquet at Don Shula's Hotel and Golf Club in the original Shula's Steak House. It was really fancy, and for many of the players, it was the first time they had ever experienced anything of the sort. We had a formal meal with linen tablecloths, ice sculptures, the whole nine yards. I wanted to do the same at Naples.

The thing is, at American, I had the time to raise the money and take care of the details to pull off something like that. There, I taught two classes a day, with the rest of my time devoted to the myriad duties a head football coach must attend to. At Naples High, as in Collier County in general, the expectation is excellence in athletics, but there is zero time given to perform the tasks necessary for excellence. It is a marvel that Collier County athletics are anything but mediocre, when you look at it systemically.

The banquet did happen, and with the help of some moms and coaches' wives, it was a tremendous success. Our players and parents loved it. They especially loved the highlight video, which Jamie Lemmond took the lead in producing. We gave each player a yearbook with statistics and write-ups of the games, and every senior received a picture of himself in his football uniform. Diana Richter, Rob's mom and Garrett Richter's wife, had come to me with the picture idea. She explained that she had purchased recordable frames, and asked that I record something memorable in each of the players' pictures. I have bumped into players or their parents years after they graduated from Naples High, and they often comment about the book and the talking pictures. The highlight videos, the pictures, and the football yearbook have become traditions of Naples High football.

CHAPTER

21

In Florida, it is impossible to compete in football, or any other sport for that matter, without year-round strength and speed training. Paul Horne reluctantly accepted the head coaching position for track and field, and Sam Dollar was really fired up every day in the weight room. We had zero chance of winning a state championship if we were not extremely technical and intentional with our strength and speed training. Our coaches were willing to volunteer their time after school in the winter, spring, and summer to make the plan work. In fact, we trained any athlete in the school who was willing to come in and do the work.

The training plan itself, however, involved a little serendipity, divine intervention, luck, or whatever you want to call it.

On September 24, 1994, I was sitting on the top row of the visitors' side of the Orange Bowl, watching the Miami Hurricanes' 58-game home win streak end at the hands of the University of Washington. As high school coaches in Miami, we were able to get a free ticket to most of the Hurricanes' home games. It wasn't many games before I discovered the best-kept secret at the now-demolished Orange Bowl. If I sat on the top row of the visitors' bleachers, I was level with the club seats of the home side. I was also able to lean against the chain-link fence and catch the cool breeze, which nobody below us had the faintest idea existed. To my left was the Miami skyline and the Atlantic Ocean beyond. To my right, on the western horizon, were the Everglades and some of the most spectacular sunsets God ever painted.

I could sit in the cool evening air and simultaneously watch one of the prettiest nighttime skylines in the world come to life, some of the prettiest sunsets on planet Earth, and some of the best football in the country.

On that particular September day, I was stunned as these upstarts from Washington (I mean, PAC-10 football from the Northwest, for goodness' sake) ran the powerhouse Miami Hurricanes out of their own stadium. And let me assure you, this was no fluke. The Huskies were dominant. I was amazed at how the heat and humidity of that September afternoon did not affect the Washington team. During warmups, I was certain that the 3:30 start time would ensure these Washington Huskies would wilt quickly in the tropical heat. Nope.

As the final seconds clicked off the clock, I knew what any coach worth his salt knows. That team from the great Northwest did not win that game on that suffocating September day. That team won that game during the previous January through July, and perhaps in the two or three years before, as they grinded with their strength coach in the weight room and on the track.

What most folks don't know is that NCAA rules allow very little contact between players and coaches, outside of football season and a few weeks of spring ball. For much of the year, it is the strength and conditioning staff that really spends time with, and gets to know, the players. The strength and conditioning staff sets the tone for the team; the best ones set an incredible tone.

As the year went forward, the sight of Miami players demoralized and beat down from that Washington butt-whippin' stuck with me. In my mind, I had seen the impossible. Early in the spring of 1995 as I was just beginning my tenure as head coach at American High, I decided to call the University of Washington and see if I could pick the brain of whoever was training the guys there. I picked up my American Football Coaches Association telephone directory and found the Washington Huskies football office number.

The lady on the other end connected me with the strength coaches' office. I didn't get an answer, so I left a message. After a couple of days I tried again, and again had no luck. On my third try, I did get a human on the other end, and asked the person if I could speak to the head strength coach or whoever was working with the football team. The voice on the other end assured me that I wanted to talk to Coach Gillespie, and that he was with players at the time, but he would give Coach the message. After another few days I called back, and this time I asked to be connected directly to Coach Gillespie.

The "hello" on the other end was one of those "this better be good because I have way more important things to do right now" hellos. If you're not familiar with that type of hello, call my cell on any game day afternoon, and there's a really good chance you will hear what that sounds like.

I told Coach Gillespie that my name was Bill Kramer, and that I was the head coach at American High School in Miami. I then tried to quickly recap my experience at the Orange Bowl and my rationale for calling. It was obvious from the background noise that I'd caught him eating, and he was multitasking even before I had called.

When I finished explaining, I asked if he would be willing to share his training philosophy and really get into the nuts and bolts of Washington's strength and speed training. He answered that he was very busy with athletes coming in, and he did not have the time. I asked him when there would be a good time and assured him that I could call any day and any time that was convenient for him. In an obvious effort to put me off, he told me they had a strength clinic for coaches each year, and perhaps I could attend the next one and have my questions answered there. I told him I would be glad to come, but that I would much rather just spend a day or two shadowing him and picking his brain. I asked him when would be a good time for me to fly in for a visit. At that point he said, "What did you say your name is again?" I told him my name was Bill Kramer and that I was the new head coach at American High School in Miami.

This is where the serendipity started. I heard him pause and then say, "Bill Kramer? . . . Did you go to Liberty?"

Talk about out of left field. I told him that I did go to Liberty, and asked how he knew. "This is Bill Gillespie from Liberty." I was amazed. Bill Gillespie had been an assistant strength coach at Liberty University when I was a football player there. It just so happened that after my sophomore and junior years, I found a local job, stayed all summer, and trained on campus at Liberty with our strength staff — i.e., Bill Gillespie.

In 1985, it was not nearly as common as it is today for guys at small schools to stay all summer and train on campus. Consequently, Bill had a limited number of guys to train, or as we liked to refer to it, be guinea pigs. Bill and head strength coach Dave Williams loved to work on new stuff during the summer, which they could then use to train the guys throughout the year.

That generally meant a lot of discomfort for us. Bill liked me because I was willing to do whatever work would make me a better player and give me a chance to get on the field. To say I was the worst scholarship player at my position is probably pretty accurate. In fact, I have often held myself up as a motivator for other guys. Look, I've said; if I can walk on and earn a football scholarship, anybody can.

With his athletes arriving for their workouts, that first conversation with Bill ended quickly, but it led to many more. I learned that Bill had been at the University of Washington since 1991 working with football, and it wasn't long until he was in charge of strength and conditioning for the university's entire athletic program. He went on to the same job with the Seattle Seahawks of the National Football League, and then went back home to Liberty University.

Bill and I stayed in touch through the years, and it is safe to say I owe him a big thank-you for helping develop the underlying philosophy of our strength and speed program. When Sam Dollar and I made the seemingly endless treks across Alligator Alley during that first winter and spring, we were able to hammer out the program that would be the foundation for our success on the football field.

CHAPTER

22

1999

The first week of February 1999, we had four players sign scholarships to play college football: defensive back James Cody to the University of Central Florida, defensive back Titus Curry to Ferrum College, tight end Roshod Hampton to Carson-Newman College, and defensive lineman Johnson Marce to Avila University. That was a big deal for our players, and I was hopeful that it would give our younger players a sense of possibility.

I can remember several times in my life looking at someone doing something, and thinking to myself that if that guy can do it, I can do it. That sense of possibility is extremely important. It is life-changing when kids get hold of it.

In February, with the banquet behind us and college recruiters off the road, it was time to get our golf tournament fundraiser up and running. It was also time to prepare for spring football. Thankfully, I had enough help from some parents that we could pull off a profitable golf tournament without it becoming my full-time job.

Each day seemed to bring less time.

With what little time I had, I reached out to the local Pop Warner youth football coaches and asked them if they would like to come to our coaches' meetings so they could learn our system and implement it. My thinking was, since most of their players would be our players, it would make us that much better if the kids had a handle on our stuff when they came to high school.

In retrospect, I realize that the way I presented it to those coaches was a major faux pas. Those guys had been dominating the area for years. They would coach kids bound for Naples High, only to see them flounder, quit, or transfer to other schools after their freshman year. In the eyes of those youth league coaches, I should have been asking *them* to coach *me* up. Here I was, some young dude from Miami, the fifth head coach at Naples High in 10 years, and *I* was supposed to teach *them* how to coach football? "I don't think so, Scooter."

The other thing that I found out really bothered them was that during my whole coaching career, I didn't come to watch the young kids play. They played about a quarter-mile from the high school every Saturday, and I never went to watch. The coaches found it downright disrespectful, and in hindsight, I understand their frustration.

CHAPTER 22

Saturday was our coaches' game-plan work day. We usually worked from 7 in the morning until 4 in the afternoon. My thinking has always been to get the work done and get home to my girls. I suppose that I could have taken the girls with me to the Pop Warner game for a bit, but the truth is that by the time I got home on Saturday I needed family time and rest. When the girls were little, Sue would put a "Do Not Disturb" sign on the front door as soon as I got home on Saturdays, and the whole family would take a power-nap and recharge.

Like I said, I figured out the relationship with the Pop Warner coaches years later. During that second spring at Naples High we had zero takers on the invitation to our coaches meetings. We began meeting in March to prepare for spring football, which started May 1. In our effort to have every coach be not just on the same page, but on the exact same line on the same page, we went through everything. That meant how we would stand in the huddle, to what our checks would be as we anticipated what our opponents would do to us. In football, check is the term used when an offense or defense changes a play, formation, or scheme based on what they see after the other team lines up. At Naples High, we trusted our players to make checks in just about any scenario and at just about any time during a game. We could do that verbally, with hand signals, or sometimes with just eye contact. That was pretty rare in high school football at that time, and made it incumbent on our staff that our players not only know their job, but the entire scheme, and how the other team is trying to attack us.

Our second March in Naples was also a time that I was really praying and thinking about what our theme would be for the upcoming season. I always had a theme for the players and a theme for the coaches' retreat too.

The players' theme was pretty easy. Our goal was simply to make the playoffs, something that had not been done at Naples High in most of our players' lifetimes. I decided to get shirts made that said only "11-19-99" in classic block numerals; that would be the date of the first week of the playoffs in the upcoming season. I felt like navy print on the front of a white T-shirt would say it all.

It was soon clear to me that, as much as we talked about leadership to our players and each other, the coaches had no clear and consistent idea of what leadership was. To some of our guys, leadership was merely hollering at somebody when they were doing something wrong. We could do much better. So while the players' theme was simple and obvious to me, I was going to have to keep praying on, and looking for, what God would have me present at the coaches' retreat — which was fast approaching in August.

CHAPTER

23

The spring of 1999 was, in most ways, easier on us than the spring of 1998. We all had jobs and places to live. We also had a consistent idea of what our program should look like and what our football, educational, and social strategies and techniques would be with our players. One of the educational strategies we employed was weekly grade checks, in season and out of season. That was new for the players and for the faculty. We would have the players carry a grade-check sheet to each teacher every Friday, and ask the teacher to give up-to-date information about how that player was performing in class. The coaches would then either provide or set up tutoring for the players who needed it. Any blank for a class on a grade-check sheet was assumed to be an F, and treated accordingly.

Players either maintained C's or higher, or had tutoring. Players who missed tutoring were given O-P-P. It was a good idea, but it did have one flaw – the onus was on the players to get those forms filled out. Unfortunately, there were a few teachers who were too busy to fill out the papers. What a drag, if you were a player with a good grade in a class where the teacher would not fill out the sheet! The comment from those teachers was generally the same; it went something like, "We do interim progress reports or quarter grades every 4½ weeks. I don't have the time to do them weekly. What if every student wanted a grade check every week? I wouldn't have time for any teaching."

It was pretty frustrating. Here we were, trying to come alongside and provide academic support, and a few teachers thought it was too cumbersome to write down how the player was doing. Thankfully, the vast majority of the faculty found it doable and helpful. I also had allies in a few super teachers. Kelley Costin, one of our English teachers, was a dynamo and volunteered to be my academic coach. Kelley's experience as a tutor at Ohio State gave her all the tools she needed. She took it to the next level by keeping tabs on all of our players' grades and standardized test scores. Kelley was stellar in the classroom and tutored our guys tirelessly. Also, Gary Brown's daughter, Barb Coleman, was tremendous with the guys needing help in English; and her mom, Sandy Brown, a retired math teacher, was terrific tutoring our guys in math.

I went to Gary Brown for a powwow about how to hopefully gain cooperation from those teachers who were not willing to fill out the forms. We decided the best bet was for me to ask the various department chairs if I could visit with their group at their next department meeting. There, I could find out if any of them had a better framework for providing academic support.

Through the meetings, we came up with a more streamlined grade-check sheet that the teachers liked better, and soon we had nearly 100-percent cooperation on grade checks. Consensus isn't always possible, but the episode reminded me that the more often we can achieve it, the smoother things will go.

On the social end of things, I combined an academic passion of mine with a social passion. I have long firmly believed that reading is the key that opens up the door to the world. I told our guys countless times that life is a vocabulary test — the more words they could read and understand, the more opportunities they would have in their lives. I have also told them countless times that we all have spheres of influence, and that it is our responsibility to be a positive influence in our community.

In Miami, I had combined the two. We had a preschool on the campus of American High where students trained to work in child care. I had organized my guys there to go and read to the kids. I wanted them to impress upon those little kids how cool and important it was to read, and I wanted my guys to know the exact same thing. I also wanted my guys to know how important their demeanor and language were around those impressionable kids who were looking up to them.

Conveniently, Lake Park Elementary School is about a quarter-mile down the road from Naples High, right next to the park where I was missing all of those youth football games. My oldest daughter, Katie, was a kindergartner in Mrs. Lewis' class. Maureen Lewis was an accomplished teacher; one of the best I had ever seen at any level. I asked her if we could bring 12 to 15 boys to read to the kinders one day each week. She thought it was a fabulous idea, and after getting the approval of Lake Park's administration, we began an annual program.

So, once a week, beginning in late January or early February, a group of our guys would don their game jerseys and head to the elementary school to read to small groups of kindergarteners. It was incredible to see the excitement in the faces of those little kids. As far as they knew, our guys were Super Bowl champions. It was also interesting to see our guys interact with the little ones. Some of our biggest, toughest guys got completely intimidated and tongue-tied around them. It was a terrific growing experience for everyone involved.

On the football end, our guys were improving in strength and speed, albeit slower than I would have liked. Sam Dollar thought it would be a great idea to have a weightlifting meet right before the beginning of spring football, and to invite local schools to come participate. It would give our guys some motivation — something more immediate to shoot for when they were working out. As we explored doing that, the knee-jerk mantra that Collier County Public Schools administrators incessantly voiced was once again repeated: "You can't do that; we've never done that before."

After dotting every "i" and crossing every "t," we moved forward with it. Only one other school chose to participate. Mark Swanson, who had moved to Collier County from Miami just a few years prior, thought it was a terrific idea. One Saturday in April, just before the traditional May 1 start of Florida spring football, Swanson's Lely High football players came over. Weight class by weight class, they summarily dominated us.

Even so, our guys were improving. They were making strength gains, competing, and rooting for each other. All of that was tremendous improvement. More importantly, Paul Horne's terrific effort with the track team had produced a district championship. That gave everyone a little more confidence, and just a hint of swagger.

Spring practice was productive; but I think most — if not all — of our staff would tell you they were pretty numb by that point. We were all very tired. The undertow of the emotion spent throughout the year, combined with all of the stress of the previous 12 months, had left us all on autopilot. That was not necessarily a bad thing. We were loving the kids, taking care of the details, and maximizing each day.

One bright ray of sunshine that spring was working with our school's new athletic trainer, Sandy Andre. Sandy had been hired a few months earlier, and she was the perfect fit. Sandy was smart, an expert in her field, and a tireless worker. I was glad she would be on the sidelines with us for our second spring game in Naples.

The spring game would be on us before we knew it. An established program from the private American Heritage School in Plantation, Florida, would expose us pretty quickly if we weren't prepared for them. While Plantation American Heritage was a much smaller private school, they had a reputation of winning, and they had a good staff of coaches. It also helped that they were able to provide financial aid to some students, and several of those happened to be football players. That game gave us a chance to have a meaningful win, something we hadn't experienced in a long time, and a chance to uncover whatever weaknesses we might have had. We discovered that our defense was pretty darn good, and that our offense was young but had real potential. We walked away with a 12-0 win.

CHAPTER

24

On the physical plant side, our next big project was to get an industrial washer and dryer. Our locker room was nasty, period. The AC was iffy at best, and the stench was ridiculous. Faculty and students consciously avoided walking anywhere near the locker room doors. I would urge the team to take their stuff home and wash it, and then I would try not to come unglued when, on any given day, a few players would leave their stuff at home. There were also the guys who didn't take their stuff home at all. "Ripe" does not begin to express it.

The fact that other county schools had laundry rooms with commercial washers and dryers bothered me. I had visited Barron Collier's facility and saw their two sets of commercial washers and dryers (complete with folding tables), so I knew a washer and a dryer were doable. I began calling local business people, explaining our plight, and asked them if they would like to contribute toward the purchase of a commercial washer and dryer. I explained that in the gym remodel, which had been done some time before, the contractor had built a laundry room with all of the hookups. The trouble was, we did not have the equipment.

My plea fell on deaf ears. I decided to get folks to actually come take a look, or smell; perhaps that would motivate them. I called Garrett Richter and asked if he could possibly swing by, as I had something I wanted to visit about; it would take just a few minutes. He agreed, and I took him to the laundry room and the locker room. I asked if he could maybe come up with a list of folks I could approach about the problem.

We weren't even in football season, so the only thing the guys had stewing in their lockers was workout clothes. But that was enough. Garrett told me he was on it, and that I need not worry anymore about it. It wasn't long before he called and gave me the good news that a commercial washer and dryer were on the way.

I went to the laundry room to make sure we were cleaned up and ready for delivery. The room had hookups for a commercial washer and dryer. It also contained two regular-old household washers and two regular-old household dryers. During my initial tour, Ernie and Gary had explained they were old and didn't work. They also told me that the district had never had the money for a commercial washer and dryer, and certainly the school hadn't, so that equipment had never been purchased.

I had never really thought about replacing the household units, but with the commercial washer and dryer coming, I decided to raise money for a couple more of the household type so we could get as much laundry done at one time as possible. Time was a premium, since it would be me and whatever coaches I could get to help do the laundry each day.

I plugged in the broken machine, pushed in the knob, and turned it — just to see if perhaps it would be an easy fix. Nothing happened. I then tried the other washer and both dryers, and got nothing, nada, zilch. I figured that the breaker had been thrown at some point, so I went to the gym panel box to try to locate the one that had been thrown. I couldn't find anything marked for that room, or any breakers that were thrown.

I decided to see if perhaps somebody had capped off the wires in the electrical outlet box. After retrieving the little tool box that I kept in the football office, I moved one of the washers and removed the faceplate of the electrical outlet.

What I saw stunned me.

There were no wires, no Romex, nothing. I quickly checked the other electrical boxes in the room. All were empty — no wiring. I had just recently completed a remodel and had put in my own light fixtures, fans, outlets, etc., so I was pretty confident about what I was looking at. It just didn't make sense.

I went one step further and turned on the water spigot for the washer hose hookup. Nothing again. I took the spigot box off to look at the plumbing behind it, and there was none. Someone had just put up a façade.

The contractor had never put in the plumbing or the electrical.

Even the drain in the floor, the big commercial one for the commercial washer, was just a hole with a drain cover and no real plumbing behind it. Once I took the drain cover off, I could see a concrete hole about five inches down that someone had painted black and fastened a drain cover over. All I could think of was, "Wow, your tax dollars at work."

I got to Ernie and Gary as quickly as I could. When they saw what I had exposed, neither knew what to say. Somehow all of that had passed inspection, and a contractor had been paid for the work. After a couple of weeks and a few phone calls, Ernie came back and told me that the contractor was from Miami, had gone out of business, and the school district had no recourse.

In the meantime, the commercial washer and dryer had arrived. Garrett had come through, and now we had no way to use them. Gary and Ernie went through the school district chain of command and explained our situation, but the district's reply was that there was no way that they would retrofit that room. The expense was prohibitive. The fact that every other school in the district had a laundry room, and equipment provided by the district, was irrelevant.

I was feeling pretty demoralized when I picked up the phone to call Garrett and explain our plight to him. My assumption was that he would just have someone pick up the equipment (which was still on pallets), get his money refunded, and that would be the end of that. But I didn't know Garrett Richter.

Before I was through explaining, he told me he had to see it for himself. Garrett was as dumbfounded as I was when he actually stood there and saw the movie-prop room with his own eyes. It wasn't a long moment when he turned, smiled, and with a slap on my back, told me not to worry about it; he would be in touch.

Garrett got with Gary and, between the two of them, they convinced the district that enough people knew about the phony room that it would behoove them to make it right. Garrett Richter emphasized that he could not return the equipment, and it was best for everyone that the room be made usable.

Thankfully, within a month of the washer and dryer's initial delivery, the construction crew showed up; they began assessing the situation and what it would take to remedy it. It was soon apparent that it would be no easy fix. Fortunately, the district administrators were now committed to seeing the project through. New plumbing and drainage had to be brought in, along with a new transformer and breaker box, because our crusty, old gym was already maxed out and could not support the higher electrical demands required by the commercial stuff.

It wasn't until all of the plumbing and electrical work was done that one of the workers noticed that the door into the laundry room was too narrow to get the new machines into the room. By that time, cutting out and bracing new double doors was just a footnote to this absolute fiasco of a situation. All we wanted was clean laundry and some small effort to slow down what was brewing in the petri dish that was our locker room.

An unfortunate consequence of our awesome new laundry room was that a few folks higher up in the district food chain did not like the fact that their initial "no" eventually turned into a "yes." I soon heard rumblings in our building, and then beyond, that "Bill Kramer gets anything he wants." I can promise you this: if Bill Kramer got what he wanted, the coaches and I wouldn't have been doing loads of practice laundry every day in fall and spring; and sorting, stain-treating, washing, and stowing all the game stuff in the wee hours of the morning after games.

CHAPTER

25

School ended and summer began. We were back in full swing with our strength and speed training. Because of the size of our weight room, we had to offer three different sessions. We made a choice to train any athlete in the school; and of course, the kids paid nothing and the coaches made no money.

This was very different from my experience in Miami-Dade County, where our coaches were paid their hourly teaching rate to train kids during the summer. Kids would sign up, either through summer school or adult education, and for every 25 kids in the class we were allowed one coach. We could even split time between coaches. That worked great, and it made sense. We were doing the same work with the same liability we had during the school year, so we got paid just as we would during the school year.

This was not so in Collier County. Football coaches were volunteers in the offseason. Our coaches were truly inspiring in their commitment to train our kids and get them better. We read the research and knew that kids who are actively engaged in the summer — who are in programs where attendance is taken and there is caring accountability — are much more likely to abstain from, or significantly postpone, risky behaviors. I am convinced that in all of the years our coaches volunteered, January through July, they had an immeasurable positive impact on our community and on the kids in it. We had another weightlifting meet toward the end of the summer of 1999, and this time several schools showed up. Naples High was able to hold its own, which was a morale booster for all of us.

Summer training had gone forward as well as it could, and slowly but surely, the coaches' retreat had come together in my mind. As I read through different material and prayed, one theme and eventually one section of the Bible stood out to me. It was John, chapter 13. Most folks refer to this part of the Bible as the Last Supper. It really struck me and stuck with me that here was Jesus, with whomever you choose to call them — his crew, his assistant coaches, his associates, his band of brothers, his disciples, his posse, his co-workers, his adopted family, his followers, his . . . you get the idea. They were the people He loved and invested in with His very essence.

Here is Jesus on what He knows is his last night with them, and He has to leave them with the most relevant, the most important, the most precious stuff that He can convey. He needs to leave them with something that they will remember.

I've wondered many times what I would do in that situation. I think it would be mostly logistics. I would have to make sure my guys understood the geopolitical structure and the socioeconomic indicators which might enhance or hinder the work we had started together. I am pretty sure I would have had everyone come up with individual short-term and long-term goals, and specific behavior changes and timelines for accomplishing them. Perhaps I would have done a collective needs assessment, where we could define necessary attributes for success, rank-order them, and determine a hierarchy for accountability.

What did Jesus do? He hitched up His robe and washed the feet of His disciples. I heard a preacher once say that this task was generally left to the newest servant; the lowest person on the totem pole. At the most critical time, Jesus became the lowliest servant.

Therein lies the beauty. It is too simple for most of us to grasp. To truly lead in a positive direction, we must first simultaneously serve.

This is where many who would be leaders get lost. As our influence grows along with our list of responsibilities, we forget that authentic, positive leadership is action, not position. It seems we often forget that we are to model what we expect of others.

How many times have we seen someone we know ascend to a position of greater access and influence (in education it is the district office; but it might be corporate headquarters, the big leagues, or the Senate), and after a relatively short time in that position, our friend changes. He or she seems arrogant or aloof.

Very often, our friend comes to believe that the position allows him or her to be served more than in the past; and consequently, they are much less interested in serving others. In some cases, we see people become more interested in keeping their new job, status, access, etc., than in living the ideals they talked about en route to their new lofty perch.

Having said all of this, history has delivered numerous browbeating, negative leaders who nevertheless have experienced tremendous success, sometimes on a global scale. This phenomenon prompted a question that our coaching staff needed to answer. Knowing that we could bully and manipulate our way to success (at least the type of success that the fans, the media, and the world love to whoop and holler about), how would we go about our business? Were we willing to be servant leaders in our homes, in our school, and in our community?

Pretty heady stuff; stuff that is difficult to wrestle with and commit to on a coaches' retreat. It's the kind of stuff that is even more difficult to implement and stay committed to when stress, fatigue, and emotions come into play during the day-in, day-out grind of real life.

The only way I've found that it works is to choose to love those around you so much that being a servant becomes part of your DNA. And "serving" doesn't necessarily mean slaving away while the other person slacks off in self-indulgent bliss. It usually means coming alongside another, and striving with them, and working with them through difficult tasks or situations in the best way you know how. Sometimes, it is simply helping with the dishes or taking out the trash.

While discussing our roles as servant leaders, Jamie Lemmond expressed a concept that I had never thought of. It struck a chord in me. After we had all committed to being the servant leaders that God wanted us to be, Jamie very simply asked, "Well, what kind of servant are you going to be when you are treated like one?"

I had never thought of that, and the truth hit me hard. When I do serve others, when I am consciously humble and/or intentionally selfless, deep down I want my wonderfulness acknowledged. I want someone to notice, and if they don't tell me, then at least they should tell themselves that I am a really terrific guy — and isn't it great of me to do whatever wonderful or menial thing I am doing.

Jamie's question still hangs in the air. "What kind of servant are you when someone treats you like one?" The example he used was one of sitting in a restaurant for dinner. What if the server came and sat with us, wanted to be part of the conversation, and wanted to have a say in whatever we were planning or doing? Generally, this would not be OK. Normally, unless we ask our server to be a part of our conversation, we would prefer them to just stand by quietly. In the event that we spill something, they would be expected to come quickly and clean up. If they want a decent tip, they shouldn't let our water glasses sit empty for any length of time. We expect those who serve to do just that, and leave us to the really important stuff – decision making, socializing, or whatever. But, you say, that is their job; that is what they are paid to do. Well, what Jesus modeled for us is that we should make serving others our job.

Pretty simple concept: serve those you love. This would start with your immediate family and expand to the folks in your world that you are choosing to love — eventually, everyone around us. The Bible says, "Love your neighbor." Remember, love is always a choice. In fact, it is the ultimate choice. I am not suggesting that I have a handle on it or have it perfected, far from it; but I do know that as God grows me, it becomes more obvious to me when I am not loving others or when I am not a servant leader.

I remember coming home a few years after the 1999 coaches' retreat and pulling into the garage, and while I didn't hear God's voice, I had the distinct impression that the Creator of the Universe was tugging at me. What ran through my head was this question: What would I say to a player or a coach who came onto the practice field with the same enthusiasm that I was about to walk into my house with? The answer was simple: they would either get with the program, or I would send them home. I wouldn't care what the reason was. It wouldn't matter what caused their fatigue or malaise. I would remind them that we must be true to our core values, and that we must fake it if we don't feel it.

That night as I turned off the engine, all I wanted to do was get in the house, eat something, sit in front of ESPN, and just chill out. I had had enough. I thought I didn't have the psychic or emotional energy to help clean up after those energetic girls, or read to them, or help bathe them, or do the dishes, or recount my day to my wife, or whatever.

Then I remembered a verse in the Bible from the book of James that tells me I have to ask God when I want something. It also tells me I need to be asking for things that are in accordance with His will for my life. When we humbly ask God for strength to love others when we really do not feel like it, He provides us that strength – but we have to ask.

Right then and there, I bowed my head and asked God to give me the energy I needed to be the dad and husband he wanted me to be when I walked in that door. He did. And He has, every time I have asked.

The times that I walked in and have been less than the husband and dad I should be are the times when I have become too complacent or busy to pause and ask God for help in doing what He wants me to do. And whatever He wants of me, I am most certain that He wants me to be a great husband and a great dad.

One of the great strengths of our marriage and then our family is something that Susie said early in our marriage. We are on the same team. Next to God, we love each other the most, and we want God's very best for each other. Regardless of what is stressing us, we can get together, go to God in prayer, and confirm with Him and each other that we love each other, and we are on the same team.

CHAPTER 26

The 1999 football season began somewhat ominously. We took the hour-and-a-half bus ride north to Port Charlotte for the Kickoff Classic, and we wound up sitting through a lightning delay that caused the game to start two hours late. In the end, our defense was stellar, and our offense was just good enough to pull out a 13-12 win. What we found during the game was way more important than the final score. I had been shuffling the quarterbacks all preseason, trying to determine a starter. As soon as Stanley Bryant, a junior, entered the game in the third quarter, I knew. He wasn't a pure quarterback; his mechanics weren't textbook. And I struggled with moving him from linebacker, where he was perhaps our best defender. But this guy fit our definition of superstar to a T; he made everyone around him better. As soon as he entered the game, everyone raised their level of play. From that point on, there was no more quarterback controversy. Stanley Bryant was the man.

Rob Richter, our other quarterback, proved that he too was a superstar. He told me he would do anything and play any position which would make our team better. Both things happened. Stan and Rob were both terrific athletes and leaders. They supported and cared for each other and their team. Both were honest, hard-working, and humble. The highest compliment I can pay is that if my girls were old enough, I would have supported them dating and marrying either of those guys.

The next week was the official first game of the regular season, and we had to travel across town to Gulf Coast High School. We felt going in that we had a really good chance of winning, as they had been one of our three wins the previous year; plus, we had smoked them in a weightlifting meet during the summer.

The game started a bit rough for us, and we were looking at the wrong end of a 7-2 score early in the first quarter. After scoring 25 straight points before halftime, we were able to call the dogs off. Duane Coleman had a terrific night, rushing for 137 yards on just seven carries; Duane's performance was a precursor to what would become one of the most storied prep careers in the history of southwest Florida.

Week 2 found us traveling to Charlotte High School. Charlotte was a perennial power, and a heavy favorite to beat us. Because of the Rosh Hashanah holiday, we would play on Thursday night instead of Friday. That meant one less day to prepare during our work week. This game had been circled mentally on our schedule since the previous spring when the schedules came out. Coach

Dollar and Coach Horne had both worked hard to prepare themselves and our guys for an epic battle. We had worked on what we would do versus Charlotte since the beginning of football camp, so the shortened holiday week was not as big a factor for us as it might have been.

In the end, it was a perfect storm. Charlotte had just had a big win against a big-time program and were scheduled to play another really tough opponent the week after they played little, old, sorry Naples. Plus, they were playing at home, and everyone knew that the Charlotte Tarpons did not get upset at their place. In fact, any smart team prefers to avoid playing football at Tarpon Stadium. Their head coach, Binky Waldrop, was a Charlotte alum and a local sports legend. He was also a great coach.

The Dollar defense did a great job, and Charlotte helped us by turning the ball over four times. Duane Coleman was stellar again, rushing for 110 yards and two touchdowns. Stanley Bryant did a terrific job of running our offense, and best of all, protecting the football. We went into the locker room at halftime up 14-0, and when we tacked on a third touchdown in the fourth quarter, the fat lady immediately began humming. Our 21-0 victory was the first time Charlotte had been shut out at home that anyone could remember.

I will never forget Paul Horne running off the field and, in his exuberance, slapping the ever-stoic Ernie Modugno on the butt so hard that it lifted Ernie off the ground. I can only imagine the handprint welt that Paul embossed on Ernie's skinny butt. A few days later, Ernie asked me to inform Paul Horne that he should never do that again.

The slap on the butt was memorable for Horne too, and not just because of Modugno's warning. It represented a seminal moment in the transformation of Naples High from a footstool in the high school football world to a perennial powerhouse.

"We just dominated them," Horne recalled. "That was the proof to our guys that, if they did what we asked them to do, they would get results. Sam and Bill looked like prophets."

The first thing the coaches had asked the players to do was go to work in the weight room. "You can't measure weak on the level we were," Paul said of the days before weight training became the norm. The second thing that the coaches asked was for the players to work hard. Horne knew the program was on the right track when players would challenge each other over their efforts in practice. "If you're not going to work hard, you'll lose a lot of respect. The players were willing to fight to win. They established a work ethic they didn't really have before. That's kind of cool; those guys established that tradition," he said.

The third thing the coaches asked was for the players to simply come out for football. "We had a ton of kids on campus here," Horne said. But even though many had played youth football, too many quit after the ninth grade. Football wasn't a popular thing to do at Naples High, like it was elsewhere. "People liked to come out to see the band," he said. "They (the students) were just tired of losing."

Through those lean days prior to the Charlotte win, the coaches believed in each other. "We knew what we were doing would work. Our players had become stubborn, high-energy young men who wanted to be great." Beating Charlotte at their place was more than just another win. It was a transition point for Naples players and coaches alike.

Horne recalls doing something the coaches hadn't done before, and to his recollection, haven't done since. They took a picture in the Tarpon gym in front of a mural of the Charlotte mascot. "It was a terrible picture. It's dark, it's blurry – but we were so proud of it," he said. After Naples beat Charlotte, a lot of people took note. "We had this upward spiral of people believing what we said."

Among the new believers were Brown, and Modugno, who had suffered through the legendary butt slap. "Gary and Ernie were happy. They were starved for success. That was a fun night," Horne said.

The Charlotte win definitely changed things for us. By the time we got back to the school, we all knew we would not be sneaking up on anybody again. Beating Charlotte was a really big deal.

The famous picture from the Charlotte gym. I am in a different shirt because I had also experienced my first Gatorade bath.

Back: Ben Welzbacher, Sam Dollar, Bill Kramer, Dan McDonald, Tony Ortiz, George Bond. Front: Paul Horne, Marlin Faulkner, Ryan Krzykowski, Ron Byington, Jamie Lemmond.

CHAPTER 27

Immokalee is a rural farm town about 45 minutes east of Naples. During the interview process, I asked Ernie Modugno and Gary Brown which local team had the best athletes. They both agreed it was Immokalee; they also both agreed the Indians had been so undisciplined in the past that they were very beatable.

Immokalee had hired a new coach a year or two before we had come to Naples; what I saw on video was very different from what Ernie and Gary described. These Indians coached by John Webber were fast, physical, and disciplined. I knew that we would have to play really well to beat these guys. On offense they were very vanilla, but as Sam explained it, the coaches were really smart to keep it simple because the players were so big and fast. They could just bludgeon people to death. I also knew these were tough kids. After learning about I-Town from Ernie and Gary, I'd made a point to drive there several times on my way to or from Naples, just to get the lay of the land. What I found was a farming community very similar to where I had grown up in Yuma, Arizona. I also found authentic Mexican food that was both inexpensive and delicious — my favorite.

The most important thing I found was tough kids – tough little kids and tough big kids. I remember grabbing some tacos from a roadside stand and then finding a little side road where I could park and eat. It just so happened I had parked right next to a trailer park, which had an entrance that served as a school bus stop for what were obviously elementary kids. The kids bounced off the bus, and no sooner had the bus pulled away, than a bunch of these little dudes reached down, grabbed a bunch of rocks and began a really fun-looking rock fight between two teams. The fight had obviously been determined before anyone got off that bus.

It took me right back to the dirt-clod fights we used to have when I was little. Nobody got hurt, there were no eyes put out, and everybody learned how to throw, avoid being hit, and talk serious smack. I also realized that none of these kids were in a hurry to get home and do their homework, and that there were no parents waiting for them at the bus stop. This was very different from my wife's description of what she had seen when she was scouting out elementary schools and bus stops in the Naples High attendance zone. While I know that "tough" is always a choice we make, I also know that some kids are forced to make that choice sooner and more often than others. These Immokalee kids were tough. That was the beginning of the undying admiration

I have for the Immokalee Indians and the community that supports them.

I was worried about us letting down emotionally and losing some of our intensity after the big Charlotte win.

That did not happen.

Our guys played a very fast physical brand of football against Immokalee. The problem was, I did a poor job preparing our offense for their defense. We turned it over four times. Yup, count 'em . . . four, just like Charlotte had done the week before against us. Teams that give the ball away four times don't deserve to win. Duane Coleman once again proved to be a super soph, rushing for 170 yards on 15 carries; but our four turnovers, anemic passing game (2 for 14), and ridiculous and untimely penalties (12 for 120 yards) proved to be too much to overcome. Naples led for the first three quarters, but the Indians scored early in the fourth quarter to take a 15-12 lead. That would be the final score.

The week after the Immokalee loss, we had no game; it was our scheduled open week. It was a long week. All of us, coaches and players alike, were having a hard time getting over the loss. The players and coaches were working hard, and while football in October is normally a grind, it seemed like things were heavier than they should have been. I preached to the players that our goals had not changed after Immokalee. We were going to play on November 19 in a playoff game, I said, and the Immokalee game had no bearing on that goal. Such is the nature of high school football in Florida. District games determine your playoff fate, and thankfully, Immokalee wasn't a district game.

Our next opponent was Bishop Verot. They were 1-4 coming off of a 49-0 shellacking at the hands of Immokalee. This was the perfect storm for an upset — an open week and an apparently inferior opponent. The game began badly for Naples. Early in the second quarter, a Verot defender picked up a Naples fumble and ran it 65 yards for a touchdown. To rub salt in that wound, we had a punt blocked just before halftime that was downed at the 1-yard line. And just like that, Naples was down 12-0 at half-time. Verot's coach was smart; he ran the ball, ate the clock, and tried to play keep-away from us. But the Dollar defense proved absolutely dominating, holding Verot to 55 yards rushing and 0 yards passing. Eventually, we had enough offensive touches to score once in the third quarter and once in the fourth quarter. We were grateful for the 14-12 win when the final whistle sounded.

Week 5 of the regular season brought us to our second district contest, this one versus a perennial powerhouse — Venice High School. Our guys understood the importance of the Venice game, and practice had a great vibe to it all week. Many of our players had played against the Venice kids as they grew up in youth football; they knew the Venice players were very physical and would love nothing more than to physically dominate us.

Meanwhile, it was becoming obvious to Paul Horne and me that our opponents were figuring out that we really could not protect our quarterback very well when we wanted to throw the ball. We always stressed to our offensive players that the number one rule of passing the football is that a quarterback cannot complete a pass from his back. If we couldn't protect him, we wouldn't have success.

Getting guys open was the easy part. The fact was that we had some really small offensive linemen. Our right tackle weighed maybe 145 pounds, and he could not bench-press his body weight.

This was 5A Florida football, not itty-bitty, private school ball, where you might be able to hide a guy that small.

The good news was that our guys had made the choice to be tough. We practiced to be fast. We practiced to be physical. There was not a guy on our team who was backing down to anyone. Paul and I decided that our best bet was to run the ball, throw a little play action, and hang our hat on a dominating defense and the triple option. Our defense was playing lights-out. Sam Dollar was proving to be a defensive genius, as well as a really good teacher and motivator.

We learned an invaluable lesson in the game: effort, energy, and enthusiasm are not enough. We found out that we must also be disciplined.

Venice drove the ball on its first possession, their mammoth linemen controlling our guys up front. They scored the first touchdown on a 32-yard run. We came back and tied the game shortly thereafter, only to have the opposition's star running back cap another Venice drive with a 29-yard touchdown run late in the first quarter.

What looked like an impending scoring fest wound up as anything but; the Naples defense stiffened and shut down the Indians from Venice the rest of the way. Our offense moved the ball at will for the rest of the game; unfortunately, poorly timed penalties would be our demise. We wound up having two touchdowns and several big gains called back; we racked up ten penalties for 80 yards. The final score was 13-7.

Once again, Paul and I each felt completely responsible for the loss. We knew our defense was playing well enough for us to win, and we were determined to find a way for our offense to hold up its end.

When we came to Naples, Sam and Paul and I made a commitment to two-platoon, no matter what. That meant we had an offensive squad and a defensive squad, with no two-way players. That had never been done at Naples, and none of the teams we faced in southwest Florida did it, either. Something else we did was play our best players on special teams. Most teams used special teams to rest their best players and get their backups some playing time. That gave us a distinct advantage on special teams.

We also believed that a player who only has one position to practice gets twice as many practice reps as those who play two positions. If our coaching was effective, our player would be a great technician. Add to that our strength and speed program, and over time, we could turn a very average athlete into a very good football player.

Another advantage of two-platooning was the ability to make significant adjustments during a game, between series. That would be almost impossible when guys would play both offense and defense. We were very dependent on being able to change things up, series by series, as we huddled with our players on the sideline.

One big disadvantage to playing guys on both sides of the ball would occur when a player got hurt — those teams lost both an offensive player and a defensive player. That made a player really tough to replace.

To many, the best part of our two-platoon system was that more kids got to play. After all, this is what every kid wants to do.

So, two-platoon football sounds great in theory, but when our fans who had never seen it watched us lose to teams who played five or six players both ways, they got fussy. I was getting hollered at from the fence behind the bench, and as we walked into and out of the stadium. I had phone calls from concerned dads and a few fans.

In the end, we stuck to our guns. As the saying goes, the proof is in the pudding; or perhaps, the proof is in the winning. Five games into the 1999 season, and we were 3-2. If our two-platoon theory was correct, the extra reps our guys were getting in practice would make an impact pretty soon.

CHAPTER 28

By 1999, the Coconut Bowl had been played for 25 years. Naples High was the first high school in Naples, and Lely was the second. Kids from both schools had attended split sessions at Naples High while Lely was being built. When the two teams got ready to play their first football game, a couple of administrators and coaches from the two schools got together and made a trophy, which the winner would get to keep at their school. It is one of the most unique looking trophies anywhere. The top of it is a coconut which is laced like a football. The coconut is mounted on the cut-off handle of a baseball bat, which in turn is mounted on a square block of the heaviest and densest wood I have ever held. A brass plate is mounted on the base, and the score of each game is engraved on it.

In 1999, Lely held a 13-12 lead over Naples in Coconut Bowl victories. The game was sure to be a defensive struggle; Lely was holding opponents to 9.2 points a game, and Naples was holding opponents to 9.4 points a game. Lely was 5-1 coming in, and Naples was 3-2.

The Lely coach was Mark Swanson, and he was a class act. Mark was the only coach in the county who reached out to me when we came to town. He asked Sue and me to dinner, and he and his wife Mary Ann had been kind and encouraging. Mark and I had kept in touch a good bit during the year, and I knew from knowing him and watching his team on film that we were in for a real test.

Mark was smart, tough, and confident, and his team played that way. The game had way more offense than anyone had predicted, and thanks to our stout D and several Lely turnovers, we had a 17-0 lead at halftime. Our running game was starting to jell, and our players were fired up. We added another touchdown in the third to go up 24 points. Lely fought hard the whole way and tacked on 14 points in the fourth quarter; but it was too little, too late.

Senior running back Anthony Denson was stellar, rushing for 189 yards and two touchdowns. The pollsters were starting to notice us. For the first time since anyone could remember, we were ranked in the Top 10 in southwest Florida.

Next up was another district opponent, Mariner. Every player and coach knew we had to win if we wanted any shot at reaching our goal and making the playoffs, and we all prepared like it. We were 4-2 and Mariner 3-3, but each team was 1-1 in the district standings. It was to be a serious challenge for our defense.

Mariner running back Jason Robinson was the leading rusher from all of Lee County the previous season. To top it off, we were on the road.

This game wasn't a contest from the opening whistle. Our defense, which had given up only 75 points in seven games, was once again stout. We held Robinson to 95 yards on 24 carries. The big story was the Naples offense, which for the first time showed how lethal and efficient it could be when it protected the ball and created some space up front. We were up 21-0 at halftime, and wound up winning 39-13.

The NHS offense accumulated 571 yards, with Stanley Bryant throwing for 194 yards and two touchdowns to go with the 377 yards our guys pounded out on the ground. It seemed as though our theory of two-platooning was working. Our guys, who might not have been as good athletically, were becoming better technically, and were in better physical shape than most of their counterparts.

Week 7 found us at 5-2 with another non-district game at home, versus an all-boys private Catholic school named Belen Jesuit out of Miami. Belen was 4-2 and was a very good, well-coached team. We could tell from video footage that these guys were extremely aggressive and demonstrative. We could also tell that they did not have the speed to run with our wide receivers, especially sophomore Bruce Gordon. Our defense had a tough time with their wing-T offense, but our offense was playing with tremendous confidence. Bruce Gordon caught three Stanley Bryant touchdown passes, and he also returned a kickoff to the Belen 3-yard-line — which led to an easy score. The game ended in Naples' favor, 47-32.

Throughout the game, our guys kept complaining about their eyes getting gouged, groins getting punched, and general nastiness whenever there was an opportunity. In fact, our guys said that Belen was the dirtiest team they had ever played. There were several personal fouls called, nearly all on Belen, and the officials were constantly warning both sides to stop the shenanigans.

At the conclusion of the game, as we were crossing the field to shake hands, the Belen side of the stadium poured onto the field. All of the parents and fans were coming down and gathering around their team. I had never seen this, but was told later it was commonplace with some private schools, especially parochial ones.

A guy that we assumed was a player's dad came up to Sam Dollar screaming and fussing in a very strong Cuban accent; his brand of Spanglish was very difficult to understand. Sam reached out to shake his hand before realizing that the guy was angry. In Dollar's thick Oklahoma twang, he said, "Sir, what are you saying?"

The angry Belen dad spat, "Never in all of my years have I ever seen such a display of poor sportsmanship."

Sam calmly replied, "Yeah, I know . . . what's *wrong* with your guys?"

I thought that angry Belen Dad was going to explode right before my eyes. His ranting became completely unintelligible and loud enough that his own folks came and moved him away. I found Sam's cool response hysterical, and I laughed until my head hurt. Our record now sat at 6-2; with a win the following week, we would assure ourselves of making the playoffs.

Andy Kent was a local football writer. He was a really good writer and a really good guy. Andy wrote a piece that week under the headline, "Golden Eagle Bleachers Lack 12th Man," which reported that while we were one of the area's top teams, we still had lots of empty seats at games. I was grateful for the article, and hoped it might fire up our fan base a bit. After all, Naples High had been playing football for 50 years. I knew that a large, vocal crowd would be a morale booster and a force multiplier, and we would need both in the not-too-distant future.

Week 9 found us at home versus a winless Sarasota High team. A win and we would be assured of a playoff spot, and even perhaps a shot at our first district championship in 16 years. Our guys came out tight, and Sarasota played with nothing to lose. Halftime found us tied at 14; thankfully, our seniors came up big in the second half and our conditioning proved to be a huge factor. We scored 17 second-half points. Anthony Denson rushed for 185 yards, and the final score was 31-21. Naples was in the playoffs; the coaches and players were ecstatic after the game.

As soon as our game was decided, everyone was asking who won the Mariner vs. Venice game. If Mariner had somehow pulled an upset, we would win the district championship outright. If Venice won, there would be a three-way tie between Naples, Venice, and Charlotte by virtue of Charlotte's win over Venice earlier in the year. Each of us had one loss in district play.

Boo. Venice won. We were in a three-way tie.

We would play in a shootout on Monday night to determine the district champion.

CHAPTER

23

In 1999, a shootout was the way that Florida high schools broke ties for the football playoffs. Basically, the teams who are tied show up and play a round-robin tournament to determine the winner. Each segment lasted a quarter plus whatever amount of overtime was required, if the score in that quarter was tied at its end. I had been a part of a shootout in my second year as head coach at American High; what sticks out in my mind is how fast it went. We went three and out, and the other team held the ball for the rest of the quarter on a long, slow, scoring drive. We got the ball back as time expired. We didn't even break a sweat. "Thank you very much. Thanks for playing. See you next time."

The Week 9 Sarasota win had guaranteed we would be in the playoffs. The Florida playoff system in 1999 allowed for a couple of wild-card bids for teams that did not finish as the district champ or runner-up, but still had very good records. By virtue of our 7-2 record going into the last week, we were already assured a playoff spot. The shootout would determine seeding for the playoffs. It would also determine if we played at home or on the road. Winning the district was huge, as we would then have a home playoff game against a very low-seeded team — in other words, a fighting chance. Going into the playoffs as a wild card was basically the kiss of death. It guaranteed an away game against a 1-seed or 2-seed team, a guaranteed powerhouse. It would be asking for punishment: "Thank you sir, may I have another?"

I was worried about the mindset of our players. Two thoughts struck me. First, Venice at 6-3 and Charlotte at 4-4 were not guaranteed wild-card spots; they would be fighting for their football lives. Our guys had already achieved our big goal; the T-shirt came true. We would be playing on 11-19-99.

The second thought was that after playing a Monday night shootout, we would have to play our big rival Barron Collier four days later without our usual preparation time. Naples had not beaten Barron Collier in 13 years.

Even so, when we watched their game video, it looked like Barron's winning streak was going to end. The fact was that they simply were not a very good football team. While records don't always determine the outcomes of games, there were good reasons that Barron was 2-7 and Naples was 7-2. Our players realized this, and were eager to get a win on the same field, where a little over a year prior, their friend and teammate had left in an ambulance.

In the meantime, we had to get ready for the shootout. We had little time to prepare for it, as the contest was scheduled for

Monday night at 7 p.m. The state determined that Charlotte was the most central spot for the shootout, so the Tarpons benefited by having a home game.

Our coaches had been working on shootout game plans all week. Now we had one day, Saturday, to put the game plans in. We also had been burning the midnight oil, preparing for Barron Collier as best we could. We knew in advance that if we played in the shootout, we would have one less day to prepare for Barron Collier.

Because Naples had the best record, we were given a first-round bye. We would play the winner of the Venice-Charlotte rematch. If Venice won and we beat them, we would be crowned district champions for the first time since 1982. That would end a 17-year championship drought.

We had brought our home and away jerseys on the bus with us, and decided to warm up wearing our white (away) jerseys. We would be the visitor if the Venice Indians won, and would be considered the home team if the Charlotte Tarpons won. Since the season matchups were what they were, we had beaten Charlotte soundly and lost to Venice 13-7. We felt pretty confident that Venice would beat Charlotte.

For the record, we would always warm up in full gear. Many teams would come out with no helmets or shoulder pads, or just helmets; they usually would have on some real tight-fitting shirts with cut-off sleeves. In our case, I did not want to embolden our opponents by letting them see us out of pads. If they saw our skinny little guys without gear, they would be convinced they could never lose to Naples High.

The format of the shootout was simple: one quarter of play, followed by overtime if necessary. Warmups were weird, with three teams needing to warm up. Since we were not playing until the first game was finished, we really didn't have a great timeline for warming up. About an hour and a half before the shootout began, we went out onto the nearby softball outfield and did the best we could to exercise.

About half an hour before the first kickoff, we exited the stadium to get back to the locker rooms. We wanted to give the players a chance to use the restroom and hydrate before the shootout started. Half an hour before game time, there was hardly an empty seat in the place, with hundreds leaning on the fence that separates the field from the stands. Every media truck in southwest Florida was there. It hit me that this was a big moment.

I made a conscious effort to be nonchalant. I knew I'd better send a confident message to our guys, none of whom had ever been in such a bright spotlight. Our pit stop did not take long, and we soon took our place in the area of the stands that had been set aside for the team in waiting. We were not far from the staging area, where we were to move as the game was decided.

From the outset, Charlotte had their way with Venice. As the quarter went on, it was obvious to all of us that we might be wearing the wrong jerseys. With a few minutes left and Charlotte with the ball, we moved our guys onto our staging area. With 20.6 seconds remaining in the game, Charlotte scored the go-ahead touchdown, and the place erupted.

We immediately had our guys start changing into the home jerseys, as it was evident that Charlotte had the game in the bag. Thankfully, Coach Dollar had already directed some of the coaches to get the home jerseys ready, so we would not waste warmup time switching jerseys. Sam also pulled out his Charlotte Wing-T defensive game plan, and started getting into his best defensive-savant mode.

Charlotte squibbed the ensuing kickoff, and Venice wound up in decent field position. With 20 seconds and 55 yards to go, a Charlotte victory seemed inevitable, but Venice would not go without a fight. They used 9.4 seconds to throw a hook and lateral that moved the ball down to the Charlotte 42-yard-line. Then, with time running out, Venice quarterback Shane Williams scrambled around, broke a couple of tackles which would have ended the game, and threw a Hail Mary pass at the corner of the end zone — right in front of where our guys were standing, ready to enter the field. The ball seemed to stay in the air approximately an hour and a half before Venice's Richie Marshall plucked it out of the air, just inside the goal line, to tie the game.

Yes, the game was tied. On their previous touchdown, Charlotte had failed to convert the extra point, and now Venice was lining up for a kick with no time on the clock. As the ball sailed through the uprights, all of our coaches began hollering for our guys to **change back** into our away jerseys.

We would now be playing Venice, just as we originally thought.

Our quarterback, Stanley Bryant, was as poised and focused as any player I had ever coached; I felt good about our chances as long as he was on the field. It had been an amazing transformation to watch Stan from the time he walked forward at the conclusion of Rusty's funeral and made a real commitment to God. He was going through a metamorphosis right before our eyes.

When I first met Stan, he was concerned about all the stuff that pop culture lies to our guys about. Pop culture teaches us lies from the time we are small boys until the time we die. Unfortunately, these lies are lethal to families; and consequently, to the very fiber of our country. From the time we start school, boys acquire status if they can demonstrate athletic ability or physical dominance. If Johnny is the fastest in the class, then he is bragged on and given status. If Johnny can beat up the other kids and impose his will, then he may or may not be bragged on, but he is certainly given status.

While we should certainly celebrate the God-given speed and strength that little kids have, those attributes are just that – God-given. Parents should acknowledge that their children's abilities are from God. When moms and dads brag on their kids and don't acknowledge the God-given part of it, they are really bragging on themselves. The implication is that the child got that ability from them, not God, and that they and their child are somehow more valuable than others.

As boys grow into men, the physical ability accolades are joined by two other status lies; and these are being told all around them, all the time, in every form of media. These are, in no particular order: having sex outside of marriage is expected and OK; and money and access will make you happy. All around us, every day — in advertising, music, TV shows, movies, magazines, and nearly everything online — our guys are taught the lie that they should have sex with as many women as possible, as often as possible.

What is interesting to me is that nearly all of the authors, actors, performers, and producers who shove this idea down our throats would be devastated if the person they love and trust were found sleeping with someone else. Yet, they continue to depict sleeping with whomever one finds attractive as the common thing to do. Subsequently, many men and women grow up with the expectation that, unless you are some sort of religious nut, you are going to do this — at least to some extent. This is a relatively new phenomenon in our country. While promiscuity and infidelity in marriage is not something new, promoting it as accepted behavior is.

The problem and the solution are the same, based on the fact that you get what you train for. I remind my students and our players all the time that, each moment and each day of our lives, we are training for something. If you eat a bunch of food and lay around on the couch afterwards, then you are training to look like a sumo-wrestler. If you constantly check your phone and post on social media, then you are training to be dependent on social media for your affirmation – as opposed to relying on God, family, and friends. If you play video games during every spare moment, then you are training to be really good at that, as opposed to developing skills and acquiring tools for successful living.

So the question remains: what are we training for? If a young man is trying to have sex with all of the girls that he is attracted to, then that is exactly what he is training for. The problem is that when he gets married, it is extremely difficult to undo that training. And so we have the divorce rate for first marriages in the U.S. at 41 percent, second marriages end 60 percent of the time, and three is not a charm – third marriages have a 73 percent failure rate. No surprise there — what did you train for?

Imagine if our guys trained themselves to love their wives from the time they are married until the time they die. Love is a choice we make. And imagine if our guys treated every girl they met like she could be "the one" – and she is, for sure, someone's "one." What would that look like? If a young man can be self-disciplined in that area of his life, then he can be self-disciplined in any area of his life. If we as a society want strong, well-disciplined men — men who can show restraint and place a high value on women — training young men to love would be a great place to start.

In the right context, sex is one of the greatest gifts that God has given mankind. The problem is that sex appeals to everyone; it feels really good. Men are especially provoked visually; consequently, sex sells. And we have a culture that worships the dollar bill.

This is a great segue for lie number three: the notion that money equals happiness. Our young men are being buried with this one.

When I talk to my guys, I call it money/access. It doesn't necessarily have to be your own money; you can just be a cling-on in the entourage to get behind the ropes. Once again, pretty much everywhere you look, wealth is celebrated and revered — in music, videos, movies, and advertising. We don't just buy stuff, we buy the best new stuff that others don't have. The best is simply not good enough if it is not the latest, best stuff. The fact that the old best stuff looks and works just fine is irrelevant. We just don't measure up without the latest, best stuff.

I often ask myself and my players this question: "What is better than having more?" The often-ignored answer is quite simple: "Having enough."

CHAPTER 30

At game time of the shootout, none of that was going through my mind. What was going through my mind was that Stan Bryant was the right guy to lead us. He had become a servant leader, and had an incredible strength in his humility. I tried to remind our guys all the time that humility is not thinking less of ourselves; it is thinking more of others.

Stan had a tremendous amount of confidence and swagger, and he was a man for others. He made a habit of setting exceptionally high standards in his conduct and speech. Stanley went out of his way to encourage and care for his teammates. Stanley was a strong, real man.

As the quarter began, with Stanley at the helm, ours was a very confident team. Venice was full of confidence as well. Beating

Charlotte as they had on the last play had them feeling that the district championship was their destiny. The quarter went fast, as both teams decided to pound the ball in the run game. We did a good job moving the ball initially, but we stalled in the red zone and had to settle for a field goal.

Venice pounded the ball at us again, and with about 15 seconds left and the Indians on the Golden Eagles' 46, it looked like Naples was about to be district champion for the first time in nearly two decades. Again, Venice made a spectacular play, a 23-yard completion that put them in field goal range at the Naples 23. The Indians had a good kicker in Adam Gold, and with 3.8 seconds left in the quarter, his 40-yard field goal knotted the score at 3. We would go to overtime.

The overtime format was simple. The ball would be placed at the 10-yard-line going in, and each team would be given four downs to score. In the event that a touchdown was scored, the scoring team could opt to kick for one point or go for two. In the first tiebreaker, Venice ran the ball for three downs before their quarterback, Shane Williams, went in from the 1-yard-line on a quarterback sneak. On our first possession, Stanley threw a hitch to Bruce Gordon, weaved through a couple would-be tacklers, and the score was tied at 7.

It was our turn with the ball first on the second tiebreaker, and after three consecutive runs, we were faced with a fourth down from our own 2. I didn't have any reason, other than my gut telling me, to go for the touchdown instead of the field goal. On fourth down, Stanley Bryant read the option, kept the ball, and found his way into the end zone. Our sideline erupted as the officials' hands went up, and the point after touchdown made it Naples 17 and Venice 10.

But Venice wasn't done. After a Shane Williams 5-yard TD run and an Adam Gold PAT, the score was tied at 17.

In the third tiebreaker, Venice's great back, Tre Smith — who would later play at Auburn — made a terrific play and made it look easy as he scored from the 10. Not to be outdone, our junior running back, Anthony "Junior" Denson, made his own great play and also scored from 10 yards out.

The fourth tiebreaker found Naples with the ball first; the stadium was going nuts. Every person was on their feet and cheering wildly. Naples fans were for Naples, Venice fans were for Venice, and Charlotte fans were for Venice. The Charlotte contingent knew that their only hope to move forward was for Venice to win. A Venice victory would give Charlotte a quarter to play against us for a shot at runner-up in the district and a guaranteed playoff berth.

I remember looking at the scene around me, and being grateful for the experience for our players and coaches. Regardless of the outcome, there was simply no substitute for this experience. Who, in their lifetime, gets to go four overtimes in a championship game? Close to nobody, right?

I cannot for the life of me remember any of the next three plays, but I do remember finding us at fourth and 1, and having to decide if we were going to attempt a field goal or try to get in from the 1-yard-line. Paul Horne and I both believed that if we couldn't get in the end zone from the 1, then we didn't really deserve to win anyway.

We called a quarterback sneak. Stanley Bryant did it once again, and after the PAT, Naples was up 31-24.

The crowd at that point was deafening. It was affecting our communication with our players, and I am certain it was affecting Venice's too. I remember seeing Charlotte players jumping up and down in the staging area, waving their jerseys over their heads, imploring the crowd to make noise. It was like the volume knob was turned to 11 and then broken off. Venice did what anyone with a brain would do. They gave the ball to Tre Smith. Once again, he found the end zone from 10 yards out. With the game knotted at 31, Paul Horne was yelling into the headset, "Next time we score, we go for two! Let's end this!"

Paul had asked me twice before to go for two, but I had said no. After scoring on fourth down twice, I just didn't feel comfortable going for two points; I didn't think our guys were in a solid enough emotional state to pull it off. I assured Paul that the next time we scored, regardless of the situation, we would go for two. As Venice lined up for the PAT, Sam asked if he could take a timeout, and I told him he absolutely could.

Sam is a genius at blocking kicks. I would have liked nothing better than for us to stuff this thing and go home. Sam went onto the field, and was in the midst of getting the block just right when Venice Coach Nick Coleman called his PAT team off the field. On trotted Tre Smith and company; Venice was going for two.

We immediately called timeout. Coach Dollar now had to switch gears and get his guys ready to defend what would be the final play of this incredible battle. Everyone in the stadium knew Tre Smith was getting the ball, and Sam Dollar knew with pretty good certainty what the play was going to be. Coach Dollar made a defensive call that guaranteed that one of our toughest and best defenders would be one-on-one with Smith to make the tackle.

So here we were, one play from the 3-yard-line; and this, for the whole enchilada. Venice QB Shane Williams took the snap and tossed the ball wide to his right, where Tre Smith caught it at about the 5-yard-line. Coach Dollar had been right, and standing between Tre and the win was our defensive end, Zach Sutter. Zach Sutter was as tough as nails, a kid that Sam had to drag to get his equipment on the last day that was permissible before practice began. But Zach had embraced the program, and now was one of the best football players Naples High had seen.

Zach had banged his shoulder a few weeks earlier, and was playing in a harness that would only let him raise his arm to just below shoulder level. Zach played the toss perfectly, containing Tre Smith. Tre was forced to cut back inside, where Zach was able to fit on him and grab hold. The only problem was, that dang harness limited Zach's range of motion. He simply wasn't able to get a firm grip on Tre, and in the blink of an eye, Tre was crossing the goal line. The air was sucked from the lungs of every player and fan in navy and gold.

The Venice players and fans were going berserk. It was the Super Bowl, minus the confetti cannons and balloons.

I knew I had a problem. In about 20 minutes, we were going to have to line up and play against a really good Charlotte team — a team which was chomping at the bit to get a chance to redeem themselves and earn a spot into the playoffs. The one thing I had in the back of my mind was that by virtue of our 7-3 regular season record, we were guaranteed a playoff spot.

In our case, we were playing for an opportunity to play anyone other than powerhouse Tampa Hillsborough, which was undefeated and ranked fifth in the state. If we beat Charlotte and finished as runner-up in the district, we would play a mediocre Pinellas County team and have a much better chance of escaping a first-round playoff game with all of our body parts intact. Charlotte was in a must-win situation. Their record made it impossible to advance without beating us; knowing that was a force multiplier for their guys.

We got our guys as composed as we could, as quickly as we could. By the time we had the Naples players composed, the Venice players composed, and actually got through the handshaking line, Charlotte was already in full warmup mode. Our first task after shaking hands was to get our guys together and think about their assignments from the Charlotte game plan. We also had to change back into our navy jerseys.

We gathered the team, and I asked everyone to take a deep breath. I reminded them that we still had work to do. The good news was, we were warmed up and ready to go, unlike Charlotte. The Tarpons had been sitting and watching for some time. I assured our guys that this gave us a distinct advantage.

I didn't talk about the fact that we were guaranteed a playoff spot. I did remind them that Charlotte was in a must-win situation, and they were fighting for their season to continue. All of their seniors would be playing with more intensity and effort than they had ever mustered in their lives. I privately hoped that they, their coaches, and their fans would put so much pressure on those Charlotte seniors that they would implode under it. I hoped they would come out tight as a drum and consequently play slow and tentatively.

Charlotte won the toss and elected to receive; we would play one more 12-minute quarter. On Charlotte's first possession, senior wingback Bruce Gipson took the ball around the left side and raced 54 yards before being knocked out of bounds at the Naples 1-yard-line – so much for them pressing, playing tight, and all of that stuff. You can't blame a coach for hoping. With less than two minutes eclipsed in the quarter, Charlotte quarterback Jeff Corsaletti took it in from the 1 to give the Tarpons a 7-0 lead.

The will of our young program was being forged, and I was proud of the way our guys responded to the Charlotte touchdown. Stanley Bryant engineered a drive, in which he completed all three of his attempted passes. The last one was a 37-yard touchdown pass to Bruce Gordon to put Naples on the board with 6:50 left in regulation.

Unfortunately, the PAT was missed, and we found ourselves once again trying to rally the troops. Few outside of football understand how demoralizing a missed extra point can be. All of the Naples coaches were determined to control what we could control. We exhorted our players to keep fighting, to win the next play, and to be the very best they could for the guy next to them. During the next three plays, Gipson was on a mission; he ran the ball in each of those plays, for a total of 42 yards. With 3:41 left in the quarter, Gipson broke loose from 9 yards out — and just like that, we were down 14-6.

I was convinced we would score and I was eager to try the two-point conversion play, which Paul Horne had repeatedly asked me to run against Venice. We were able to move the ball, but time was against us. We were soon out of timeouts. With under five seconds remaining and the ball on the Charlotte 13-yard-line, we once again found ourselves in a fury of sound and energy that was on the edge of overwhelming.

I called a pass play we all believed in. As the huddle broke, I hoped against hope that we had the tools we needed to make this play. As the ball was snapped, the Tarpon defense pressured Stan almost immediately; he scrambled and made an incredible play. With Charlotte defender Brandon Angelini hanging from his back, Stan's final throw found the open space in the back of the end zone. Unfortunately, our receiver was unable to track it down, and the ball landed on the turf, incomplete.

Once again, our guys had to watch utter mayhem as the Charlotte players and fans rushed the field and lost their minds. Our guys mostly stood or fell or bent over wherever it was they happened to be; most of them with their mouths open, some crying. Sheer disbelief was our trophy of the day.

As we got our guys composed and in the handshaking line, I had two indelible impressions. First, I was grateful that our coaches and players had that opportunity on that stage. There is no substitute for what legendary University of North Carolina women's soccer coach Anson Dorrance calls the "competitive cauldron." Second, I knew that while we had given a terrific effort and had no regrets, we could have had more in the tank and more in the toolbox if we had treated each day in the offseason as if it were a shootout. The fact is that our players had never before played as hard, been as focused, or been as completely committed as they were in that shootout.

Therein was the problem. We needed that kind of effort, energy, and commitment to be our normal level, not the occasional high-water mark. As I shook hands with legendary Charlotte head coach Binky Waldrop, I knew right then and there exactly what our theme for the ensuing football season would be: "For Naples High, Every Day Is A Shootout."

My epiphany did nothing to ease the ache from losing both games of the tiebreaker. The bus ride home was miserable. We'd brought sandwiches from our school cafeteria for after the game, but there weren't many guys eating. Everyone was pretty bummed out.

We were right there. We could taste victory. In the end, instead of being the cream of the crop, we were simply the cream of the crap. I had to get our guys through their funk as quickly as possible. We had to line up and play Barron Collier in four days – we had a short work week to prepare for a team we hadn't beaten since 1986. Thirteen years is a long time.

We got back to the school and had the usual tasks. Hurt guys needed to be assessed by the trainer; equipment needed to be put away; laundry needed to be sorted, destained, and washed. I got home late, and the girls were in bed already. I gave Sue a big hug, and she gave me an even bigger one. I could tell she was disappointed for our guys. No one roots harder for Naples High football than Susan Kramer. I went in as I usually did, and kissed the girls goodnight. It always takes my breath away to see my babies sleeping. In that moment, they were the closest thing to angels I have ever seen.

CHAPTER 31

Naples vs. Barron Collier was not a friendly rivalry. It was one in which the losers felt they were victims, and the winners felt they were some master race. To get a sense of perspective, a little history from Brent Batten might help; a little history and perspective that I did not have the week of the last regular season game in 1999.

Naples, Florida, began as a wilderness outpost in the latter half of the 19th century. Inlets interrupting the miles of white sand beach provided shelter for fishermen working the area's waters. Promoters — hoping to build winter tourism — came up with the name based on its climate, said to be similar to that of Naples, Italy. In 1887, Kentucky newspaper magnate Walter N. Haldeman purchased much of the land under what is now Naples and set about a series of improvements, the most notable of which was a T-shaped pier extending into the Gulf of Mexico. The lack of roads into Naples made this pier the favored arrival and departure point for the seasonal residents who comprised the bulk of the population. A year later, the first school opened in a rented house.

In 1911, Barron G. Collier, who had made his fortune in streetcar advertising, bought over a million acres in and surrounding Naples, on the belief that it could one day be developed similar to Florida's east coast. Barron Collier promised to spend more than $1 million of his own money to build the Tamiami Trail, a road linking Naples to Miami. As a reward, the 1923 state Legislature created Collier County, which had been part of neighboring Lee County until then, and named it after him. The road opened in 1926, but the growth that Collier envisioned didn't happen – at least not then.

Barron Collier's vision of growth for Naples began to come true in the 1960's, and by 1973 Lely High — named for the development company that provided the land for the campus — was added east of downtown Naples. Five years later, another high school, named for the advertising mogul whose heirs still owned most of Collier County, opened its doors to the north.

The early years weren't kind to the Barron Collier High School football program. When it opened, Barron Collier had no football stadium. Its home games were played at either Naples or Lely. Butch Manley, Barron's first principal, said that was a problem from the start. "You play football to bring a sense of purpose to your school. How do you do that when you're playing away all the time? It was kind of demoralizing."

More demoralizing were the results on the field. Scheduling smaller schools as opponents, Barron managed to win three games its first year in existence. Against stiffer competition over the next two years, the program went 0-20, Manley recalled. He singles out a 77-7 loss against east coast powerhouse St. Thomas Aquinas as one of the low points. Another low came in Barron's first meeting with Naples, a 53-7 shellacking in which Naples wrapped up the scoring by kicking a field goal. "That put a bad taste in our mouths," he said.

As a growing school, Barron Collier was able to add teaching positions every year. That meant it could attract coaches and assistants by offering them not only the football job, but a classroom job as well. By 1984, the gap was narrowing. Naples was up 10-3 late. Barron Collier scored and was poised to tie the game – only Barron Coach Dave McCarney wasn't going to settle for a tie. He went for two and made it. Then a flag came out. Barron had 12 men on the field. They lost 10-9. Manley said he found McCarney walking alone on Goodlette-Frank Road near Naples High after the game. He had to talk him into the car and calm him down. "I guess that's when I realized the rivalry had gotten pretty intense," Manley said.

The 1986 school year brought yet another coaching change to Barron Collier High. Before incoming coach Dave Tanner took the job, Manley told Tanner, "I'm tired of being everybody's homecoming game." After nine years of football frustration, while being competitive with Naples in the other sports, Barron Collier's team under Tanner finally broke through with a win against Naples. It was the start of a 10-game winning streak, in which the tables were turned from those early years.

Without the growth experienced at Barron, the Naples program was stagnating. Promising players who had attended elementary and middle school in Naples' zone began showing up on the Barron Collier roster, leading to the suspicion that Tanner was illegally recruiting players. In spite of investigations by the school board and the state, the allegations were never proven. Manley said it was more a matter of players from broken homes choosing to live with a parent in the Barron district over living with one in the Naples district.

"All of that was difficult for the average person in the community to understand," Manley said. Nevertheless, the sight of former Naples prospects excelling in Barron's blue and white aggravated the Naples faithful, especially after Barron began reeling off wins in the manner that Naples had a decade earlier.

"Each time the shift happened, the tendency was to pour it on a little bit," said Gary Brown, the assistant principal — and later principal — at Naples High when the rivalry was building. "Over time, hard feelings developed." Brown says that personalities also factored into the intense Naples-Barron Collier rivalry. Manley was a former college football player at Purdue and competitive by nature, as was Dan White, the Naples principal from 1980 to 1993, who played quarterback at Akron University.

"That's how it started; the personalities of the two principals," Brown said. Manley doesn't dispute the fact that the personal conflict that he had with White played into the rivalry, spilling out particularly onto the football field. "Without question, Dan and I were competitive," he said. "In retrospect, it wasn't good.

It not only created a problem with the schools; it created a problem in the community, and a problem with the school board."

As intense as the local rivalry was, it was just that — local.

Says Modugno, "I still remember the first interview with Bill Kramer. Bill said, 'I've never heard of Barron Collier. If you're hiring me to beat Barron Collier, you're hiring the wrong guy. I'm here to win a state championship.'" Adds Brown, "He couldn't believe there was such a rivalry between Naples and Barron Collier. We weren't even in the same district. To Bill, the district is what matters. This was kind of new to him."

CHAPTER 32

As Barron week 1999 began, I still didn't fully grasp the level of animosity between the two schools. What I did know was, Barron was a 2-7 team and Naples was a 7-2 team. There was no way we should lose to these guys. What had happened in the years before didn't matter.

Normally, we review the video of our Friday night game the Saturday morning after the game. The coaches are in by 7 on Saturday mornings; we grade every play and write up grade sheets for the players. The players came in at 9 or 10, depending on what time we had finished up the previous night. (Away games could find us getting off the yellow "cheese wagon" buses in the wee hours of the morning.)

When the players arrived on Saturday mornings, coaches gave them their grades. Then, together in position groups, we dissected the game — play by play. After that I would take the players to the field; they would do an aerobic run, stretch, and go home.

Things were different as we passed the *Welcome to Naples* sign that night after the shootout. Because it was a Monday, we all had school the next morning — which threw our regular Saturday schedule out the window . Everyone was pretty tired. It had been a long season, and we were now going into our last regular-season game. We were looking forward to a heated backyard rivalry, followed by a playoff game versus behemoth Tampa Hillsborough, a team the pundits would favor by at least 28 points.

Before heading home, Sam, Paul and I powwowed and decided we would forgo watching the shootout video; our time would be best used getting the players prepared for Barron Collier.

Barron did have some outstanding players, namely Chris Resop and Renald Joseph. Resop was a big, strong-armed quarterback who would go on to a terrific career pitching in Major League Baseball. Joseph was a strong, fast back who could shake your boots off in the open field.

Tuesday's practice went better than I expected. We had come out of the shootout healthy, and our guys knew what was ahead of them. They understood that Barron had an extra day to prepare, and that BC would do whatever they could to keep their win streak alive. We had all seen their coaches — and many of their players — in attendance at our shootout, and they were definitely taking notes.

We were at least as determined to end the Barron Collier win streak as they were to keep it. Our seniors especially knew that this would be a chance to get a monkey off our back – a monkey that their older brothers and cousins could not shake. Our seniors had been 4 or 5 years old the last time Naples had eked out a 3-0 win versus BC. Our coaches felt confident. We knew we should win the game; if we didn't give it away with uncharacteristic turnovers, we would.

By Friday, our guys were a quiet and confident crew. It was calming to our coaches to see our players' demeanor. They expected to beat Barron, and it wasn't going to be a big deal when we did. Or so I thought.

The game was at Barron Collier, and by the time the ball was kicked off the place was packed. Naples fans were hoping to see the demons exorcised right in front of their eyes, and Barron fans were expecting to see the upstarts put back in their place.

On our first play from scrimmage, Stanley Bryant read our triple option perfectly, wound up keeping the ball himself, and scampered 35 yards. Paul and I wanted to pound the ball, running it right at the BC defense, and we did just that. Plugging along at 3 or 4 yards a clip, we were soon inside the Barron 20-yard-line. As one might expect in a rivalry game, the Barron defense stiffened. What I did not expect was Naples to miss our attempted field goal. The change of possession gave the Barron offense the ball at their own 20, and also gave the Barron defense a good dose of confidence.

That was exactly what I didn't want to happen. In rivalry games, it is said, you can throw the records out. The reason is that the players and coaches of the underdog team are going to bring more passion, effort, and focus to their preparation and play than they do in any other game. What I didn't want to happen was for us to stall on offense, turn the ball over, or miss field goals. That kind of play would allow Barron to hang around, gain confidence and momentum, and fuel the fire that burned in their underdog belly.

Thankfully, Coach Dollar, Coach Byington, and Coach Lemmond had our defense ready to go. Our guys got after Barron and forced them to punt the ball back to us. We started deep in our own end, and again, we were able to pound the ball until we stalled in the red zone. This time, we were successful on a 32-yard field goal and took the lead 3-0.

As our defense took the field, I asked Paul Horne if we could protect the quarterback. Barron Collier was loading the line of scrimmage and playing straight man-to-man coverage in the secondary, just daring us to throw. Paul thought we would be fine in pass protection.

After the next defensive stop, the plan was to get the ball to our best wide receiver, Bruce Gordon; we did just that. A couple of Bryant-to-Gordon passes and a couple of Duane Coleman runs got us to the Barron 9-yard-line. We called a play-action pass to Bruce, and just like that, we were up 10-0.

But the BC football team had no intention of going quietly. On their next possession, they rode Resop's arm and Joseph's legs to a 75-yard drive. It culminated in a 30-yard touchdown pass from Resop to wide receiver Josh Fuqua with 1:34 left in the half.

The last two minutes of the half or the last two minutes in a close game are my favorite part of any football game. The time crunch puts a lot of stress on both teams, and it is always interesting to see how coaches and players react to all the tension in this competitive cauldron.

In our case, Stanley Bryant was superb. With nine seconds left in the half, he and Bruce hooked up on a nice little slant and go. Stanley's perfect pump fake caused the corner to bite, and Bruce wound up catching the ball with no defender in sight. At the half, it was Naples 17 and Barron Collier 7.

The second half was all Golden Eagles. The first touchdown after the break was Duane Coleman from 2 yards out. Although Bruce Gordon didn't score again in the game, he did catch nine balls for 141 yards, and kept several drives alive with clutch plays. Duane finished the game with 138 yards on 23 carries, becoming the first Golden Eagle in years to break the 1,000-yard rushing mark in a season. The future looked bright, as Duane and Bruce were both just sophomores.

Two fourth-quarter events really bothered me. Early in the fourth quarter, I heard a voice behind me, and I realized that someone was urgently saying, "Coach . . . Coach . . . you gotta . . . ," I turned and saw a grown man I did not recognize; he was telling me that the tight end would be open if I called a particular play. I looked around and realized there were actually **several** men on our sideline who had no business being there. They were mixed in with the players and the coaches, talking to guys, hollering to players on the field, fussing at officials. I went straight to Ron Byington, who I knew would fix the problem. I told Ronnie that those guys had to be moved; they could not be on our sideline. In short order, the sideline was cleared, but it was bizarre to see those fans on our sideline.

The second disturbing development in the fourth quarter was when our running back, Anthony Denson, broke free on a long run. With no defender near, he decided to turn around at about the 10-yard-line and jog backward into the end zone. The officials' flag appeared instantly, as that was obvious unsportsmanlike behavior. I was livid. There was no excuse for that. Ant forced me to both pull him from the game and give him OPP at practice during the coming week.

As the game came to a close, Barron tacked on a couple of irrelevant touchdowns. Our last score was also irrelevant, except that it was a linebacker's dream. On the final play of the game, with Naples up 37-21, Naples linebacker Garrete Perrone intercepted a Barron pass and returned it 35 yards for a touchdown. The final score was Naples 43 and Barron 21. Barron Collier's streak was over.

CHAPTER 33

The teams lined up to shake hands, and coaches and players alike were well behaved. I was the first to go down the line shaking hands. When I came to the end of the line, Naples Daily News reporter Andy Kent was there. He asked if he could talk with me right then, before I met with my guys on our end of the field. He needed to make his deadline. Andy knew that at the conclusion of every game, after we shook hands with our opponents, I would meet with our guys near the 10-yard-line for a few minutes. I told Andy that if we could make it fast, I would talk with him first. I really liked Andy; he was a terrific young reporter who obviously loved sports. He reported on prep stuff, but he also covered the Tampa Bay Buccaneers for the Naples paper. He did a great job at both. As I talked with Andy, our guys finished shaking hands and began jogging down to where we would meet.

I don't recall what I was talking about while Andy took copious notes, but I do remember the look on his face when he gazed up from his notepad and said, "Oh boy, this isn't going to be good." I turned to see that a bunch of our fans — probably 100 — were mixed in with our football team in the visitor's end zone, just below the goalposts. That was not the problem. The problem was that on the goalpost uprights themselves were a bunch of Naples fans, and a bunch of Naples players. They were all riding those goalposts like a Mardi Gras float.

Before I even got over to the goalposts, first the left, then the right side gave way, bending under the weight of the Naples fans and players. Simultaneous with the bending of the goalposts was the arrival of Collier County sheriff's deputies. The crowd on and around the goalposts dispersed immediately. Now the goalposts were bent in a lonely **"W"** and had their own private security detail.

The irony of this was immediate. Naples finally had a W at Barron Collier. I hollered to our coaches and players to get lined up; I wanted the players to get their helmets on and get in two lines, as we always do when we enter or exit a field. We were going to have to walk 100 yards through the parking lot in order to get to the locker room, and I was afraid we had just stirred up a hornets' nest of Barron fans. Our guys started to get in order, but the way out was blocked by one bunch of fans who were exiting the game and by another bunch who wanted to stay and see the mayhem.

I turned to see the Barron football team running towards us. They were obviously angry. I hollered out for our guys to turn around and leave their helmets on. I certainly didn't want this to escalate, but we darn sure were not going to get bum-rushed from behind.

Thankfully, the Barron players stopped about 15 yards from us, and their coaches did a good job of corralling their guys and getting them back to their side of the field.

It was a tense moment when the two teams were standing facing each other. I was glad no punches were thrown. Still, there was a lot of verbal jabbing going on. I hollered out for our coaches to space out along our two lines and get the kids back in the locker room. We were in a bit of a logistical jam. We had all of our equipment, including training supplies, football stuff, water coolers and bottles, video stuff, and audio stuff on our sidelines, and we needed it all to stay safe and get back to the school.

Normally, we had several coaches immediately break down the sideline equipment and start loading it into equipment vans. This time, we were going to have to do it with one guy, and use the rest of our staff to get the kids into the locker room. I asked Paul to get as much done with the equipment as he could. I knew Paul was imposing enough to discourage anyone from messing with our stuff, and he was smart enough to both diffuse any hostility and figure out the fastest way to get our gear home, intact.

The rest of the coaches followed the plan, spreading out around the two lines of players as we walked towards the locker room. We needed to get the kids in and out, and ready to get on the buses as quickly as possible.

My next thought was of Susie and the girls. I had last seen them by the fence behind our bench. I headed that way, in the opposite direction of our football team. I heard my name called; looking to my left, I saw two women double-timing it towards me from the Barron side of the field. One I recognized from church. I figured I could pause a moment to find out what the church gal needed, and then catch up with Sue.

It didn't work out that way. As soon as I stepped towards the ladies, they let go with a simultaneous tongue-lashing that I wish I had an audio recording of. I was not expecting it, and all I could really do was offer my apologies and try to move on as quickly as possible. The women were having none of the apology. I remember one of them saying, "And you call yourself a Christian!" They went on to tell me that they were going to talk to our pastor, and they made it clear that if they had anything to do with it, I would no longer be welcome at church. With that, I'd had enough. I excused myself and hit a fast jog to find Sue and the girls.

I had last seen Sue and the girls, along with my mom and stepdad, standing with Gary Brown and Ernie Modugno by the fence behind our bench. I had silently mouthed and motioned for Sue to stay with them. I figured that both of those guys were going to want to touch base with me before any of us left. I had no idea how far away Sue had parked.

Looking through the crowd heading into the parking lot, I saw Sue with Gary Brown. Sue was holding one of the girls with the other two in tow, my mom and stepdad close behind. Interestingly, this was the first time that my mom and stepdad had visited us in Naples. Mom had only been to one of my games in high school and had not been able to see any of my games when I played in college, so this was a big weekend for us.

I hugged all of my girls as quickly as I could, and began walking with them in the general direction of the van. Sue said she was parked about as far away as possible while still being on the school property. Very often, by the time she cleaned up after the pregame meal she prepared each week, and then hustled home and got our girls ready, she would make it to the game just before kickoff. At away games, that could result in a long walk to a parking space.

All of the adults were keenly aware that what had just happened was not good, but no one mentioned the fact that half of a stadium of people were pretty angry at whoever was supposed to be in charge of the guys on the goalposts. I asked Gary if we could find Joe Scott or another youth relations deputy to walk my family to our van. I did not want any problems for them, and I know that fans can be ridiculously irrational. The crowd was thick with mostly Naples fans at the place we were walking, near the visitor bleachers. However, unfortunately, Sue would have to walk across the parking lot, and would be in the middle of Barron fans in short order. Thankfully, Sue saw friends who were going in her direction and she joined them, herding along three little girls and two in-laws.

No sooner had Sue left than Barron Collier Principal Ray Baker appeared from out of the crowd. Next thing I knew, he was going off on me. I am not sure what he said at first; I just know he was yelling, red-faced, sweat-soaked. He was not happy. I do remember the end of it, and it was this: "This is your fault! This is all your fault! We never had any of these problems before you came to town!"

At that point, we were not principal and opposing coach — we were man to man. My impulse was to knock this joker out. Thankfully, I used my better judgment; instead, I said in a firm, even tone, "Look at yourself, Ray. You are supposed to be in charge here. How 'bout you show some composure." Ray looked at Gary Brown and said, "Did you hear that, Gary? Are you going to let him talk to me like that?" He was right — I should not have been disrespectful to him; my ego was definitely running my mouth.

I headed to our locker room, and found our coaches standing outside the door in the corridor that separated the home and visitor locker areas. I thought this was a good idea until it occurred to me that we needed someone inside with our players. I asked the coach closest to me if we had any coaches in with the players. I was told there was a lot of smack-talking going on between the two teams as they were coming into the locker rooms, and the coaches thought it best to stay in the hallway to keep everyone separated. Fair enough, but we still needed someone in the locker room.

As I entered the locker room, it sounded like a frat house party. Guys were singing and dancing and whooping and hollering. I noticed that the cups we used for Gatorade were all over the place, as was the Gatorade itself. It was obvious that guys had been using it for a "champagne" bath, like they saw on TV after big sports wins. It was also obvious that several shower curtains had been torn down, and it looked like a couple of the metal locker fronts were dented in. Maybe things were that way before we got there, but I had my doubts.

My priority was still to get our guys off that campus as safely and quickly as possible. In a very short moment, the players noticed I was there, and the place quieted down. I told all of the guys to grab their stuff; we were heading out. Normally, our team leaders cleaned up the locker rooms we used while on the road. We would bring our own trash bags and did our best to leave the rooms how we found them — better in some cases.

My new plan B was to get our players on the bus, and then send a couple of coaches back to clean up the locker room. Afterward, those same coaches would head out to the field to help Paul get all of our gear back to the school. They could ride back to our school in the equipment vans, so the buses wouldn't need to wait for them.

As the players exited the locker room, our coaches spread out around them. The players walked in two tight lines out of the building and into the parking lot. We could see our buses as they made their way to us through the traffic logjam. When the buses finally arrived, we got our guys on. We were immediately gridlocked.

Whenever we traveled, I sat in the front right passenger seat on the front bus; the front bus was always designated the offensive bus. That position allowed me to communicate with the bus driver and to make sure we agreed on the best route. After a late game, it also put me in a good spot to talk to the driver in case he started to doze off. I wasn't in the seat more than a minute when I saw Gary Brown walk up to the bus and motion for me to step off.

Gary told me I had to see the locker room; he said that the players had messed it up, and the custodians were mad. I told him I had seen it and that our coaches were coming back to clean it up. What I didn't know was, as soon as we left the locker room, the custodial staff had gone in. By the time our coaches assigned to the cleanup detail had returned to the locker room, they were met by Ray Baker. Evidently one of the custodians had gone and found him, and brought him to see the mess. Principal Baker had simply told our guys to leave, and they did — going straight out to see if they could help Paul. When Gary and I arrived at the locker room, Ray was there. If possible, he was angrier and liked me less than he had in the parking lot.

As Ray and Gary ushered me into the locker room, I tried to explain the plan I had, but Ray was having none of it. I soon realized that any explanations I had were falling on deaf ears. As quickly as I could without infuriating him further, I said that my guys were waiting for me, and that we needed to get those busloads of kids back to Naples High. I knew as I walked out of there that I had not heard the last from Ray Baker.

CHAPTER 34

I got back on a silent bus. I broke the silence when we got to the Naples High parking lot, letting everyone know we were meeting immediately in the blue gym. We called our auxiliary gym the "blue gym," because of the color of the synthetic floor; the main gym had a wood floor. I told them not to go into the locker room or anywhere else — straight to the blue gym. "Immediately" meant largely ignoring the herd of fans lined up to welcome us home. Our fans were really fired up about the win. And I guessed, the aftermath too.

As soon as our bus stopped, I jumped off and made my way through the well-wishers to the spot directly behind the offensive squad's bus, where the defensive players' bus would pull up. Sam Dollar also always sat in the front right passenger seat of the defense's bus, so he too could communicate with his bus driver and keep him awake. Sam had obviously told the defensive guys to tighten up, because as I stepped on the bus, it was completely quiet with every eye on me. I gave them the same message I had given the offensive players.

As I made my way from the bus toward the gym, I noticed the size of the crowd. I also noticed there were a lot of adults, not just the usual high school kids. Regardless of their age, these fans were FIRED UP! I pushed through the melee, focused on getting my guys together. I wanted to make sure that none of this stuff escalated. Upon entering the gym, I realized that a whole bunch of fans had entered ahead of me with our players.

I shooed the fans out. Once we had the gym secured and it was just the coaches and players, I let the guys know that the stuff after the game was an embarrassment. I wanted them to realize that beating Barron was never on our goal board, and that the real stuff was going to happen the next Friday night in Tampa. I also told them that because of their stupidity after the game, everyone had OPP. I told them we had an entire school community really mad at us, and that we were going to have to make it right.

The last thing I told them — and I made sure that each guy heard and understood, and responded that he had heard and understood — was that under no circumstance should any of our players go to the Barron Collier side of town. That meant they were not to go to Sports Authority, Applebee's, or any other store or restaurant in that area until further notice. I expected every player to go home, eat, go to bed, and be back at school for video at 9 the next morning.

It was actually relatively early when Paul Horne and I headed out from the coaches' office. Among many other things, Paul was our video guru, and after every game he made sure that the tight and wide angles of our game video were matched up, interleaved, and ready for each of the coaches when they walked in the next morning at 7 o'clock. In this case, Paul didn't have any tight (end zone) views to match up with the wide (sideline) views like we normally had. The post-game mayhem saw to that. Bill Spencer, our videographer in the end zone, should have had a good view. His video camera was set up on a scaffold a few yards behind the doomed goalposts.

O-line coach Dan MacDonald, who also was a Collier County sheriff's deputy, told the story this way. "After the goalposts were bent and the deputies came to guard them, one of the deputies noticed Bill Spencer and his camera up there. He told Bill that he wanted the videotape as evidence. Bill told the deputy that the video was Coach Kramer's, and consequently not his to give; whoever wanted it would have to ask Coach Kramer for it. The deputy told Bill that he really didn't want to have to arrest him for obstruction of justice, to which Bill quickly replied, 'I didn't say I wouldn't give it to you.'"

In the end, the end zone video wasn't any evidence at all. Bill had stopped the camera at the conclusion of the game. Eager to celebrate with the team, he was already packing up when the goalposts were bent. And so Paul had no tight view to prepare for the next morning, and he and I were out of the office earlier than we normally would have been.

As we walked out the air was still humming. Band members and cheerleaders, students and parents, were all milling around, simply loving the moment together. I had a new appreciation for the word "revelry" . . . and for the word "rivalry."

Sue and my mom and stepdad were all up when I got home. Sue and I had come to the same conclusion; this was not going to be good. There was no way that the Barron Collier administration, coaches, and parents were going to let it go. Mom was her sweet self; perhaps a bit naïve about the whole thing.

I am sure that my stepdad had an opinion, although he was keeping it to himself. He had been on his best behavior on the trip. The truth is, the reason he and mom had never visited before — the reason they hadn't seen me play in high school or college — was because from the time he had married my mom when I was 5, he simply did not like me. Growing up, I had a hard time figuring that out, but once I did, it gave me a tremendous amount of peace.

There was always an air of anticipation for our Saturday morning video sessions. Coaches were eager to see what they had taught well and what they had failed to teach well, and players were eager to see themselves improving and making plays. On that particular Saturday, players and coaches alike were stoked to see the video; rumor had it that at the end of the wide-view video, we would see the goalposts being bent in living color. By the time the coaches showed up to grade the video, Paul had already made copies for us to grade, along with another copy that we would trade later that day with our next opponent, Tampa Hillsborough.

As we graded the video, it was obvious to me our team had played hard and mostly smart, and that we had improved dramatically in a year. What the video did not show was who had instigated the whole goalpost debacle. It seemed to be spontaneous, but it was hard for me to believe that it had happened without some forethought. I had to believe that someone had come up with the idea, and I was hoping against hope that it wasn't any of our players.

At some point in our video review with the players, I got a call from Ernie asking me when would be a good time for me to meet in Gary's office. He said one of the bosses from the school district had called Gary, wanting the original wide view of the video tape, and I should bring it with me. I told him we could meet around noon. By noon, the players would be gone and our trade tapes from Tampa Hillsborough would be at the school. I figured it would be efficient for me to meet with Ernie and Gary while our coaches ate lunch and began entering the Hillsborough data into the computers for analysis.

Before letting the players leave, the last thing I did was assemble everyone in the blue gym again, and explain in no uncertain terms that they were not to go anywhere near Barron Collier. That side of town was off-limits. They needed to find somewhere else to shop and eat until further notice. Naples was big enough that no one needed to go anywhere near that place. I assured them that Coach Byington had put the sheriff's office on high alert, and that deputies were looking out for any Naples football player who strayed anywhere near Barron Collier High School.

CHAPTER 35

My meeting with Ernie and Gary was matter-of-fact and efficient. Gary had to ask the question, and I assured him that neither I nor my coaches knew anything about the idea to damage the goalposts beforehand. We all knew my guys had messed up, and we would have to make it right. We watched the end of the game on the video, and did our best to identify the fans and players that had been on, or had pulled on, the goalposts. I assured Gary and Ernie that I would punish our guys before practice each day in the coming week. I also assured them that our guys would do whatever fundraising was necessary to fix the damage. Gary and Ernie figured we would have to make a written or verbal apology to Barron, and I said I would write something up by Monday. Gary told me that the district administration had asked for the video, and he really didn't know what was going to happen on their end.

I asked what the worst-case scenario was. Gary and Ernie both agreed that the worst case would be that all the kids involved in bending the goalposts would be suspended. I told them if that happened, we would have to forfeit the playoff game in Tampa. One of them asked if we might be able to put junior varsity players on the field, so we could field a team. I told them I would not be willing to do that, as it would put kids at serious risk for injury. Tampa Hillsborough was loaded with really big, fast, strong players; it was absurd to think that we could put our JV on the field with them.

One interesting side note: on the front page above the fold of the Naples Daily News that weekend was a big picture of the fans at the University of Arkansas riding the goalposts for all they were worth as they tore them down after a big win versus the University of Tennessee.

I made up my mind that all I could do, was all I could do. We would prepare for the upcoming playoff game assuming that we would have all of our guys. We would prepare for the game by giving it the respect it deserved. We would need to play our very best to avoid being embarrassed by arguably the best team in Florida.

I wasn't back in my office very long when the phone rang. On the other end was Rob Richter. I figured that whatever it was Rob needed was important; this former quarterback who had turned into a jack-of-all-trades for our offense had become a strong leader for our team.

The stress in his voice was obvious. He explained to me that he had called me because his dad was out of town, and I was his next choice. He was at Barron Collier with several of his teammates, and Rob was afraid they were about to be arrested and taken to jail.

Rob told me they had gone onto the field to take a picture of the bent goalposts and had been seen by a Barron Collier football coach. The coach had detained them and called the sheriff's office. He wanted them arrested for trespassing. I told Rob to hold tight, and I would be right there. I hung up and immediately called home. I asked Sue to look up Scott and Lynn Salley's phone number. Scott was a captain in the Collier County Sheriff's Office, and his wife Lynn worked in the attendance office at Naples High. Both of their kids had attended Naples High, and from the first moment we stepped on campus, the Salleys had befriended us and had informally adopted our girls. Lynn and Scott Salley were two of the coolest people God ever created.

Lynn answered the phone. I asked for Scott, who wasn't there; Lynn gave me his cell number. I got hold of Scott and explained the predicament to him. He told me to sit tight. He thought it best that I not go to Barron, as my presence would only inflame the situation. He told me he could not guarantee anything, except that the boys would be treated fairly. I asked him how my players could be trespassing when the public had access to our track and fields whenever we weren't using them. Again, Scott told me he would head over to Barron and look into it.

I was livid. I could not believe that my guys would defy me like they had by going over to Barron's field. Not just to that side of town, but back to the actual stadium – unbelievable! When I spoke with Rob, I had asked who was with him, and he told me he was with three teammates. The first was Mark Kovacevic, a hard-hitting defensive back who was a guy we all knew we could count on. Mark was serious about his commitment to his team and coaches. Next was Victor Cabral, one of the best players to come through Naples High. Big Vic played defensive line and also happened to be the battalion commander for the Naples High Junior ROTC. Vic was the ultimate yes-sir, no-sir guy, and we simply didn't have a more responsible student in the building. Last was Cam Bulloch, one of our largest guys. Cam was physically imposing and played offensive line, and he also happened to be our student body president. If I'd had to pick four guys I knew I could count on to do as I asked, and stay away from the Barron side of town, it would have been those four guys.

As I sat there in our janitor's closet football office, I could not wrap my mind around it. I obviously did not have the influence over my players that I thought I did.

In the meantime, we had a playoff game to prepare for. As I pushed "play" on the VCR, I tried to push thoughts of four of our best players going to jail out of my head.

After about an hour of watching video of the behemoths of Tampa Hillsborough trouncing various opponents on film, the phone rang. It was actually nice to be distracted for a moment from the biggest, fastest team I had seen since moving from Miami. There was nothing remotely close to this Hillsborough team in all of southwest Florida. The more I watched them, the more evident the difficulty of our task became.

Scott Salley was on the other end of the line. First, he told me that no one was going to jail. He said that as soon as they realized who Rob Richter's dad was, they backed off of that idea. One of Rob's sisters had gone to Barron Collier, and Rob's parents had done much to support that school. Scott went on to explain that the boys had climbed a locked fence to get on the field. When confronted by a coach who was outside the fence, one of the boys had actually told him to hold on a minute while he proceeded to adjust the padding on the goalpost — to frame it better in the pictures he was taking.

Needless to say, that was not an appropriate response.

The short version was that all the boys' parents were called except Rob's, since they were out of town. Everyone was told that the incident was not over. Barron Collier would take a couple of days to determine how they would pursue our players' misbehavior — whether through the courts, the school administrations, or both.

My mind kept coming back to the notion that this should have been a happy time. A terrific season, a playoff game; we all should have been really happy and stoked for the week to come. Instead, we had a stark reminder of how fast things could change when we got outside the margins. How many DUIs are earned on the night of a celebration? How many times do work relationships which are really positive and productive get out of bounds, and unwind marriages and families?

The Bible clearly says that we are to guard our hearts; we have to be vigilant to stay inside the margins placed by God. When we get out of bounds, whether during good times or during trials, we can turn good into bad, and bad into worse in a hurry. What I did not know was that this thing was going to get a lot worse before it was going to get better.

CHAPTER
36

On Sunday, we went to church as usual. I didn't see the church ladies who wanted me out, but I did feel a bit conspicuous as I sat there. It was reassuring after the service when Pastor Hayes Wicker put his arm around me and told me he was praying for me, and encouraged me to stay the course. After church, I took the girls on a walk down the street to Gary Brown's house.

The girls and I would often go for walks — and later, bike rides — in the neighborhood, and those often wound up at Gary and Sandy Brown's. The Browns always had a smile and a hug for our girls, and all of my girls were in love with their little cocker spaniel. In fact, for years, the only thing that Courtney asked Santa for was a puppy dog of her own. Unfortunately for Courtney, other than with stuffed animals, Santa did not hook her up.

Gary assured me of two things: first, this little crisis was going to have to run its course; and second, this little crisis would surely run its course. He had been in education a long time and had seen all kinds of different situations, and he knew that eventually the school and the community would move forward. Gary Brown was trustworthy and calm; his reassurance was a great comfort for me.

I also took solace in the fact that I knew — beyond a doubt — God had me in that place at that time for a reason. While I didn't necessarily understand the reason for all of what was happening, I knew I was learning how to deal with stress and developing self-control all at once. I also had all of my girls. Those little girls didn't care what the score was; who liked dad, or who didn't like dad. All they knew was that daddy was either home or not, and when he was home he was either their happy, fun-loving dad, engaged with his girls — or he was something else. I wanted to be the husband and father God intended me to be, and that sure wasn't going to happen if I allowed the stress to bend me.

Susie was steady as a rock through it all, not just responding to, but by anticipating the needs of everyone in the house. She has done that for our family since day one, and continues to do it today; I simply do not know how she does it. What I do know is that I love her desperately, and I am grateful that God put her in my life and by my side.

On Monday morning, Ernie came to my guidance office to tell me the district was doing an investigation, and said one of the assistant superintendents was going to come at the end of the school day and interview the coaches. I reminded him that each Monday we met with the team in the auditorium immediately after school to give out our player-of-the-game awards and to review opponent video.

He told me that the kids would have to wait in there until the interview was done. He said that we would find someone — an administrator or a coach who wasn't at the Barron game — to sit with the kids, but every coach who was at that game would be in the principal's conference room immediately at the end of the school day. I asked him what he thought it would entail and how long it would be. While he had no idea about that, he did know that a vocal group from Barron wanted me fired.

At the conclusion of school, I quickly ushered our guys into the auditorium; our coaches who had been in Tampa scouting Tampa Hillsborough the previous Friday would sit with them until the meeting with the district bigwig was over. As I headed down to the principal's conference room, which was adjacent to and had a connecting door to Gary Brown's office, I was praying for God to give me peace and patience. The irony of the situation was not lost on me. Here is this football coach coming to town and telling everyone he was taking the job because he felt led by his Creator to take it; yet in his second season, his players are so out of control that they bend an opponent's goalposts and tear up their locker room and showers. *What a fraud, what a hypocrite; this guy must be a scumbag.*

Our coaches arrived within moments of each other, and we talked in muted tones about what was going on and what was possibly going to happen. We were all worried we might have to forfeit the upcoming game, and we were also worried that the meeting was going to go long and cut into our preparation time. Gary and Ernie entered, and Gary introduced an assistant superintendent who was with them. This was as stressed, worn, and tired as I had seen either Gary or Ernie since Rusty Larabell's death the previous year. I thought about both events that had occurred on that field, and I wished I had never seen or heard of Barron Collier High School.

The assistant superintendent, Dr. Morris, began by telling us how disappointed the district was in the behavior of our team, and that included coaches and players. He said that the only way for the situation to heal was for our coaches to come clean and tell the truth about what really happened. He said he had eyewitness accounts from people, stating that they had heard our coaches encouraging our players to tear down the goalposts.

Dr. Morris assured us that it was a serious situation, but also said it would go better for any and all of us if we cooperated and simply told the truth. He then said he was going to give us a few minutes to discuss it among ourselves. Soon, he said, he would be back to hear from whichever one of us was willing to be honest and tell him exactly what happened. At that, Dr. Morris, Gary, and Ernie went through the door connecting the conference room to Gary's office and closed the door behind them. As the door closed, I was sure I knew what the answer would be, but I had to ask the question.

"OK guys, this is a serious deal. Did any of you guys know anything about this, or encourage anyone in any way to tear down the goalposts?"

The words had barely left my mouth when Paul Horne half-heartedly raised his hand and said, "Yeah, it was me. I told them to tear the goalposts down." I felt the blood drain from my face; in an instant, my heart froze and my chest became so tight I could hardly breathe. All I could muster was, "You what?" Paul immediately broke out in a cheesy grin and said, "Nah man, just kidding! C'mon, this is stupid! Like any of us had anything to do with this!" As the room broke out in laughter, I felt my cheeks flush with embarrassment. Paul really got me that time . . . hook, line, and sinker.

I reminded everyone that it was serious and asked the question again. All of them said that they knew nothing about it, and that they would have come to me immediately and squashed it if they had known. I encouraged everyone to just keep telling the truth; I assured them, while we would be OK when the smoke settled, there was a very real possibility this would affect our playoff game.

The truth was, it already was affecting the game. We should have been preparing our kids for the game of their lives, and instead we were in conference with a district administrator. In the back of my mind, I was afraid we would at the very least lose the guys who had gone on the picture-taking tour of Barron Collier Saturday morning.

The door opened, and in came Dr. Morris — alone this time. He looked around the table, and then asked all of us if any of us had something we wanted to say. He said he was in there without Gary so we could feel free to say whatever we needed to. He reassured us that he was a friend and an advocate for any of us who would be forthcoming.

I took the lead and began with a full apology. I explained in detail what had happened at the end of the game. I assured him that none of us knew anything beforehand, and that each of us was shocked and appalled at what had happened. I told him that if any of us had any inkling of what might happen before the event occurred, we would have quashed it immediately.

I also took responsibility for underestimating the intensity of the rivalry; I explained to him that before I had come to Naples, I had never heard of Barron Collier. I went on to say that they were simply not a very good team, and as far as our coaches were concerned, there was no reason why anyone should be so fired up about beating them.

I found out later that this last editorial remark probably did not help my cause, as Dr. Morris's wife happened to be an administrator at Barron Collier. Lest we jump on the bias bandwagon, Dr. Morris's connection to Barron was a godsend. The superintendent at the time, Dan White, had been the previous principal at Naples High, and it was not a quantum leap to imagine folks would claim he was biased as the penalties for the fiasco unfolded. Dan White was smart to assign the investigation to a guy with Barron Collier ties.

After I finished my apology and explanation, Dr. Morris addressed the group again. He said he simply did not believe what occurred was random, and he was determined to find out what had really happened, up to and including the events of the previous Friday night. He then asked the question again. He wanted the truth, and he wanted to know which of us was going to be man enough to tell the truth. None of us said a word. Dr. Morris then said he had interviewed a cheerleader who was in the line shaking hands at the end of the game, and that she saw and heard a Naples High coach say, "It's time for mass destruction; go get the goalposts!"

We all glanced around the table and looked at each other. All of us had the same thought: "Who on earth talks like that?" I wanted to say to the good Dr., "Really? It's time for mass destruction? Are you listening to yourself? This is a credible witness to you?" Thankfully, none of us gave in to the urge to question what he'd said. Dr. Morris next informed us that he would go around the table, look each of us in the eye, and ask the question. He expected us, as Christian men, to answer honestly and tell the truth about what had happened at Barron Collier.

As soon as Dr. Morris explained what he was going to do, Ronnie Byington slapped the table, stood up, and said, "This is bullshit! I don't have to sit here and listen to this." I said, "Ronnie, come on, bro." But I doubt he heard me; Dr. Morris was much louder, as he said, "You sit back down, mister; we aren't done here yet."

The fact was, Ron was done. He paused for a moment, looked our assistant superintendent in the eye, and said, "Well, I'm done. I don't work for you, and I don't have to stay here and listen to this." With that, Ronnie turned to me with absolute sincerity and said, "Sorry, Coach, we told him the truth. I'm not gonna sit here and be treated like a liar." One small irony: Ron Byington was a Barron Collier graduate.

As Ron left the room, Dr. Morris was obviously angry; his face was flushed, and he spoke in a terse tone. He assured us that Coach Byington would be dealt with later and told us he was going to get to the truth. He pressed us again, and as each of us said we did not know anything about the incident, I couldn't help but look at my watch and rework the practice schedule in my head. We still had a playoff game on Friday, and we were falling farther behind.

At last Dr. Morris was done, and we were dismissed. As we filed out of the room, Gary Brown walked in and told me he would talk to me after practice. I felt really bad about the stress he was going through. I have always felt that my job is to make my principal's life easier. Clearly, I was failing in that regard.

As the coaches walked into the auditorium, we found a rather stoic lot. A number of players hollered out, "Sorry, Coach." I could see they were truly sorry about the trouble they were causing the coaches. I also had a sense that if they had it all to do over again, there was not much they would have changed about what went down the previous Friday night.

I told the guys everything I knew to that point. I explained to them that we were going to get two things accomplished that week. First, each day, I would punish them for the stupidity of the previous Friday night; and second, we would prepare to beat the best team in the state of Florida. We headed out to practice, and the determination in the demeanor of the players was obvious. These guys had become a team, and whatever happened now, they were going to face it as a team.

Practice began like every other practice, although it took a moment for me to muster enough enthusiasm to holler out, "Great Day . . . Today!" As soon as stretching was over, any similarity between that practice and all previous practices disappeared. The first thing I had the guys do was two 300-yard shuttle runs for time. We did those once a week at the conclusion of practice, as lactic acid conditioning. Players lined up on the goal line by position, and then would run to the 25-yard-line, touch the 25, and run back to the goal line. They would do that six times; hence the name, 300-yard shuttle run.

The first one isn't bad. Athletes are allowed three minutes for a rest interval (approximately a 3:1 rest interval), and then they do it again. Within three minutes, lactic acid can begin to build up in the athletes' system. It will sit in the muscles, causing them to shake and feel weak; it will pool in the stomach, causing many athletes to feel nauseated. Many people feel the effects of lactic acid after walking quickly up a few flights of stairs or sprinting through an airport to catch a plane. Our guys were feeling it after one shuttle; that makes the second timed shuttle significantly more difficult.

The shuttles were just a warmup. Next, we got in lines and did something I had made up years earlier when I coached women's track and field — something I called the Big 21. The Big 21 was quite simple: the coach calls out the cadence, and as a group, the team does 21 push-ups, 21 sit-ups, 21 mountain climbers (hands on the ground in front and alternate jumping and switching your feet from front to back), and 21 jumping jacks. Each player must count out loud and stay in unison with his teammates. That was followed by the same exercises; only 20 of each, and then 19 of each, and so on. By the time we get to zero, the athletes have done 186 of each exercise. It was not a big deal, per se; however, when they had a good bit of lactic acid built up, were in full football equipment, *and* had to count and stay in unison or start over, it could become zero fun. By the time we got through the Big 21 everyone was gassed, and we had been at it for well over an hour.

The first time we had to start the Big 21 over, I hollered out, "Well, was it worth it now?" After a few seconds, someone hollered out, "Hell yeah, it was worth it!" Many times, the boys had to start over from 21 during Monday's Big 21. On several occasions, we were down to single digits when we restarted. Each time the boys started over because someone didn't keep up or someone had failed to count out loud, I would ask the same question – "Is it worth it now?" By the ninth or 10th do-over, the entire team was saying in unison, "Hell yeah!"

There was a weird balance to it. These guys had determined that they would do whatever was asked of them to pay the penalty for their behavior. They had also decided that whatever was asked, it was worth it. We spent the last 30 minutes of practice doing an extremely abbreviated version of what a normal Monday would look like; at the conclusion of practice, we were officially way behind in our preparation for Tampa Hillsborough.

I never took pleasure in punishment, and I never made it personal. I often explained to my players that a lot of coaches get discipline and punishment confused. I have heard many coaches at all levels talk about how they had to discipline a player. The fact is, they weren't disciplining a player, they were punishing a player who didn't have the self-discipline required to keep the commitments he made. What we did that Monday evening was definitely punishment, and it was a huge waste of everyone's time.

Before I left school that night I swung by Gary's office, but he wasn't in. I stopped by his house on the way home, and he told me he and I would be going over to Barron Collier the next morning to talk to Ray Baker and offer an apology. There really wasn't much else to say. When I finally pulled into our driveway, my three little girls didn't care a bit about all the junk at work. All they knew was that daddy was finally home, albeit rather late; and it was time to play, or read books, or do something fun.

CHAPTER

37

The newspaper on that Tuesday morning had the story on the front page above the fold. The article said that Gary and I were going to go to Barron that morning and apologize to the school via their in-school TV. I wasn't looking forward to it, but I realized that it was the next step in getting the ordeal behind us.

The paper also ran an op-ed piece in that particular section, which called for "Time Out." It called for a dialogue that looked to the future and would not dredge up past incidents. The author of the piece believed that it was time to reframe the rivalry and make it a lasting productive process.

When we arrived at Barron Collier, we walked immediately to the principal's office. There was a small reception area where Ray Baker met us, and he took us straightaway into his office.

Ray walked behind his desk and sat, as he offered us each one of the two chairs opposite his desk. The conversation began with both principals commenting about the need to put the contention behind us, and how in time the bad feelings would all heal.

Next, Ray turned to me and said, "Coach Kramer, I do have one question for you. You have repeatedly said that this game wasn't a big deal to you, that you had no idea who Barron Collier was, and that this rivalry meant nothing to you." "Yes," I told him, "It's true." Ray then leaned forward and said, "Well then, tell me this, Coach — why did you give your team T-shirts at the beginning of the season with the date of our game on them?" Ray was intense. He thought he had me, and he was ready to pounce.

What I said next did nothing to soothe him. I explained to him that I did give T-shirts out at the beginning of the season, and that they did have a date on them. But the date on the shirts was not the night of the Barron Collier game, 11-12-99; the date on the T-shirts was the next Friday's first round playoff date, 11-19-99. I explained that our goal from day one was to play in the playoff game in three days. Beating Barron was not on our list of goals. I probably went too far when I reiterated that I had never heard of Barron Collier two years earlier, and as far as I was concerned, the Barron game was just a late-season game against a weak, non-district opponent.

Ray sat back for a quick moment and collected himself. He then looked me in the eye and explained that he was going to bring the Barron Collier student body into the gymnasium and have Gary and me apologize to them.

No sooner had the words come out of his mouth than I said, "That's not going to happen." It was one thing to go into an empty

TV studio and talk into a camera; it was another thing entirely to stand in front of a couple thousand teenagers and try to say anything. A gym full of kids could be a security nightmare, and as we had found out the previous Friday, only a few knuckleheads could cause something bad to happen.

Ray was not happy with my answer. Turning to Gary Brown, he said, "Did you hear that, Gary?" At that point, my immaturity took over. I leaned forward in my chair and said, "You don't need to talk to Gary. I am sitting right here. If you have something to say, you can say it to me, man to man. I am not going to go into a gym full of kids and humiliate myself for you or for anyone else. I don't even work for you. If Gary wants to fire me, he can fire me, but I ain't doin' that."

Gary put his hand on my shoulder, and in an even tone let it be known that no one was going to be fired; I'm guessing he said it as much for Ray as he did for me. Gary then asked Ray if it would be OK if I left the room, so that the two of them could talk in private. Ray nodded, and I left.

In a few minutes, Gary came out. He told me we were heading to the TV studio, and that he would do a video apology himself. As I stood outside the TV studio while Gary was apologizing in front of a camera, I realized I could learn a lot from Gary Brown. Like Tony Dungy, there was a strength in his humility and calm demeanor. It wasn't that he didn't get fired up about stuff, it was that he had the discipline and self-control to work through a situation without inflaming it. He had the ability to see the long-term, versus the here and now.

Before practice on Tuesday, I went to Ernie's office. I explained to him that I really needed to know if we were going to play on

Friday or not, and that I also needed to know if we were going to have any players suspended. He told me he didn't know, but said he would do all he could to find out something. Ernie also told me that he, Gary, and I would be going to the school board meeting on Thursday night to offer an apology. He said that we would need to bring a few players, and asked me who I thought would be best. I immediately thought that Cam Bulloch and Rob Richter would be perfect. After the meeting in Ray Baker's office, I certainly was not looking forward to standing in front of a school board. But once again, we were seeing forward progress, and we needed to get the situation behind us.

It was tough, going to a practice field and preparing for a game that might not be played, with personnel that might not be available. Nonetheless, I conjured up "Great Day . . . Today!" and we did all we could to control what we could control.

The coaching staff was great through it all. Sam and Paul took the lead on enthusiasm, and all of the coaches did all they could to encourage our guys and bring positive energy. Tuesday's practice was a carbon copy of Monday's, except for two things. First, practice started on time, so we had time to get more done. Second, our guys did a much better job of the Big 21. That meant we finished the punishment phase of practice much more quickly, and we were able to get into the preparation phase much sooner. That combination ensured we got a lot more real football stuff done on Tuesday.

Wednesday morning's paper once again had the story on the front page, above the fold. I was beginning to realize I really was in small-town America. At American High in Miami, our team buses had been shot at while coming home from a game, and it didn't even make the news. Here in Naples, bending goalposts was front-page, above-the-fold, and the lead story at 6 p.m.

The article talked in general about the meeting in Ray's office, and said that Gary and I delivered a videotaped apology. As I read the article, I thought Ray Baker did a great job of being positive in the newspaper, and it was obvious to me he wanted to move forward without beating us up verbally in the press.

After lunch on Wednesday, Ernie came to my office and closed the door. He told me that we would be able to play at Hillsborough and no one would be suspended from the game. Ernie told me the Florida High School Athletic Association, or FHSAA, had ruled in accordance with their bylaws. If we didn't play, we would be responsible to pay Tampa Hillsborough what they would lose in revenue — an estimated $21,000. Our school district had no interest in giving away that amount of money. Ernie went on to say that a memorandum was just being released from the superintendent's office, and that it would run in the paper the next day.

Ernie left, and as soon as I could tie up my guidance counselor obligations, I got on the phone and called Todd Toriscelli. I'd met Todd and his wife Chris at FCA Coaches Camp at Black Mountain, North Carolina. Todd was the head trainer for Coach Dungy and the Tampa Bay Buccaneers. At Black Mountain, Sue and I had the privilege of spending time with the Toriscellis and with Clyde and Debbie Christensen. Clyde was also on staff with Coach Dungy. These were tough, competitive men who exuded humility and selflessness; these were the kind of men I wanted to be.

The Toriscellis were incredibly kind and gracious people. In fact, when Todd found out we were only a few hours away in Naples, he immediately told me to call and stop by anytime we were in the area. I wasn't sure if my visit could include our entire football team, but I figured it couldn't hurt to call. Todd picked up after a couple of rings and was the same guy he had been at camp. I told him we had a playoff game coming up, explained the odds against us, and asked if perhaps we could swing by One Bucs Place to see the facility. I suggested that maybe he and one of the players could share some words of wisdom to motivate our guys.

Todd told me that we were welcome to stop by on our way to the game, but the Bucs would be off at the time we would be there. He said that a couple of his rehab guys would be around, and he would see if he could get one of them to talk to us.

I headed straight to the weight room and told Sam the good news. We would be playing on Friday, and we were going to visit the Tampa Bay Buccaneers facility. Sam was fired up. As the coaches filed in to change before practice, the word spread like wildfire, as did the energy level. We had a game coming up on Friday, and we had all of our bullets in our gun. The fact that we had a .22 and our opponent had a bunch of fighter jets was irrelevant. We knew what we had to do, and that was both inspiring and a relief all at once.

Practice that Wednesday afternoon was much the same as Tuesday, albeit my "Great Day Today!" was much easier to project. The players were positively giddy, especially the over-the-fence gang who were counting their lucky stars. The punishment phase to start practice was not even a speed bump, as these guys knew they needed as much prep time as possible. Naples High was in the playoffs for the first time in nearly two decades.

Thursday morning's paper had the story front-page, above the fold, for the third consecutive day. An op-ed piece ran, suggesting that the school district look no further than the student Code of Conduct, urging the district to treat the situation as it would any other act of vandalism and property destruction. That was a significantly harder line than Tuesday's op-ed. I reminded myself that, first and foremost, the goal of the newspaper is to sell papers.

The Naples Daily News also had the memo from Dan White printed in its entirety. The gist of the memo was that we had failed to supervise our players appropriately. It said we would have to hold fundraisers to pay for the damages, and the over-the-fence gang would have to do eight hours of after-school detention. Interestingly, the total nut to crack financially was $275. The goal-posts had been fixed by putting jack stands underneath them and bending them back to their original shape; that left a few shower curtains, a few dented lockers, and a broken sink fixture to repair. I was certain that seeing the total amount to repair the damage had minimized the response from the district. We had already told the players that we would host a minimum of three car washes as part of the punishment for the stupidity; I had anticipated having to buy new goalposts.

I arrived at school early Thursday morning to see Ernie; before I got too comfortable, he reminded me we still had to go to the school board meeting that night and face the fire. Ernie assured me there were going to be some extremely irate and irrational Barron fans on hand.

Barron Collier had not cornered the market on irrational fans. At one point during the week, I had taken a phone call from a husband and wife who were interested in purchasing new goalposts for Barron Collier. These Naples fans had offered $2,000, way more than enough for new goalposts, and they told me they would make the check directly to Barron Collier or the Barron sports booster club, or however BC wanted the check made out. The only proviso was that they could keep the old goalposts. They were eager to mount them in their front yard.

CHAPTER 38

Practice on Thursdays was generally a walk-through with an emphasis on special teams substitutions, but we had to do much more than that, as we still had punishment to take care of. We also needed to work on game plan stuff, which we had not had time to finish during the week. Once again, our guys sailed through the punishment, and the vibe at practice was terrific.

However, I saw that the season, the stress from the shootout, and the week of uncertainty and punishment were taking a toll on both the players and the coaches. Our guys were tired. I hoped against hope that we would have the physical and mental energy to play well. Win or lose, I wanted us to play well, and I was hoping that the visit to the home of the Tampa Bay Bucs would be just what the doctor ordered.

Ernie, Gary, and I rode together that night to the school board meeting. Ernie had insisted on driving, which was fine with me. Ernie Modugno was a car aficionado and always had an incredible ride, either a Mercedes or a BMW, and it was always one of the top-end models. Riding with Ernie was a treat.

As we drove to the meeting, we talked about what the order of events would be, and both Ernie and Gary tried to give me an idea of what to expect. I knew I had at least four folks at home pulling for me; Sue and the girls would stay home and watch it on local cable TV.

This meeting would be one of the highest attended in the history of Collier County Schools. I was told later that it was also the most-watched local program in the history of Collier County local cable programming.

We arrived nearly half an hour early, and the place was already packed. The meeting began with regular board agenda items; the last item on the agenda was the incident at Barron Collier. No one in the room gave a hoot about the regular agenda items, and the tension was palpable as each agenda item was checked off.

In short order, the school board chairperson brought forward the incident at Barron the previous Friday. After a short overview she introduced the Naples High administration, as well as Cam Bulloch and me, to offer our apologies. We all said basically the same thing: the incident was regrettable and an anomaly. We would raise the money for reparations, and as far as Naples High was concerned, something like this would never happen again. We emphasized that we would like to move forward and do everything possible to grow a positive relationship and friendly rivalry between the two schools. When we were done, the floor was opened up to public comment.

The Barron faithful were having none of our apology.

For over an hour, they lined up to lambast us. In their view, the punishment did not fit the crime. One after another, the BC crew begged the school board to reconsider and come down heavier on Naples High. Three of the folks stood out to me. The first was one of the church ladies who had confronted me on the field; the one I had not recognized. As she spoke, she mentioned that her son was a senior captain on the Barron Collier football team, and the on-field confrontation after the game suddenly made sense to me – she was a mama bear protecting her cub.

The second speaker that stood out was one of the BC cheer-leaders. She said that seeing those goalposts torn down at the last football game of her cheerleading career was the most traumatic event of her life. I wanted to stop the meeting and give her an award for Least Traumatic Life in the History of the World.

The last speaker that really stuck out to me was a Barron football player. He pleaded and begged for the school board to reconsider and suspend us from the playoff game. He said that anything less would ensure that the wound would not heal, and that he would not be surprised if Barron students took matters into their own hands.

I wanted to give him an award too. His would be the Most Whiny and Soft award. The goalposts had nothing to do with the outcome of the game. If this cat was indicative of the players at Barron, it was no wonder they finished the season 3-7.

The meeting concluded with each school board member con-demning the behavior the previous Friday night and accepting the sanctions as presented in the memo by the superintendent. The school board chairperson did the same, and the meeting was over. I was immediately approached by Barron parents and students who wanted to fuss at me, exact a personal apology, or both.

Ernie and Gary headed toward the door, and were either greeting supporters or fending off detractors along the way. I moved with them, and we made our way out of the boardroom. The hallway was packed; I had no idea that the crowd was as big as it was. The boardroom was a theater-style room, with the board members seated at the front end and theatre seating facing them. The room probably held a couple hundred, with standing room. There were at least that many in the hallway and beyond, and those folks had come to say their piece.

They were not happy. They were not happy about the goal-posts. They were not happy about having to stand outside of the meeting. And they were not happy about not getting a chance to say their piece – for many, the main reason they were there. Within a few steps, I found my back to the hallway wall, surrounded by Barron students, parents, and fans.

The crowd around me was being pressed by those behind them, and I had to stand with one foot in front of the other and my arms bent at 90 degrees, with my hands in front of me, in order to maintain any semblance of personal space. I had been convinced that a sincere apology would defuse the situation. I was wrong.

Some of the folks backed off as I looked them in the eye and apologized, but the vast majority wanted me to suspend all of the players involved and forfeit the playoff game if need be. In the view of those folks in the hallway, there was only one right thing to do, and that was whatever they thought was the right thing to do.

The crowd was big enough and loud enough that within a few minutes, sheriff's deputies arrived and escorted me out of the building. I quickly caught up with Ernie and Gary. As Ernie started the car, I told my bosses I was done apologizing. I told them that the truth was, I had done nothing wrong. I had done all that anyone could have done, up to and including Friday night. I told them I was moving forward, and while I was still all in at Naples High School, I was definitely done apologizing.

Friday's paper had the story front-page, above-the-fold for the fourth consecutive day. It also ran an op-ed, which was a rather scathing assessment of how the district was handling the incident at Barron Collier. The op-ed said that Dan White's decision ignored a countywide code of student conduct that expressly forbids vandalism, and declares zero tolerance for violence on school property. So much for resolution.

As of Friday morning, there had been 15 letters to the editor regarding the goalposts; about 10 were from folks on the Barron Collier side of the fence. The newspaper continued stoking the fire with another four op-ed pieces and an editorial cartoon over the next several days. The letters to the editor would continue until January 21; in the end, there would be more than 70 printed in the paper.

It didn't help matters when the newspaper ran a story on January 19 about a local T-shirt vendor located in the mall across the street from Naples High. The article had a picture of an employee holding up a T-shirt which had the screen print of a picture of the Barron Collier goalposts bent in the shape of a "W". At the top of the picture was the score: Naples 43, Barron 21. At the bottom were the words, "What?! What?!" Evidently, when Rob Richter's camera was confiscated, the memory card was not.

Thankfully, the grainy handheld video from the Barron stands, which had been the first story on all four networks during every time slot on nearly every day that third week in November, had run its course. While it was taking longer than anticipated, Gary Brown was right again — the situation would eventually go away. On the front page of the November 19 sports section of the paper, above the fold, was a picture of Anthony Denson going after a loose ball. There was a big article about Naples High going up to play the best team in Florida. Finally, we were back to football.

The infamous goalpost picture, taken by Rob Richter.

CHAPTER

39

As we boarded the charter buses to head to Tampa, I said a quick prayer and thanked God for the opportunity our kids were about to have. I hoped that through this experience, any of our guys who hadn't already grabbed hold of God would make real, meaningful commitments. I was grateful for the coaches I was privileged to work with, grateful for the charter bus (a serious upgrade from the cheese wagons we normally rode in), grateful for a chance to visit Todd and the Bucs facility, grateful for a playoff game to play, and grateful for these knucklehead players who were giving me the experiences of a lifetime.

As we neared Tampa, the terrain changed. We were only a couple hours north of home, but the trees were different here. In fact, I could see that some had leaves that were changing into fall colors. It wasn't a drive up the Appalachian Trail, but there was definitely a change in scenery. I realized that these were the first fall leaves that I had seen since my playing days at Liberty. One more thing to be thankful for.

As we pulled onto One Bucs Place, I was struck by how pedestrian the place was. There was a small sign confirming that this was where the Tampa Bay Buccaneers trained, and several nondescript buildings which looked like portables and trailers. I kept the team on the bus and headed into the main building to find Todd.

The pleasant lady behind the desk rang him, and in a short moment we were ushering our guys off the buses, through the hallway, and into the locker room. Whatever the place looked like from the outside was irrelevant to our guys when they saw the names above the lockers of the pros they watched on Sundays. Mike Alstott, Derrick Brooks, Warrick Dunn, John Lynch, and Warren Sapp were the favorites. Our guys had cameras out and were taking pictures in front of those lockers. Everyone was amazed at the boxes and boxes of shoes and cleats in every locker. How many pairs of shoes can one guy wear?

After a few minutes, Todd took us outside to the practice fields, where he and a couple of the injured guys talked to our players about the opportunity they would have in the upcoming game. They told us that our against-all-odds challenge was a microcosm of what each of us would face at various times in our own lives. Our players — and coaches — were all eyes and ears, and each of us left there with a renewed sense of possibility and commitment. I have often said that in order to be inspired, we need to be willing to be inspired. We were inspired.

Hillsborough High School is one of the oldest schools in the southern United States. It had its first students in 1882 and was moved to its present location in 1928. The red brick building is beautiful and distinct in Florida. Architect Francis Kennard's Gothic Revival design is truly something special for the students in Tampa Bay.

Our guys were somewhat starstruck by the size and grandeur of the campus. It was obvious that there were a lot of people taking a great deal of pride in that campus. Such pride often makes for a formidable opponent.

It is interesting how much you can learn about a school just from walking around the campus. You can usually tell what is important to the school, and if there is a culture of accountability and attention to detail. That doesn't mean you are always going to win against a pigsty school or that you'll always get smoked by the Louvre Lions. But let's just say that walking onto this immaculate campus home of an undefeated, and now No. 1-ranked, football team in Florida was a wee bit intimidating.

As the guys were dressing in preparation for pregame warmups, I took a stroll to verify that the coaches were finished setting up the field. As usual, everything was set up perfectly. We were controlling what we could control.

I walked over to Ryan Krzykowski, and as we mused about the beautiful school, we saw a guy walking toward us. He was coming from the direction of the concession stand, and he was making a beeline for us. For the uninitiated, the coaches/players box on a football sideline is sacrosanct. Once the teams show up and the sidelines are set up, people outside the program are expected to steer clear. Our new pal obviously did not know this. He walked an arm's-length from us, waved the Styrofoam cup in his hand towards us, and said, "Best coffee in Tampa . . . and it's only 50 cents." He then looked squarely at Ryan and said, "Football game tonight; don't be scared."

I'll admit, Ryan Krzykowski was a young-looking 20-something coach, but he was dressed like a coach and had a clipboard in his hand, so I understood when Coach Krzykowski waved his clipboard at the guy and said, "I'm not scared. I'm not playing." Our interloper didn't miss a beat, immediately replying, "What's the matter . . . chicken?" and then made the clucking sound that most boys have mastered by the time they're in second grade.

As Coffee Guy clucked down the sideline away from us, Ryan tried to explain to him that he was a coach, but I am pretty sure Coffee Guy couldn't hear a word over all the clucking he was doing. I was torn between the hilarity of the scene and the realization that Coach Kryzykowski's new friend must have come there pretty often to get coffee, and that he might just have known what he was talking about.

Our guys went out for warmups as per our usual schedule. The Hillsborough team didn't appear to be very intense and was obviously not intimidated by the upstarts from Collier County. In fact, one of Hillsborough's running backs actually came out to midfield and laid down on his side with his arm propping up his head, just chillin' out and watching us warm up. As we always did, we concluded warmups 30 minutes before kickoff, and headed back to our locker room.

I was mulling over what I would tell our guys. I am a firm believer that you can't win a game with a pregame pep talk, but I also think that plenty of coaches lose games with the pregame pep talk. With that in mind, I decided to leave the obvious out of it. I didn't talk about being underdogs or the tumultuous week we all had. I didn't mention that all of us were pretty much on empty in terms of emotional energy. I sure didn't give the old "We Are About to Shock the World" speech.

I avoided the tried-and-true "Seniors, This Is Your Last Game" talk, or the similar "Underclassmen, We Owe These Seniors, as This Is Their Last Game." Instead, I talked about some of the technical stuff we had emphasized in practice that week. Jamie Lemmond, our special teams coordinator, was convinced we could both block a punt and fake a punt if we executed the game plan. I knew that if our guys did exactly what we had coached them to do, we had a chance to win. I also knew that if they did anything other than what we had coached them to do, we would get smoked.

We left the locker room and lined up to enter the stadium. As we entered, I could see that Hillsborough had not taken the field yet. Their cheerleaders had a banner pulled open at about the goal line on the opposite end of the field. I guessed that they were waiting for our guys to get out there, so we could watch them run through the banner. We hustled to our sideline, and I had begun putting on my battery-pack belt and headset when I heard one of our players near me say, "Smoke . . . cool."

I looked up to see the banner and the area all around it immersed in smoke. There were several men with what looked like fire extinguishers spraying smoke all over the place. The players were completely obscured. And then the earth shook.

I didn't know where these monsters were when we were warming up, but some of the largest, most agile men I have ever seen came pouring out of that smoke and onto the field. Evidently, Hillsborough only allowed the little guys to go out and warm up before the game. Or perhaps these freaks of nature simply didn't need to warm up. Or maybe they just told their head coach they didn't want to warm up, and there was nothing he could do about it. Regardless, I stood and stared with the rest of our crew; nonchalance was not an option. Hillsborough's mascot is the Terriers. I thought at that point it should have been the Terrors.

In preparation for these Terriers, Sam had worked on a defense with a personnel group that we had not used all year. Basically, we were completely selling out to stop the run, using more linemen than we normally did, doing our level best to make them beat us some other way than by bludgeon. Our guys came out fighting their tails off. With the score still tied 0-0 in the first quarter, Duane Coleman blocked a Terrier punt, which we recovered on their 37-yard-line. Jamie Lemmond knew his stuff.

That gave us a spark, and six plays later Stanley Bryant ran an option play pass to perfection and found Bruce Gordon in the back of the end zone. With the extra point, Naples was up 7-0 on the best team in Florida. The massive Hillsborough stands, which had been rocking during the Mount Saint Helens entrance, were now remarkably quiet; even the crickets were taking a break.

As with all great teams, the spark which ignited the underdog team also ignited the favored team. Eight plays and 66 yards later, the score was tied. Our guys were still fighting their tails off, but the size, speed, and strength of the Hillsborough team were more than a match for the technique, toughness, and togetherness of our Naples squad. At one point in the second quarter, as Paul and I hunkered with the offense, a conversation with 6'1", 165-pound right tackle John Harris started like this: "Hey Johnny, we are getting killed on the backside by Snell."

It just so happened that the guy lining up in front of Johnny that night was a 6'2", 300-pound, All-American named Shannon Snell. The reason Shannon Snell lived in Tampa was that his father, Ray Snell, had ended his long NFL career by playing several seasons for the Tampa Bay Buccaneers. We knew we couldn't run right at Shannon, so the game plan was to either read Shannon Snell in the option game so we didn't have to block him; or, run away from him, and just get a body in his path to slow him down. Either way, we didn't want to have to block him.

When we tried to read him, he basically tackled everyone in the backfield, sorted out the ball carrier, and mauled whoever that was. When we tried to run away from him, he ran right through the guy trying to slow him down and mauled us from the backside.

"So Johnny, what can we do to buy just a little time with Snell?"

"I don't know, Coach; I've tried everything."

"Johnny, can you get your hat across?"

"Coach, I am, and he just runs right through me or over me or whatever."

"OK Johnny, how 'bout this? Don't even try to block him. Just grab him, hold him; try and tackle him. I don't care about the penalty, let's just see what we can do to stop him one time."

"Coach, that's what I'm already doing."

Hillsborough dominated the scoring of the second quarter with 13 unanswered points, but the play on the field was not as dominant. We were actually getting first downs and moving the ball, and the Dollar defense had allowed only two long touchdown runs — one on fourth and two. I told Paul as we went in at halftime that when I first saw those Hillsborough guys, I thought it possible that we would have a running clock at halftime. In Florida, if a team leads by 35 points at halftime, the clock runs continuously for the remainder of the game. That rule shortens the game dramatically, and it is commonly called the mercy rule.

The final score of 36-20 gave us confidence and hope as we loaded up for the trek back home. I must have fallen asleep as soon as I hit the seat, and was still tired when Paul Horne woke me up back in Naples. So much for staying awake and talking to the bus driver so he wouldn't fall asleep.

CHAPTER 40

The fatigue didn't end there. It was the wee hours of the morning when I got home that Saturday morning, November 20, 1999. I peeked at the girls and snuck into bed, and before I knew it, I was hitting my alarm. We arrived in Naples so late that I told all the coaches just to go home. Somebody got the team laundry started, but it had to be finished. And there was still a bunch of game gear to be stowed. In addition, I had a pile of work in my guidance office which had to get done. On top of all that, I had an awards banquet to organize, and college recruiting was a constant itch that no amount of scratching could relieve.

Over the next few weeks as we approached and then passed Thanksgiving break, I found myself becoming more and more cynical and angry about the hours I was spending at work. It had been almost two years of insane hours, and the wear and tear was starting to show. I found that I was having to really force myself to be positive and enthusiastic at work, and I felt constant guilt as I spent weekends and nights — as well as Thanksgiving, Christmas, and Easter breaks — at the school. I was always either wearing my guidance counselor hat or my football coach hat. In my worst moments, I would remind myself of the big pay cut I had taken for this misery. The football and the guidance work was all getting done, but I was failing as a dad and a husband.

I began feeling like a visitor in the house. The girls loved me being home. It was a healing experience to get their hugs when I came home each day, but there was a weird dynamic to it. If there was a decision to be made, or any bump in the day-to-day, I would weigh in — and the girls would tell me that they would ask mommy because she would know. On occasion, there were challenges or problems at home that I should have known about and should have been involved with, but I would find out after the fact. I was either at work, or — worse yet — I was home but still absent. I began praying about a resolution, and as we went through Christmas of 1999, I came up with one prevailing answer – I could not do this any longer.

By the end of Christmas break, I decided that after I returned from the AFCA convention the first week of January, I would sit down with Gary Brown. I would let him know how I felt about my situation and see if he had a solution to my problem. I had come to Naples on the premise that, as a guidance counselor, my schedule would be less demanding than if I were a classroom teacher. In Miami it had been doable. I had only taught two classes there, and one of them was the football weight training class.

I was guessing that the only option Gary could give me would be a full teaching schedule. While that would be less than what I was doing, I didn't believe I could be an effective coach and teach full-time too. I continued to pray on it and comforted myself in the fact that God had a plan for my life, and that He was not going to leave me hanging.

CHAPTER 41

2000

In January of 2000, the AFCA convention was in Anaheim, California. One of my personal must-do recommendations for any football coach is to attend the American Football Coaches Association National Convention. This annual convention brings together thousands and thousands of college and high school coaches from all across America. The convention lasts for four days, and is an intense, focused experience. Days begin early and end late. Speakers begin at 7 in the morning and continue on the hour until late at night, with many different program options occurring simultaneously. Coaches have a menu of items that includes: the ABC's of PR or media relations; heat illness prevention; the latest on concussion prevention and diagnosis;

standardized test preparation; NCAA recruiting rules; implementing character education through football programs; time management; motivation; professional development; every manner of strategy and technique; and the list goes on and on. There are countless committees which meet to discuss everything — from rules, to sanctions for members breaking rules, to the nuts and bolts of playoffs.

A poignant part of the convention each year is a number of massive job boards where coaches who just got fired and recent college grads post their resumes. Generally, when a head coach gets fired, he is able to find a job as an assistant pretty quickly. His experience makes him really valuable, and there is a fraternity within the coaching profession which is exclusive to head coaches.

Head college coaches also sign multiyear contracts, and those who are fired generally have some money coming to them — at the very least, a buyout of the remainder of their contracts. But assistant coaches rarely have such a parachute when the head man gets fired. They either hope that their head coach will be asked to run another program and then will take at least some of the current staff with him; or, they hope to catch on with the new head coach — who may or may not clean house. If those two options don't work, then perhaps they can find another school with a staff in transition where they might catch on.

I can't count the number of times I have seen a guy who was on staff at a top-flight school the previous season scrambling to find any job that would help him feed his kids after his school's staff was fired. I mean, for example, who could predict that a starting quarterback **and** an All-American linebacker would both sustain season-ending injuries the first week of the season? That scenario would virtually assure that the team would not meet the expectations of the fans and school administration, and would likely result in the coaching staff being fired.

The convention also hosts a sea of vendors who set up in a massive hall in the convention center with the latest technology for helmets, computer software, video editing, training room supplies, stadium construction, on-field training equipment, strength and conditioning equipment, and lockers. Vendors also offer stadium and campus graphics, artificial turf from every manufacturer, team T-shirts, the latest in mouthguards, and on and on and on.

As a young coach, I was able to see and hear many greats of the game: Tom Osborne, Ara Parseghian, Tom Landry, Eddie Robinson, Bill Yeoman, Bill Walsh — and that list goes on and on. In addition to the conventions' featured coaches, guest speakers have included President George Bush Sr., United Nations Ambassador Andrew Young, General Tommy Franks, and New York Mayor Rudy Giuliani.

The AFCA convention rivals any professional organization's convention in the country. When I first came to Naples High, I was amazed that the folks at the school or the district office were unfamiliar with the AFCA convention. We began to look into it, to see if our coaches could be given temporary duty for the three school days they would miss while attending. It was either Ernie or Gary who told me that the district basically felt like the convention would just be a bunch of coaches hanging out and getting drunk. While I was not naïve enough to think there was no drinking going on at the conventions, I would have invited any of our district personnel to go with me, any year. They could have seen for themselves what a must the convention is for every coach in America – if they could have kept up.

For our staff, the most important piece of going to the convention was our opportunity to get information about our players to college coaches who had scholarships available. We would come to the convention loaded with video and transcripts, and we would hard-sell our guys to as many of the thousands of college coaches in attendance as we could. Through the years, we had many, many guys offered scholarships as a direct result of our efforts at the AFCA Convention.

We got back home from the convention late Wednesday night, and I made sure I got to school early Thursday morning. I had been keeping up with my email as best I could while we were in Anaheim, but I always inevitably got buried when I returned from missing some days of school. I also wanted to find time in my day to get to see Gary about my assignment the following year; something had to give.

I thought it was convenient when one of the first emails I opened was from Gary Brown, asking me very simply to swing by his office when I had a chance. I imagined that it might be a perfect segue into what had been burdening me for way too long. But when I did get a chance to see Gary, I didn't broach my topic at all. He told me he had been contacted by someone at the district office. They had a complaint that I or one of my coaches had denied transfer papers to one of our players, a sophomore named Jimmy, who wanted to leave our school.

I told Gary I had no idea what he was talking about. I had worked during Christmas break to catch up on my counseling and football stuff, and I had been the Lone Ranger at the school.

I had left for the convention before the end of Christmas break. Consequently, I hadn't seen any of our players yet, nor had I seen any of the coaches who didn't go to the convention.

Gary said that he was told one of the coaches that didn't go to the convention was involved. With the goalpost incident so fresh, and knowing there were at least a few people with influence in the district who would have loved to hammer me, I asked Gary how best to handle the situation. He suggested that I call Jimmy down and get his story and then move forward from there.

I was very interested in getting the story. Jimmy was one of our best young athletes and had a legitimate chance to earn a college scholarship. In addition, he was thriving in his classes, involved in student government, and was even active with the drama club. I figured that it was all a misunderstanding, but I wanted to find out.

I checked Jimmy's schedule, and per my standard operating procedure, made sure I called him to the guidance office during one of his elective class periods. I did not want him missing time from an academic course. When he showed up, Jimmy was obviously uncomfortable. He avoided eye contact and exhibited just about every version of closed body language. This was odd for Jimmy; I thought he and I had a strong relationship. He had been injured during the football season, and I had helped him and his mom navigate doctor's appointments and rehab. This reticent Jimmy was new to me.

I told him what I knew. He admitted to me that he had tried to get an application for school choice or an out-of-zone waiver from the office, but they had been out of them. I asked him what any of our coaches had to do with his idea of transferring. Jimmy told me they had nothing at all to do with it; he just had to go back by the office and pick up the papers.

I then asked him what was going on; why on earth would he want to leave Naples High School? Jimmy explained that during Christmas break, he had been hanging out with his cousin and his cousin's friends, all of whom played football at Barron Collier. They had told him how bad they wanted him to play football at BC. He also said it would be the last chance for him to play with his cousin, who was a rising senior; and he said that playing for BC would give him a chance to play at Disney World's Wide World of Sports. Barron Collier was scheduled to play a game there during the upcoming fall season.

I could not believe my ears. I asked Jimmy if he was seriously considering transferring, and he replied that he just didn't know what he wanted. I asked him what his mom wanted, and he said that she wanted him to stay at Naples High. I wondered if his cousin and Disney World were the real reasons that he wanted to leave us. I saw the carrot being offered, but I wondered if somewhere there was a stick. Had one of our coaches or players said or done something that offended Jimmy?

I sent Jimmy back to class and headed down to Ernie's office. I wanted to get Ernie and Gary together, lay the situation out, and figure out the best way to move forward. Ernie and I headed to Gary's office, and thankfully he was available. I told them what I had learned from meeting with Jimmy, and that my first priority was to make sure none of my coaches or players had done something inappropriate. Very often, the head coach is the last one to know about hazing or bullying. There was also the remote possibility that Jimmy really wanted to transfer. As ingrained and involved as Jimmy was in our program, I felt that if he was so selfish and uncommitted that he would turn his back on his school, his friends, his teammates, and his coaches, then good riddance. Don't let the door hit you in the tail.

We all agreed that the next best course of action was to talk to Jimmy's mom and find out what she knew, and see where she was on all of this. Jimmy's mom was a nice lady who really loved her son. She had immigrated to the U.S. from Haiti, and her strong accent and sometimes-broken English made it a challenge to understand her. Thankfully, my ESOL (English to Speakers of Other Languages) counselor position came with a couple of very capable translators. Jimmy's mom knew the story and said pretty much everything Jimmy had said. She emphasized that she wanted Jimmy to stay at Naples High, and she asked me to talk to him to help him understand that it was best for him.

As I made my way back down to Ernie's office and the two of us moved on to Gary's, I was struck by the gap in this little fiasco. How on earth would anyone at the district administrative level know that any of this was going on? And just as soon as I finished detailing my conversation with Jimmy's mom, I asked that very question. Both Gary and Ernie said they didn't know, and we all agreed that we didn't like it. The meeting ended; the next step for me was to make sure Jimmy had whatever papers he needed. I was also going to press him a bit more, to make sure none of our coaches or players were driving him away through some action that was inappropriate.

For his mom's benefit, I took a page from the decision-making unit taught in our health classes, and decided to have Jimmy write down the pros and cons of transferring. The maddening thing about this situation was, here we had a current Naples High football player, a student who lived in our school zone, who was thriving at our school. But he was considering a transfer in order to play football at another school – something that was expressly forbidden by both our state rules and our district rules. The district knew about it, but instead of condemning the move immediately, the district seemed to be trying to facilitate it.

I called Jimmy down to my office the next day and pressed him to make sure none of our coaches or players had done anything to offend him. He said the opposite was true, that the coaches and players were great. I asked him — for the sake of his mom — to make a pros-and-cons list, and I also finally asked him if he had contacted anyone from the district about transferring. Jimmy was really vague when answering that last question. He said he had talked to someone at the district, but he didn't recall who had called who first.

I sent Jimmy on his way, and figured that the little saga would sort itself out before too long. I couldn't imagine the district administration approving his request anyway. He had no reason to transfer, other than that he wanted to play football at Barron Collier, and moving to play a sport was expressly forbidden by the district and the FHSAA. I went on to the next thing on my to-do list, satisfied that I wouldn't have to spend any more time on the Jimmy transfer.

I had some other surprising news that January, too. A letter came to me at school with a return address that I did not recognize. The author wrote that I did not know him, but he knew I was the Naples football coach. He said he'd had an encounter with two of my players and that I should know about it.

He went on to say that he and his wife had retired and moved into the trailer park just north of the high school many years earlier. He wanted to tell me that one evening during the previous month, just a few days before Christmas, there was a knock on his door. The two kids at the door introduced themselves and told him they were from the Naples High Fellowship of Christian Athletes club. They had a poinsettia for him with a card attached that wished him a Merry Christmas and gave a short version of the nativity story. The man told them that he didn't want the plant, but the kids explained that they weren't selling the plants; they were giving them away to folks in the trailer park as a Christmas gift.

As I read the letter, I remembered that Jamie and Mandi Lemmond had organized that FCA project. Their gang had brought wagons and used the track team's hurdle carts to haul poinsettias to give to folks in the neighborhoods north of the school.

Our friend who wrote the letter went on to tell me that in the previous year, his wife had become ill and passed away. He said he had struggled mightily since his wife's death; in fact, on the evening that those Naples High athletes knocked on his door, he was planning on ending his life. After his visit with the kids he went inside, read the card, and did something he had not done in a long time . . . he prayed.

After his wife's passing he had abandoned his faith; that abandonment had taken him to a dark place. But since the evening that those FCA kids knocked on his door, he started faithfully praying and reading his Bible. He still missed his wife, but his heart was healing and he had a renewed purpose. He was walking in the light. He closed his letter by asking me to pass his sincere gratitude on to those kids and the folks involved in spreading that Christmas cheer.

I was really encouraged by his letter; it reminded me of John 8:12, where Jesus says he is the light of the world. It also reminded me that we just never know what is going on behind the scenes with the people we encounter each day.

CHAPTER

42

Within a week of my meeting with Jimmy, I was contacted by Peter DeBaun from the Collier County School District administrative offices. He asked me when a good time would be for him to come and meet with me regarding Jimmy's transfer. I gave him my earliest next appointment that fit his schedule, hung up the phone, and headed to Gary's office.

When I told Gary who had just called and asked for an appointment, his face flushed. He told me that Peter DeBaun was the district's lead personnel investigator, and that he usually spent his time following leads on the big stuff; i.e., employee drug use and inappropriate contact with students. I told Gary that Mr. DeBaun said he wanted to meet about Jimmy; both Gary and I felt like there had to be something more. Gary assured me that he would call people he knew at the district office, and would find out what the meeting was really all about.

I made sure to see Gary first thing the next morning, and he did not have any news. He'd tried to find out, but if anyone knew anything, no one was saying anything. As the date of our meeting moved closer, I tried to move forward under the old adage, "no news is good news," but I wasn't really believing it.

Peter DeBaun was of medium build with dark hair and glasses, a nondescript, regular-looking guy. Nonetheless, he had the air of an investigator about him. He just seemed like what I imagined a guy doing that job would be like. While he was poker-faced, he was also extremely professional and courteous, so much so that I never felt very comfortable with him. He asked me very specific questions about my relationship with Jimmy; when I first heard anything about Jimmy wanting to transfer. He asked for details, right down to what class it was that I had called Jimmy from in order to speak with him.

I answered all of his questions, and at some point toward the end I said to him, "OK, so let me get this straight. I have a student who lives in my school zone and plays football for me. He is thriving at our school academically, socially, and athletically. At my principal's direction, I talk with him and his mother about why he would want to leave my school — and I am being investigated for recruiting?"

Peter DeBaun pretty much ignored that, and then I said, "Has anybody noticed that it is expressly forbidden for kids to transfer schools to play a sport at another school? If we're going to do an investigation, shouldn't someone be investigating the guys that are trying to get him to transfer to the other school?" At that,

Peter DeBaun told me his job was to gather information for the superintendent and write down the facts that he found; whatever would be done with that information was out of his hands.

I had a couple of calls from Peter DeBaun over the next couple of weeks as he looked for a little more detail. Each time, I pressed him for the real motives and for information about the person or people behind the investigation. Each time, he was his cool, professional self and stuck to his script. In early February, Peter DeBaun came by my office again. Evidently, there are an infinite number of ways to ask the same question. Once again, I answered the questions with the same answers. One really convenient thing about telling the truth is that you don't have to remember what you said. And once again, I pressed him to tell me what the heck was really going on, and finally got a chink in the armor. He looked at me and said flatly, "I have a teacher smoking dope with students, and I have a teacher who I think is sleeping with a student. The fact that I am here with you, investigating this, is embarrassing."

In that moment, I realized the investigation was simply petty and vindictive. Someone with juice at the district level was still ticked off about the goalposts, and they were going to make sure I was punished — one way or another. As he left, Peter DeBaun said he didn't anticipate that he would be contacting me again; he would finish his report and have it to Dr. Morris within the week.

CHAPTER 43

February and March were going as well as they could. With spring football beginning May 1, I felt like every day with our guys had to be maximized academically and athletically if we were to win a state championship. On the academic end, I was working hard to get our guys going in the classroom. I did our standard planner and flashcard checks, where the boys would bring me their up-to-date planners and 10 vocabulary flashcards each week for grading. I was also working with them on using the Princeton Review curriculum for SAT and ACT test prep.

We spent a lot of time rehearsing the test and taking practice tests. As I had done at American High, I taught the guys how to aim for a target score and then prepare for that score by first eliminating portions of the test they would not answer.

That allowed for more focused time to answer the portions they needed to perform well on. I taught them how the SAT and ACT tests are designed, and covered strategies for eliminating the bad answers and solving for the correct answers. It isn't enough to fuss at guys to get good grades; we have to give them the tools.

My days as a guidance counselor that second spring were more palatable, but they were no less cumbersome. They were easier to take in that I had a better idea of the ins and outs and the ergonomics, but the sheer volume was overwhelming. Once again, our ESOL department was selected to be audited. Missy Zeliff, our lead teacher for ESOL, saved our bacon; she was smart and tireless, and I was grateful for her.

The conversation that I needed to have with Gary Brown regarding my teaching schedule wound up being really easy. The district had decided we were going to the 4x4 block schedule, and they were doing everything they could to convince the teachers in the district that it was simply the best for everyone.

I remember seeing PowerPoint slides of the research data on the 4x4 block schedule, which proved how the model was absolutely best for students. The 4x4 model is similar to college, where students go to four classes a day, every day, and earn a full credit for each class in 18 weeks. In the second half of the year, the student would have four new classes; therefore, they could earn eight credits a year. A few years later, it was amusing when the district tried just as desperately to convince us that seven classes a day was absolutely the best thing for kids. Welcome to the bureaucracy and politics of education.

The new class schedule meant we would need a few new teachers. So, I figured that it would be perfect timing to have my schedule conversation with Gary, and one late afternoon toward the end of March, I found him alone in his office. I came to the point pretty quickly. I remember saying, "Gary, I can be a great football coach or a great guidance counselor, but I cannot do both any more. I am losing my family. You did a national search for a head football coach and wound up finding me. If you wanted to hire a counselor, you would post on the internet and interview the first five who sent decent resumes, or hire someone from within the district. You need to let me know what you want me to do."

Gary assured me that it would be way easier to replace a counselor than a football coach; all that was left was to figure out what my teaching schedule would be.

We came up with the plan that I could teach personal fitness and health for first and second block, have the third block be my planning period, and then teach a combination study skills and weight training class for the fourth block. We also figured that since all freshmen have to take the personal fitness and health course, we could schedule as many freshman football players as possible in my first period. Second period would be random kids, and fourth period would be as many of the JV and varsity football players as we could schedule in that class. We both thought it was a good idea. With the insight I had as a counselor, I knew that if we were willing to do the work, we could make the schedules work. Heck, the marching band had a class; so did ROTC and the cheerleaders. Knowing there would be some relief with my next year's schedule gave me an extra little boost as I led the charge for all of us to finish the school year strong.

By early April I had pretty much forgotten about the "recruiting" investigation, assuming that truth and common sense had prevailed. Jimmy seemed to be thoroughly engaged; he was working hard athletically and academically.

Unfortunately, my false sense of security was just that. Reality hit when I got a call from Gary, asking me down to his office. I sat down and he got straight to it. He told me that Dr. Morris had called him and had concluded the investigation. He said Dr. Morris had a letter of reprimand for me. I was going to have to sign it as acknowledgement of wrongdoing, and the letter would go in my personnel file. Gary also said that he didn't foresee any disciplinary action being taken, as long as I signed the letter. If I refused, I could be terminated.

I was angry, and I told Gary there was no way I was signing any letter. I also told him I was going to get a lawyer, and that I wanted to see the report. Gary didn't discourage me from getting a lawyer, but did ask me to sleep on it, which I agreed to do. He too thought I was being railroaded.

I went back to my office, picked up the phone, and called the American Football Coaches Association's office in Waco, Texas. I knew I was a nobody, but I also knew they had some sort of legal division that members had access to. At the very least, I thought, I might get some good advice.

I told my story as quickly as I could to the lady who answered the phone; she was kind and patient, and asked me if I could hold for a moment. I was on hold, praying silently that God would give me wisdom, when I heard, "Hello, Coach Kramer" in an absolutely unmistakable Southern baritone. It was the executive director of the AFCA, Grant Teaff. The head honcho, the big dog, the grand poobah was on the other end of the phone. This was unbelievable. This guy is a bigtime. He is friends with the greatest coaches in the game – not to mention highly successful leaders all across the country, from all walks of life. He also has one of the greatest voices ever; he could narrate a Disney movie and bring you to tears, or narrate football highlights and bring you to cheers . . . he is one of a kind.

I explained my situation to Coach Teaff, and he told me I should meet with the superintendent and demand a copy of the investigator's report first. Coach Teaff told me Florida had a Sunshine Law. He said that if the superintendent didn't give the report to me, I could order it just as a media person would, and the district would have to produce it. He asked me to get it, read it, and call him back. He also said that if it described what I had told him, and if they still wanted to make me sign or be fired, he would have a lawyer in Naples in the blink of an eye. He told me it would become a media event. I thanked Coach Teaff and asked him if I could drop his name with Dr. Morris. His baritone "Absolutely!" filled me with confidence.

When I got home and told Sue about the day, she was not happy I was being treated unfairly. My wife loves me more than anyone in my life ever has, and she is protective of me. She didn't like the idea of me signing a letter of reprimand one bit. Sue and I were both really encouraged and amazed by the interest and effort that Coach Teaff was giving my situation. Sue comforted me more than once by reminding me that God was in control, and that I had done nothing wrong.

CHAPTER

44

As I sat in the reception area waiting for the assistant superintendent, I was at peace. Enough time and prayer had passed; I knew God was going to handle this situation, however it turned out.

I entered the office, and Dr. Morris and I exchanged greetings. I didn't want him to get into whatever he was going to start with, as I thought that what I had to tell him could possibly change things. I also did not want to waste anyone's time. I asked him if I could take a minute to get him up to speed on some stuff that had transpired, and he said I could. I recounted my meeting with Gary Brown and the conversation that I had with Grant Teaff. When I was finished, I asked him if I could see the investigator's report and offered to meet with him another time if he couldn't produce it. I also mentioned that I could go through whatever procedure was required by the Sunshine Law to obtain the report.

I don't know if he was angry or not, but I got the sense that maybe Gary had given Dr. Morris a heads-up. He slid the report across his desk and told me I could read it, but that I would have to sit there and read it in his office. I would not be allowed to take a copy. I began reading, and there it was in black and white — the conversations I had with Peter DeBaun, in detail, along with interviews with several other people at both Naples High and Barron Collier. Of course, interactions with Jimmy and his mother were included too. It was weird to see my conversation in black and white from my listener's perspective, and it was impressive to see the detail that had gone into the report. There were dates and times and specific emails that I didn't know he had. He even found exactly what class I had called Jimmy from to speak with him, what times he had left and had returned to class, and there was a notation that the teacher had approved of him leaving class.

I was glad to find that the report corroborated everything that I said. I guess I expected some contradiction or a different version of events. I felt vindicated when, at the end of the report, Peter DeBaun wrote that not only had I done nothing wrong, but it seemed pretty evident that people with an interest in Barron Collier football were recruiting Jimmy.

I set the report down and looked at Dr. Morris. He told me that all I needed to do was sign the letter that he was sliding across the desk to me, and then we would be through. I looked at what was obviously a letter of reprimand, and was completely baffled. "Why on earth would I have a letter of reprimand?" I asked. The report clearly stated that I did nothing wrong, and if anyone should have been investigated, it should have been the somebody at Barron Collier.

I can remember, clear as day, Dr. Morris's response: "It is not the job of the investigator to draw conclusions; his job is to gather facts and write the report. It is my job to figure out what really happened, and... I don't think your intentions are altogether altruistic." I had no idea where he was going with his line of reasoning; I just sat, dumbfounded, and listened. Dr. Morris went on to tell me that when I was arranging tutoring for Jimmy, helping him or his mom fill out insurance forms, or giving him a ride to the doctor or to physical therapy, I was only doing that stuff because I wanted him to play football for me. And then the quote of the day: he said that by doing all I had done for Jimmy, I had "encumbered his decision for school choice."

I could not believe what I was hearing. "So," I asked, "when I have a player who needs medical care or academic help, I am supposed to ignore him? And, you are mentioning school choice; he lives in our school zone and plays football for us already. What does that have to do with school choice? The rule clearly says that students may not transfer to play a sport." But Dr. Morris didn't want to hear any of that, and he really did not have to offer me a rationale for anything. He was clearly irritated. He told me the investigation was complete; I needed to sign the letter and then the case would be closed. I politely told him there was no way I was going to sign the letter, and that I was willing to go to both Coach Teaff and the media with the investigation and its findings.

Dr. Morris told me that we did not need to get the media or anyone else involved. He said that it would be bad for the district, bad for football, and bad for all of the people involved — especially Jimmy. He concluded by telling me that the letter would not go in my professional file; he was going to take the unsigned letter and keep it in his personal file in his desk drawer. He finished by saying that he would be keeping a close eye on me.

I left and headed straight to Gary Brown's house. He did not seem a bit surprised, but he did seem relieved. We were both glad to have that situation behind us. I felt bad for causing Gary stress, and I didn't want him to get messed with by his bosses. Once again, I thought about how my job was to make the principal's job easier. I didn't feel like I was succeeding.

Interestingly, Jimmy was not at the first spring practice on May 1, 2000. We had issued equipment the previous week; Jimmy had come and picked up his stuff, and everything seemed copacetic. I normally would have been chasing down one of our guys who missed the first day of practice, but I was gun-shy with Jimmy. I didn't even blink when he didn't answer after I called his name while taking attendance.

The next morning, Jimmy's cousin walked in the open door to my guidance office and said, "Hey Coach, did you hear about Jimmy?" I told her I hadn't heard anything; all I knew was that he had missed the first day of practice the previous day. His cousin went on to tell me that he was at Barron Collier, and he was playing football there — much to her chagrin.

She also said that someone had gone to Jimmy's house two nights earlier with transfer paperwork. All of the paperwork was completed and OK'd, so that he would not miss the first day of spring practice at Barron Collier. I could not believe it. I went to my computer and there it was, plain as day. When I looked up Jimmy, it showed that he now attended Barron.

I really did not care. We had a whole bunch of guys who believed in us and what we were doing. Our coaches were growing to love each other and our players, and our players were growing to love each other and their coaches. If Jimmy didn't want to be at Naples, it was his loss.

An interesting footnote to this story: many years after my meeting with Dr. Morris, I was shopping at Lowe's when an older gentleman came up to me and said, "Hey Coach, you got a minute?" I assumed that it was one of our fans, about to give me some advice or looking for an inside scoop. He introduced himself with the disclaimer that I might not remember him; then, he told me he was Tom Morris. He went on to apologize. He told me he had followed our program through the years, knew a lot of people who knew me, and that he had been wrong all those years ago. I told him there were no hard feelings, and that I hoped I would see him at a game.

That Lowe's encounter was a good reminder to me — I do not want to define people by their worst moment, their biggest mistake, or their one affront. In the verse right after the Lord's Prayer, Jesus tells us that our Heavenly Father will forgive us as we forgive other people. I need to remember this.

CHAPTER 45

One of the guys I was looking forward to watching that spring was a lanky freshman named Josh Greco. Josh had never played organized football before; he played basketball and baseball.

I was in my guidance office early in Josh's freshman year, when our guidance director, Evan Flamer, came in and gave me Josh's name. He told me that I might want to connect with him. He told me Josh was a good kid from a rough situation, and because he was an athlete and I was a young coach, I might want to make myself available to him. He added that Josh had recently lost his dad by suicide, and said Josh's mom was struggling.

I thought it would be awkward to call Josh down to my office; maybe just a bit too formal. Fortunately, within a couple of days, I was able to bump into him. He was called down to the office for something else, and it gave me a chance to shake his hand and get an eyeball on him. Josh was about 6 feet tall, with jet black hair, broad shoulders, and big hands. I didn't talk to him about his dad at all; I found out later it was his stepdad who had died, but it was the only dad he had ever known. He didn't talk much that first meeting, and I didn't press him. But I did let him know that I was available for him if he ever needed to talk about anything.

As the year went on, I occasionally bumped into Josh at lunch or as I walked through the gym during basketball practice. He was a very level guy; never loud and never emotional. He was more mature than his freshman brethren. Josh even made the varsity basketball team as a freshman — something very rare at that time at Naples High. Josh didn't play much in games, but I saw him play plenty in practice. I loved what I saw.

I had not gone to basketball practice to see Josh; I had gone to watch our basketball coach. I like to watch coaches coach. I have learned a lot about coaching from some really good coaches. I have also learned a lot about coaching from some really bad coaches.

Fortunately, we had a legend in our head boys' basketball coach, Tommy Smith. Since the weight room was attached to the gym, I had plenty of opportunities to watch Coach Smith work. I didn't stay long, but I spent two or three minutes watching basketball practice nearly every day as I was walking from the weight room.

That freshman kid Josh Greco stood out to me. He didn't play many minutes on game night, but in practice he gave the upperclassmen fits. Josh was extremely athletic, extremely competitive, and extremely smart. He also possessed the key ingredient for any great athlete: he was unflappable under pressure. He hadn't played football his freshman year, but the more I watched him at basketball practice, the more convinced I was that Josh Greco could be a championship quarterback. I told him just that when I approached him about playing football.

Just after Christmas break, I was in the guidance office and got a call from Peggy Sadelfeld. Peggy would call me on occasion when her Home Ec class was cooking something particularly delicious, or anything that could be classified as Mexican food. I would run over to her class and grab a plate. It was always terrific. It just so happened Josh Greco was in her class that day. I asked Peggy if I could talk to Josh for a minute, and she agreed.

As he shook my hand and said hello, I said to him, "Do you know what you are?"

His facial expression was somewhere between amused and puzzled as he said, "No, what am I?"

"You," I replied, "are a state champion quarterback."

I asked Josh if he had ever played football, and he said that he had not, other than some pick-up games in the neighborhood or at the park. I asked him if he had played quarterback in those games. He told me he had not, but said he would sometimes go outside at his house and throw a football over his house from the front yard to the back yard — back and forth.

I assured him that was good enough, and told him that I would teach him everything he would need to know. It was my experience that having a blank pallet to work with is much better than trying to break bad habits. Josh really was a newbie when it came to football. This was most obvious when he showed up for his first day of spring football practice wearing his metal baseball spikes. I told him it wouldn't matter that first day, as he would only be conditioning, but I advised him that he'd need to be in some rubber cleats by the time we started contact in practice.

My "Great Day... Today!" at the start of practices that spring was heartfelt and delivered with gusto. We were improving each day and having fun doing it. Our work in progress was making progress. Because so many young players had played the previous year, we had much of the team returning during the spring of 2000. It was energizing to see the boys really begin to understand the effort and tempo that was necessary for Naples High to compete for a state championship.

It was also really encouraging for me to get to work with Stanley Bryant and Josh Greco. Those two guys were everything you could ask for. They were great students and great teammates. The fact that both of them were gifted athletes was icing on the cake. I was really fortunate to have Stanley Bryant on our team, because he was an incredible mentor to the younger players — Josh Greco in particular. Stan was also one of the few guys that three of our best players would listen to. Stan had grown up with Duane Coleman, Anthony Denson, and Bruce Gordon, and while all of those guys were tremendous athletes, I would be lying if I said any of them were low maintenance.

None of them were particularly motivated in the classroom. Stan did all he could to help me move his pals forward, but I still had to work constantly to motivate them to work in school and hold them accountable when they refused. It was like pulling teeth to get them to understand that they would find life much easier, and success much more attainable, if they would prepare and compete in the classroom the way they did on the football field.

Another prod for our players and coaches each practice that spring was our upcoming spring game date with Bradenton Manatee. We would be at their place for our spring game – and playing at Bradenton Manatee was no joke. The two-hour trek north up I-75 would be a great test for us. Manatee was an established powerhouse in Florida — and in the country, for that matter. I knew that if we could hold our own against them, we could hold our own against anyone.

CHAPTER 46

Entering Hawkins Stadium can be overwhelming. It is big, and it is old, but not worn down. It is old and well kept, and there are so many state, regional, and district championships painted on the scoreboard that it's intimidating to read them all. Our guys had the Hillsborough experience from the year before in the bank, and that certainly helped. But there was no help to be found when Manatee's mammoth, fast players took the field. I am pretty sure that the ground shook and local seismographs started bouncing as those players warmed up. Our guys were obviously doing everything they could to ignore the size and speed across the way in the red helmets, but that was pretty much impossible.

It's also impossible to simulate size and speed in practice, so it took us a while to catch up in the game. With about a minute left in the first half, we found ourselves down 17-0. Manatee was having their way in every phase of the game. On what we anticipated as the last play of the half, Stanley Bryant connected with Cleannord Saintil on a great throw and catch. Time expired as Cleannord ran for his life down the sideline. A Manatee defender tackled him out of bounds at the 10-yard-line, and as luck would have it, there was a roughing-the-passer penalty against Manatee on the play. The rules allowed us one untimed down. With the penalty assessed after the catch, we had first and goal from the Manatee 5-yard-line. One Anthony Denson 5-yard run later, we headed into the locker room with the score 17-7.

We really needed the confidence boost that the score at the end of the half gave us. As we gathered in the locker room to figure out how to fix things, our players and coaches felt a sense of possibility. We also really needed that halftime break to catch our breath and regroup. It was obvious that we were physically outmanned at just about every position; yet, there was still a sense of optimism in the humid locker room air.

The task at hand was to find a way for us to win. We had to be more technical than they were, so that each guy individually would have a chance to win his individual battle. We also had to win tactically with play-calling that gave the unit on the field an advantage as a group. One of the strengths of our staff was halftime adjustments, and our players now had the knowledge, strength, and confidence to implement those adjustments.

The second-half start was very different from the first. We received the opening kickoff, and the fans had not yet settled back in their seats when Anthony Denson found room on the dive off of our triple-option veer; 64 yards later, the score was

17-14. On Manatee's ensuing possession, the Dollar defense did what it would become known for, getting the ball back for the Naples offense, and it forced a Manatee turnover.

With Manatee a little shell-shocked, the Golden Eagle offense picked right up where it left off. Stanley Bryant and Duane Coleman showed the fans what the pitch phase of the triple option looked like, as Coleman took the pitch 62 yards for a Naples score. We now had the lead, and the full attention of the Manatee players, coaches, and fans. And consequently, those Manatee Hurricanes did what great teams do. They refocused and came storming back. The third quarter ended with Manatee retaking the lead, and the score was 38 for the Bradenton Manatee Hurricanes and 28 for the Naples Golden Eagles.

The fourth quarter continued to be a slugfest, with both teams keeping their starting players in the game. While we did close the gap to three points, we would never regain the lead. The final score, with Manatee winning 44-35, was a disappointment for all of our guys. All of our coaches and players knew that if each individual guy had coached or played just a fraction better, we would have won the game. That mindset was a quantum leap for the Naples High football program.

Our summer workouts began immediately at the conclusion of the school year. Once again, coaches volunteered their time. The coaches' commitment and selflessness were obvious. Any one of our guys could have spent that same time making money to help pay summer bills... bills for which there was no school district paycheck help from June to August.

Especially during summers, kids are much more likely to forgo or postpone risky behaviors if they are working hard to keep their bodies in physical shape. It also helps if they have a place to belong, with someone checking to see that they are there each day. Our coaches knew that and were committed to helping our young people.

During our first year, our Team Committee had come to me and asked if we could have some sort of accountability system for guys during summer workouts. I asked what they had in mind, and after bouncing it around with them a good bit, we came up with what was affectionately called the Mile High Club. Players would be allowed 10 workout days off during the summer. For every day they missed beyond the 10 they would have to run a mile after practice within a prescribed time. Players would not be allowed to dress for a game until they completed their mile highs. There were no exceptions; the worst-case scenario was when a player would have a custodial parent in another state. In that case, I would sympathize with them and give them a great workout to take with them — which, when completed, would ensure they would be able to finish their thirty or forty mile highs.

The idea was, if you and I were going to buy a car together, we would both need to be equally invested in order to share the care equitably. If I gave $200 toward the $1,000 car and you gave the other $800, chances are you would not want me to drive the car on the weekends. You would probably figure that I could use it maybe Tuesdays and Wednesdays. So, if I wanted to be a full-fledged equal partner, I would have to be equally invested.

That equality of investment created an incredible synergy. Each guy on that sideline and in that huddle knew every other guy had invested as much as he had; this eliminated much of the petty jealousies that normally exist on a team.

The plan was an easy sell and agreed upon by the team, in part because of the way the team leadership was set up. I found early in my athletic career that coaches rarely knew who the real leaders in the locker room were. Captains were usually selected because of their athletic ability or because of their ability to kiss up to the head coach or coaching staff. In contrast, our Team Committee was made up of six players who would be chosen by the team.

The players were given the team roster as a ballot and asked to choose six teammates they trusted — guys they could count on every game night, in the community, in the classroom, and in the weight room. I asked them to pick people they could trust to decide consequences for players who messed up, guys they could take instruction from, and individuals that they would trust on a weekend trip with their sister. I would also tell them that if they didn't know anyone on our team that fit that bill, the problem was with them, not their teammates.

The Team Committee had nothing to do with how fast a guy ran or how high he jumped. The Team Committee had everything to do with authentic servant leadership.

CHAPTER 48

Three things happened during that summer of 2000 that were really beneficial to our team. We had several players go to camps — either the FCA Leadership Camp in Black Mountain, North Carolina, or the Kanakuk Kamps near Branson, Missouri. Several of our coaches and their families were able to go to the FCA Coaches Camp, which was also in Black Mountain. In all cases, scholarship money made it possible. For players and coaches, that time of study, reflection, and fellowship had long-term positive results; in fact, for some of our guys, the results were life-changing. At Black Mountain, we were at camp with high school coaches, college coaches, NFL coaches, and their families.

For years, I had been challenged by Ken Sparks, the head football coach at Carson-Newman, to go to Black Mountain. As usual, Ken Sparks knew what he was talking about. To this day, I don't know what provoked Ken Sparks to take me under his wing and mentor me, but I am grateful that God brought him into my life. Ken Sparks was the real deal; a man's man who loved God, and as a result, loved those around him.

On the mountain, it doesn't matter what level you coach or how much money you make. In fact, the high school coaches often had it way more together in their spiritual lives — and consequently in their marriages and their parenting — than many of the college and pro guys.

I remember many guys from camp through the years, but Clyde Christensen, Bob Sanders, and Tony Dungy all stood out to me. These were guys coaching at the highest levels of football who were great husbands and fathers. They all went out of their way to pour their positive spirit into coaches they came in contact with. There are many other guys through the years whom I have also admired and want to emulate, but I spent a lot of time just watching these three. What I saw was authentic love. I saw servant leadership in action.

CHAPTER 49

As fall camp approached in 2000, we had a great motivator to train hard. We were told that our third game, a September 8 rematch with Charlotte High School, was going to be carried live on the Sunshine Network throughout Florida and several southeastern states. It was the first time anyone I asked could remember two southwest Florida teams appearing live on regional TV. The network guys said they thought it was the best game in the state on that night.

If the previous season was any indicator, the game would be a dogfight. We had a convincing win during the previous regular season at Charlotte, and they had returned the favor in the shootout during the last week of the season. The upcoming game, live and in color, was going to be epic and our players knew it.

With all of the **"EVERYDAY IS A SHOOTOUT!"** T-shirts our guys wore as a constant reminder, we didn't have many lulls in our workouts. On the occasion when there was a lull in a summer workout session, we reminded our guys about playing Charlotte on TV, and they responded with increased effort and energy.

The theme for the coaches' retreat in the late summer of 2000 was obvious to me throughout the 1999-2000 school year. While much of the school was enthusiastically supporting what we were trying to do with our program, there was still a small group of folks who did what they could to make our lives difficult. For many of our coaches, that nagging problem was having a cumulative effect, and it was not healthy for them or for our program. In addition, we had experienced several instances of coaches disagreeing and losing their cool with one another; I had to make absolutely sure we could reconcile these differences. Our theme for the coaches for the 2000 season was simply: Forgiveness.

Our coaches' retreat centered around some simple and heavy truths. As long as we carry unforgiveness toward someone, we are bound to that person. We cannot be free from them until we forgive them. As Nelson Mandela said, refusing to forgive someone is like drinking poison and expecting the other person to die. It just doesn't make sense. And perhaps the most important part is: just as we want God to forgive us, He wants us to forgive others. Not always easy, but always necessary. For the record, if I forgive someone, it doesn't necessarily mean the relationship between me and the other person is restored. That person may continue to hate me. What it does mean is that the relationship between me and my Creator is restored.

Another interesting thing happened just before the start to the regular season in 2000. The Naples football team appeared in the two big sports writers' preseason polls. Well, maybe not actually *in* the poll as we didn't make the top ten, but we were in the "also getting votes" section. Few could remember the last time they had seen that.

Our first game was the Kickoff Classic against Port Charlotte. Kickoff Classic is the name the Florida High School Athletic Association gave to preseason games in Florida. We treated them just like a regular season game; the only difference was the state got a cut of the gate receipts.

Port Charlotte had a really big, athletic quarterback named Anthony Hargrove. He also played safety on defense, and we were hoping we could tire him out enough on defense so he wouldn't be as effective on offense. Going into the game, we weren't exactly sure how that was going to work. Our starting quarterback, Stanley Bryant, had banged his knee the week before and wasn't playing. Anthony Denson, one of our starting running backs, had twisted his ankle and would not be available to play either. Thankfully, we had Duane Coleman in the backfield, and sophomore quarterback Josh Greco had demonstrated in practice that he was a really special athlete. I was eager to see how Josh would perform in a game.

Josh Greco did not disappoint. By the beginning of the fourth quarter, Naples High was up 38-0, and we were playing with a running clock. Josh Greco had thrown for 164 yards and two touchdowns, and Duane Coleman ran for 132 yards and three touchdowns on only nine carries. Our defense dominated, start to finish, and held Anthony Hargrove in check. I doubt that we had anything to do with it, but Hargrove later wound up changing positions. He would have a long and distinguished career as a defensive end in the NFL.

Josh Greco was a competitor, and like all great competitors, he wanted to play. He was a little edgy as we prepared for the next week. Josh never said anything, but his demeanor told me that he thought he should be starting the upcoming game against Gulf Coast. But Stanley Bryant was a competitor too; the senior returning starter was not going to just let that young whipper-snapper take his position.

At Naples High, we made it very clear about who was going to be a starter or who would play, and who would not. Coaches watched practice videos and graded each player on every play. Before every scheduled practice, players got a grade sheet which showed their grade for each play. Before practice each day, coaches and players spent about half an hour watching the video together. Any disputes about the grades were settled while watching the video. That system ensured that each player would know exactly what he was doing right and what he needed to improve.

Our standing rule was that the guys with the higher practice grades would start. If two guys tied, we deferred to the younger guy. The only exception was, in the event of a tie, we gave the older guy the nod to start **if** he was a previous starter. In the case of Stan and Josh, Stan was the guy who scored a little higher in practice, and he was the returning starter.

There were some players who were not going to play unless we were winning by a lot or losing by a lot. The good news is we often won by a lot, and many nights everyone on the team got to play.

The Gulf Coast game verified what the practice video had told me. Stanley had an incredible night, completing 13 of 20 passes for 296 yards and four touchdowns. He also carried the ball six times for 61 yards and two touchdowns. For his part, Josh Greco was a terrific teammate, communicating with and encouraging Stanley throughout the game. As usually happens, the competition between these two players made both of them better players.

My challenge the week before the Charlotte game was to keep the main thing the main thing. The hype surrounding the game would have been a distraction if our coaches and players had allowed it. The Naples Daily News and all of the television networks made a good effort to publicize our game with Charlotte; the school was buzzing in anticipation. The excitement on campus was really cool unless you were the coach, trying to make sure your players were focused on their studies and practice. In the end, our players and coaches took the increased media attention in stride. We had a very focused workweek. Consequently, our team had earned the confidence we shared heading into the game.

The crowd arrived early at Staver Field on that hot and humid Friday night, the first week of September 2000. Both sides of the stadium were fired up. It was impossible for coaches, players, or fans not to notice the production semis, the cameras on scaffolds, and the television trucks that were covering the game. Charlotte had fantastic fans who followed their Tarpons en masse to away games. As a result, our stadium was bursting at the seams by kickoff.

From the outset, it was all Naples. The defense forced two Charlotte fumbles, and the punt block team did its job. The Naples offense took full advantage, and at the end of the first quarter the score was Naples 18 and Charlotte 0. The only blemish on the stellar first quarter was Naples' inability to convert on three PATs. Halftime found us up 32-8, and after a Naples score in the third quarter, the fat lady was singing loudly.

The final score of 39-14 was more than we could have hoped for against a talented and well-coached Charlotte Tarpon team. Duane Coleman was spectacular, with 126 yards rushing and 70 yards receiving. Stanley Bryant was his usual terrific self, with 140 yards passing and 46 yards rushing. The Naples defense was strong, creating six turnovers and setting the tone for the game from start to finish. The best part of the win was that we were 1-0 in the district standings and Charlotte was 0-1. In Florida, where all that mattered for the playoffs was your team's district win-loss record, that was huge. We would not have much time to celebrate, as we would travel to Immokalee the following Friday night to take on a very talented squad.

The Tuesday of Immokalee week found the Naples High School football team ranked in the Top 10 in the state football poll for the first time in a very long time. I clipped the poll results from the paper and posted them on the bulletin board in the locker room. However, I also explained to the players that while it was cool for folks in the state to notice us, the only poll that matters is the last poll of the year. Being ranked No. 9 after two regular season games was simply a starting point. I also told them that if we stumbled even a little bit, our name in the poll would disappear immediately.

Immokalee coach John Webber was a smart and hard-nosed football coach. He loved the kids who played for him, and John was a very intelligent human being. The thing John was best at was creating an "us against the world" mentality in his teams. That mentality was never more intense than when Immokalee was playing Naples. John Webber had each guy playing as if he believed someone had a gun pointed at his mother, and that an Immokalee win would be the only thing that could keep her safe.

Undefeated Naples took the field at undefeated Immokalee's packed Gary Bates Stadium on a mid-September Friday night. The heat and humidity were stifling. Nevertheless, Naples came out of the chute firing on all cylinders, and went into halftime with a 28-13 lead. As we headed into the locker room at halftime, I was torn. While I was pleased with our first-half performance, I sensed that our guys thought the game was already over. Unfortunately, I did a really poor job of changing their minds.

The second half was all Immokalee. Immokalee's great bruising running back Walter Campbell was a man among boys, and the three turnovers Naples gave away provided way too many opportunities for him to prove that. By the time our guys realized we had to match the effort and intensity of those Immokalee Indians for four quarters, there were only about three minutes left in the game, and we were down 35-31.

Thankfully, the urgency of the moment relit our fuse. Stanley Bryant led the Golden Eagles' hurry-up offense down the field like poop through a goose. With 47 seconds left in the game and with us third and goal from the 4-yard-line, I was convinced we were going to get the win and get out of Immokalee with a tough lesson learned. In football you can never relax, no matter what the lead may be. If players or coaches relax, not only is the outcome of the game in jeopardy, the health of the players is in jeopardy. If one player is playing at 80 percent and another is playing at 100 percent, the first player has a much greater risk of injury. It's important to play with 100 percent intensity and focus at every snap. In the end, Naples' fourth turnover just outside the Immokalee goal line gave us that painful lesson — but no win.

We were out of the poll immediately. Immokalee went from not appearing in the poll to No. 3 in their classification — from the outhouse to the penthouse for them, and vice versa for us.

CHAPTER 50

Week 4 found us at 2-1, facing a 2-1 Chaminade Madonna team out of Broward County. Chaminade had a terrific coach and a bunch of terrific players. They were led by running back Jerry Seymour, who would go on to rush for more than 2,400 yards and average nearly 22 yards per kick return at Central Michigan. They also had a guy named Jon Beason on the team who was pretty good; and by pretty good, I mean he went on to be All-Everything at the University of Miami, the 25th overall pick in the 2007 NFL draft, and second in the voting for NFL Defensive Rookie of the Year. After coaching against him, I was not surprised when he was later selected to several Pro Bowls. At one point, he signed a deal making him the highest-paid middle linebacker in NFL history.

I wish I'd had all that information from the future before we played Chaminade Madonna. Our guys saw a small private Catholic School that, like us, was 2-1. While we worked hard that week in preparation, there was no edge to us. Many of our players and coaches didn't understand that some small private schools had the money to scholarship really great players and invest a ton in their football program. Chaminade was doing just that. Head Coach Mark Guandolo had been at several schools and knew how to win state championships; Chaminade had recently hired him to win one for them. In the end, the Chaminade Wing-T offense was too much for us. We found ourselves on the short end of a 41-35 final score.

We took two great lessons from that game. First, our players needed to do exactly what we coached them to do. Great teams will expose an opposing player who is not disciplined in technique and assignment. Second, it was important to not turn the ball over. Both teams had three turnovers for a net zero in takeaways, but turnovers add a randomness to the game that is sometimes impossible to overcome. In our case, we turned the ball over close to our own endzone which led to Chaminade scores; Chaminade turned the ball over a long way from their end zone, and we were unable to sustain drives long enough to score.

Two weeks into the season, we had been 2-0 and ranked in the Top 10, coming off the biggest win in recent memory — and on television, no less. Four weeks into the season, we were 2-2. Polls and games on TV were now a distant memory.

Week 5 found us preparing for the Bishop Verot Vikings, another private Catholic school, this time from Fort Myers in Lee County. The bad news that week was that Stanley Bryant had taken a hit to his knee, and it was pretty sore. The good news that week was that Josh Greco was chomping at the bit to be our starting quarterback.

The players and the coaches were all tired of losing, and it took no effort to get our guys focused and practicing with intent that week.

The game itself on that sultry Friday started out all Naples. Josh Greco was stellar, and we raced out to a 28-0 lead. The well-coached Vikings from Verot never gave up, and when we put in some backup players, they took full advantage.

In the end, the final score was Naples 42 and Verot 21. Josh Greco threw for 278 yards and three touchdowns. Bruce Gordon scored three touchdowns; the first two were passes from Josh Greco. The third Bruce Gordon score was on a Bishop Verot onside kick attempt. From his front line position, Bruce cleanly fielded the kick, and proceeded untouched past the stunned Vikings kickoff team into the end zone.

As we approached the midpoint of the football season, things at home were much better than they had been the previous two years. I was still working a ton of hours, but being in the classroom was way more manageable than being a guidance counselor. Interestingly, two counselors were hired to handle the assignments that had buried me during my two years as a counselor.

Susie and the girls were settled in, and I was able to spend more time being a dad and a husband on the weekends and at night. Sue's parents, Duke and Angel Sistrunk, were our biggest fans. They faithfully made the trek from Fort Lauderdale every week during football season to support the Golden Eagles. To Duke and Angel, "support" did not just mean that they were fans in the stands on Friday nights.

To those two beautiful people, "support" meant helping to manage the girls, the grocery shopping, and the cooking that Sue did each week for the pregame meal that served 80 to 100 people.

CHAPTER

51

During the end of September and the beginning of October 2000, the local sports pages had many people following the story of Lely head coach Mark Swanson. On September 8, Lely played at home versus Lee County powerhouse Fort Myers. Mark Swanson was a fiery and intense competitor; he was also a really successful coach who loved his players. On that particular night, the half-time score was 21-0 in favor of Fort Myers. As Mark headed into the locker room, the lack of focus and energy in his team was obvious. In an effort to get his guys' attention, Coach Swanson walked into the locker room, grabbed the nearest helmet, and threw it down a bank of lockers. The helmet bounced around, and somewhere down the line it banged into the side of a player who was sitting on the floor leaning against a locker.

Coach Swanson then walked up to one of his guys, grabbed him by the shoulder pads, and pulled him close in to emphasize the point he was making. Namely, that it was completely unacceptable for that player, or any player, to first ignore and then intentionally undermine what coaches were telling players during a game. Grabbing a player for emphasis has been done by coaches since the beginning of time, in every sport known to man. The helmet hitting someone was bad luck, or bad aim, or both.

The problem? On most teams, not everyone got the same playing time. Sometimes, a backup player had an axe to grind. In Mark Swanson's case, a disgruntled player with influential parents simply could not bear the abuse that his poor teammates were being subjected to. So it began.

A Lely player's parents complained to the administration at Lely High School and also to the district administration, and someone called the newspaper so they could do their job too. The job of the newspaper is to sell papers, and the job of the school district is to prevent legal liability and negative exposure. In Mark's case, both groups went to work diligently.

Because of my experience with "Goalpostgate," I called Mark as soon as I read about his predicament. I told him that I was thinking of him and praying for him. I invited him over to hang out, or talk, or just to get away. Mark took me up on my offer; a few days later, we were able to sit on the couch in my family room and spend some time sorting it all out.

There were articles in the paper, editorials, and letters to the editor. Most of the letters to the editor were positive, although there were enough negative ones to make anyone mad. Mark described what happened. As he had told the district folks and the paper, he was trying to find a way to light a fire under his troops — nothing more. Mark's version was corroborated by his coaches and by the players. It's interesting that the player who was hit by the bouncing helmet wasn't complaining at all. The motor behind the boat was a backup player's parents who wanted their son to play, or play more. When Mark told the story, he was clearly upset — not necessarily for himself, but for his wife and three kids. The Swanson family had followed dad's lead and were all-in for Lely High. They had actually purchased a dog and named it Lely, for goodness sake.

This was Mark's first head coaching job. He had picked up and moved his young family with the intention of being a vital part of the fabric of the Lely community. When Mark and I first talked, his biggest decision was whether or not he should resign his position as head coach. Administrators were pressing him a bit by telling him that if he resigned the football position, the investigation would end, and he could just continue on as a math and economics teacher at Lely. By all accounts and evaluations, Mark Swanson was an outstanding teacher. The locker room outburst was the first-ever-negative-anything in his career. The admin folks also said that if Mark did not resign from football, the investigation could become a long and drawn out process. There was even a remote possibility he could lose his teaching job over it.

Mark and I agreed that the only course of action was to spend time in prayer for the foreseeable future and trust that God would give direction and peace. Within a few days, Mark came to the conclusion he should resign from football and have it over with.

I told him that as soon as circumstances would permit it, there would be a place for him on our staff at Naples.

Mark's football resignation did not bring closure. The district administrators were going after his job, and his school administration either couldn't, or wouldn't, do anything to prevent that. At one point, Mark was informed that he was in jeopardy of losing his teaching certificate altogether.

Coach Swanson is a really loyal and committed guy; it was inspiring for me to watch him cling to his faith and his family throughout the administrative process. Mark had peace and confidence because his process was prayerful and faithful. In the end, after the investigators and lawyers and mediators were through, Mark Swanson kept his teaching certificate.

In late September, I got a phone call from Gig Senini. Gig worked for Riddell, the equipment company where we bought our helmets and shoulder pads. Gig was a Riddell boss who worked out of Atlanta, but he was conscientious enough to follow up on us little guys. That great customer service was one reason that, in addition to our regular equipment, we had recently purchased home and away uniforms from Riddell.

Gig called to ask if I was interested — or knew anyone interested — in being a Riddell rep for South Florida. I am sure that phone call didn't qualify as a miracle, but I am convinced it was a godsend. The match was obvious; Mark Swanson had coached on the east and west coasts of South Florida. Mark had terrific people skills, was a really hard worker, understood what coaches needed, and taught both math and economics.

Sure, there were lots of guys like that running around for Riddell to choose from — Mark began working for Riddell on

Halloween that year. Not only did the job fit Mark to a T, it gave him a schedule that was flexible enough to allow him to coach both his daughters in youth basketball, coach his son in youth football, and eventually join our staff at Naples High.

When I was still in college, I remember my sister Sharon telling me that life is a series of trade-offs. You can't have everything, but you can always try to trade up. Mark Swanson definitely traded up.

CHAPTER

52

Week 6 of the football season found 3-2 Naples traveling up I-75 to play at 11th-ranked and undefeated Venice. Most of the players on our team had been on the field the night of the shootout the previous year, and we all — coaches and players — knew the buzz saw that we were about to walk into. The knowledge of that buzz saw did not motivate all of our guys as much as I had hoped.

On Monday of Venice week it was business as usual, with our guys going to class and then lunch; and then the last period of the day, most of the team had a weight training class with Coach Dollar and me. When attendance was taken for class that day, both Bruce Gordon and Duane Coleman were missing. Having seen both of them earlier in the day, I knew they had been in school. I hoped that they were somehow excused, because an unexcused absence would not be good. It would especially not be good for Bruce, as our attendance rule was clear: one unexcused absence, and a player would not start the next game; two unexcused, and he would be suspended for a week. This was Bruce's second unexcused absence. For Duane it was numero uno.

Coach Dollar took over the class, and I walked quickly to the attendance office with the hope that both players had been called down for something or checked out for something. No dice. My mind immediately began working on a game plan that allowed for us to miss our best running back for at least the beginning of the game, and our best receiver for the whole game.

As I took attendance at practice, I looked up to see number 3, Duane Coleman, in full gear, jogging across the field to get in his stretching line. Unfortunately, there was no number 15 jogging with him. I didn't address the issue with Duane until after practice, but the short version of the story was that Duane and Bruce had gone to their academic classes and then left campus at lunch to go hang out with a couple of girls. Duane managed to make it back to practice. Bruce did not.

Bruce would have an obvious consequence; he would be suspended for our most important game of the season. I knew I had to hold Duane accountable, too; I decided pretty quickly that Duane would have O-P-P and miss the first quarter of the game.

I let the coaches know Monday after practice, and on Tuesday, I told the team what the consequences would be for both Bruce and Duane. I emphasized that the rest of us were going to have to stand in the gaps that these guys had created because of their bad decisions.

Bringing Duane in after the first quarter did create an opportunity for a special play. My great idea was: on the first offensive play of the second quarter, we would pitch the ball to Duane as we might if we were going to run a speed option. Duane would then tuck the ball for two steps, pull it from under his arm, and throw a pass to the wide receiver. The receiver would have instructions to stalk block the corner, release down the sideline, and catch a touchdown pass from Duane.

I figured that when Duane Coleman entered the game, Venice's whole defense would key on him. All he would have to do is lob the ball to the receiver — who, according to my plan, would be completely uncovered.

The end of the first quarter found us down 7-3, but a tremendous effort from our punt block team gave our offense the ball on the Venice 13-yard-line. Every guy on the Naples sideline knew what was coming. Evidently, every guy on the Venice sideline did too. Duane took the pitch on the right side, but the defense did not sprint to him. The Venice defense read it as a pass play all the way, and completely covered the receiver. Duane threw the ball, and it was intercepted easily. Many of our fans let me know they thought that was the stupidest play call ever. No argument from me.

We managed two more really poor plays. The first was in Venice territory, as Stanley Bryant was pressured while making a quick throw to Bruce's backup. That guy, who had not played much at receiver, didn't realize that the ball was thrown backwards, and as such was a live ball — the same as a fumble. As our guy stood a few feet from the ball on the ground and watched it for what seemed like an hour or so, a Venice player, who understood the rule, scooped up the ball and ran as far and as fast as he could before being tackled. It was the Naples 16-yard-line. Four plays later, the great Venice and soon-to-be Auburn running back, Tre Smith, made the score 14-3, Venice. I had obviously done a poor job of teaching the live-ball rules of football.

On Naples' next possession, the Venice Indians stopped the Golden Eagles cold, and we were forced to punt from our own 27-yard line. Somehow, one of our coaches inadvertently signaled a fake punt call to our punter's personal protector, who just happened to be Stanley Bryant. Stanley summarily set up in the punt formation, took the snap, and threw the ball to no one. Stan was the only person on the field who knew it was a fake punt. Of course, the fans assumed I called it. While I didn't call it, the play was definitely my responsibility. *"Kramer, you idiot, what are you doing?!"*

Valid question.

It was now first and 10, Venice on the Naples 27. This time it took just two plays for the great Venice-soon-to-be-Auburn running back to score, and now we were down 21-3. My ears were ringing with *"Fire the coach."* I soon realized it was just me, talking to myself.

Thankfully, our players didn't see it that way. We came out of that halftime locker room, and for the first time that night, every coach and player was all-in and willing to do whatever he could to fight for the guy next to him. There was zero finger-pointing. Instead, there was unanimity in our love for and belief in each other.

At one point early in the second half, offensive lineman Chris Knapp came off the field holding his hand. Chris was strong, and he was one tough dude. Our odds of winning would slim considerably if Chris Knapp was not in the game.

Soon after Chris' exit, our offense stalled, and we punted. That allowed me to head over to where Chris was huddled with our trainer, our team doctor, Paul Horne, and several of his teammates. As I leaned in, I could see that Chris' pinky finger was bent at a right angle and then bent again at another weird angle.

Our team doctor, Mike Havig, confirmed my suspicion when he told both Paul and me that Chris was done for the night. His pinky was dislocated, and he needed to get to a hospital to have it reduced. Mike thought it probably needed surgery, and reducing it on the sideline could permanently damage the finger.

As soon as the words came out of Dr. Havig's mouth, Chris grabbed his pinky and pulled hard, moving his hands up over his head as he pulled. Before I realized what had happened, Chris Knapp held his hand straight out at no one in particular, and yelled, "Tape it!"

Voila. His pinky was straight; and while it was admittedly swollen and painful to bend, it was able to bend. After a few more tests on it from Dr. Havig, Chris was taped up and ready to play. Chris Knapp was strong and determined, and while I didn't necessarily agree with the risk he took, there was no denying how much he inspired his teammates.

The second half was all Naples.

With 13 seconds left in the game, and with the score Venice 28 and Naples 26, I had no choice but to go for the 2-point conversion. I was convinced that we would tie the score, go into overtime, and continue the second-half domination in overtime.

I was proud of our guys' resilience. This win would help fade the scar that Venice left on us during the previous year's shootout.

We called our bread-and-butter triple option. The play was built for situations like that, and is mathematically unstoppable when executed properly. As the ball was snapped, the mass of humanity in that goal-line scrap made it impossible to distinguish who had the ball or where it was. As the whistle blew, a Naples player wound up breaking loose and tumbled into the end zone. The side judge came running in and dramatically signaled that the runner's forward progress was stopped, and therefore he was down. Whatever happened after that was irrelevant. Ball game.

It was a long, quiet ride on the bus back to school that night. We had accumulated 330 yards of offense to Venice's 247. Each team had three turnovers, and in the chaos that turnovers create, we got the short end of the stick. We had effectively lost the district championship. At 3-3 and with a loss to undefeated Venice, our only hope for the playoffs was to win the district runner-up spot.

It was another trip from the penthouse — after the Charlotte win — to the outhouse, after the Venice loss. Instead of proving we were the cream of the crop, we were proving to be the cream of the crap. The responsibility and the fault were mine. I simply had to do a better job.

CHAPTER 53

Our next game was versus Lely in the 27th Annual Coconut Bowl. With Mark Swanson no longer at the helm, the Trojans were now led by Merv Ward, a former Lely head coach. Helped by an unchallenging schedule, Lely's record was identical to that of Naples at 3-3.

This was the rubber match in the Coconut Bowl series. Each school had taken the trophy home 13 times. To make things only marginally more interesting, the game was to be played on Friday, October 13, under a full moon. To say our coaches and players were a little edgy was an understatement.

It is commendable that Bruce Gordon asked to speak to the team during Monday's practice. His apology was really rough around the edges; it was also really sincere and honest. The vibe on the team seemed to be the same one I was feeling. *Come on back, Bruce, but we will know what you are by what you do, not by what you say.*

What we did on that Friday the 13th was completely dominate Lely. If not for a 91-yard Anthony Denson touchdown run being called back, Naples would have amassed more than 400 yards in the first half alone. As it was, we went into halftime winning 35-0, and the second half found the mercy rule in effect beginning with the kickoff. With a running clock, we played as many of our back-up guys as we could, and the final score wound up Naples 35, Lely 15. The Naples defense was spectacular, allowing only 81 total yards and creating four turnovers.

Our next game was against another district foe, Cape Coral's Mariner High School. We would face the winless Tritons at home. I can still hear Coach Dollar trying to fire up our guys that week in practice.

"Y'all know how hard it is to go undefeated?"

"Well, it is just about as tough to go defeated!"

"Think about it, how many defeated teams can you think of?"

I don't know if it was because of his logic or a pitiful 0-8 Mariner squad, but the Dollar defense allowed 13 total yards in a 57-0 rout that wasn't nearly as close as the score.

Game 9 would find us taking the 113-mile trek up I-75 to Sarasota High School. The Sailors were 4-4 on the season and stood at 2-2 in the district. A win for Naples would assure us of the runner-up spot in the district and stamp our ticket to the playoffs. Sarasota was fired up, and although Naples amassed over 400 yards of offense, several big goal-line stands by the Sailors kept them in the game. With less than a minute to play and a

30-28 lead, we lined up to punt the ball back to the Sailors, giving them one last chance to win the game. The punt snap was good, but our punter did not handle it cleanly, making it Sarasota's ball. It was first and 10 from their own 49-yard-line. Thankfully, the Naples defense answered the bell, and on fourth down, defensive lineman Francisco Clervoix sacked Sarasota QB Thomas Berkery to preserve the win for us.

It was a mostly quiet bus ride back to Naples. Our guys were proud of making the playoffs for the second consecutive year, but each of us knew that with a little more focus, a little less selfishness, and a little more attention to detail, we would have been district champions.

Our final game before the playoffs was against 2-7 Barron Collier. The Cougars should have been 4-5, but they had been forced to forfeit two games earlier in the season for playing two ineligible players. In their defense, the error was a clerical one, which they self-reported immediately. It was a shame for the rest of the team to have to give away two wins; it seemed to be demoralizing for the Barron Collier players and their coaches.

Our workweek was crisp that first week in November. The tropical weather had finally relented, and of course our guys were happy to have the Cougars at home after "Goalpostgate" the previous year. With the added incentive that their buddy Jimmy was playing running back for Barron, I did not have to say "Go" that week. It did occur to me that at some point I would need to say, "Whoa!"

Naples came out focused and fast, and jumped to a 13-0 lead six minutes into the first quarter. Barron answered less than two minutes later, with a 37-yard touchdown by — you guessed it

— Jimmy. That touchdown run pretty much sealed Barron's fate. Our defense was on a mission, individually and collectively, to keep Barron's offense out of our end zone. While they did move the ball effectively at times, the Cougars did not score again.

With just over two minutes remaining, our free safety, Mike Whooley, intercepted a Barron pass and scampered 93 yards to make the final score Naples 54, Barron Collier 7. The defensive score was just enough to allow us to set the all-time single-season scoring record at Naples High, with 393 points in a regular season. I thought it was really cool that a defensive score put us over the top.

Naples was now 7-3 and gunning for its first playoff win in 19 years. In more than 50 years of football, Naples High had an all-time playoff win-loss record of 4-5. We found some encouragement in the fact that our three losses were all in close games, to teams with a combined record of 29-1.

CHAPTER 54

Our draw in the first round of the playoffs was 8-2 Bradenton Manatee. We needed all the encouragement we could find; Manatee was a perennial state powerhouse. They had an all-time playoff record of 33-12, had won four state championships, and had played in several other title games.

Manatee's head coach, Joe Kinnan, was a legend throughout the state and in much of the country. Unfortunately for him and for us, he had just announced that he had been diagnosed with prostate cancer and would retire at the conclusion of the season, whenever that happened to be. To say that his players were playing with abandon is an understatement. They did not want to lose their coach.

Normally, I would not want to have played a team in the spring that we had a chance of playing in the playoffs. In the case of Manatee, I was glad we had. Our guys were already past the bigness of the stadium and the energy from their crowd. By that point in the season, we were actually starting to develop a consistent following of our own. When we were home, the home stands were full; on the road, the visitors' stands were full. No one would describe our fans as loud or intimidating, but they were there and that was a really cool change. Fans would have nothing to do with the outcome of this game anyway.

Friday, November 17, 2000, proved to be a cool fall evening — perfect football weather. Both teams were as prepared as they could be, and both teams gave their best effort. Manatee moved the ball effectively from the outset. Our guys fought for all they were worth, but the size, strength, skill, and speed of the Manatee players tipped the balance in their favor. The game plan that week pulled out all the stops; I was not going to leave anything in the bag on that one. Stanley Bryant jumped out of the gate hot, completing his first six passes of the game. Our little guys on defense were fighting their tails off against those beasts from Manatee. As we jogged into the locker room at halftime, down 14-7, I was really proud of our guys. Both teams had played nearly mistake-free in the first half. The fans were getting their money's worth.

As the game wore on, our guys wore down. The bigger, faster, stronger guys from Manatee were really wearing on us. Naples played well, committing just one penalty and losing just one turnover. We did all we could to keep it interesting, successfully converting a fake punt and a halfback throwback to the quarterback. It was simply not enough. Manatee rushed the ball for 327 yards and five touchdowns, controlling the ball and the clock for a 35-20 win.

After the game, all the media wanted to talk about was the size disparity between the two teams. I was happy to hear Duane Coleman tell a reporter after the game that the remedy was for Naples to work harder in the weight room during the offseason to get stronger. He didn't buy into the talk about how much bigger Manatee was. Our constant message of "control what we can control" seemed to be sinking in.

CHAPTER

55

Thanksgiving was a restful time for the girls and me. It was the first time in a long time that I hadn't spent a vacation in my guidance office. We spent a few days in Fort Lauderdale at Duke and Angel's. It was the perfect place for me to rest and recharge.

The state finals in 2000 were at Ben Hill Griffin Stadium, aka the Swamp, on the University of Florida campus in Gainesville. Venice had played really well throughout the playoffs, winning close games. They beat defending state champion Lakeland, 34-30; a desperate Manatee team, 24-21; and a ridiculously talented Ely team, 24-20. No one was really talking about it, but all of our guys were aware of Venice's march to Gainesville. We had played those guys really close, and after four playoff wins, the same Venice

Indians — a team that we maybe should have beaten — were going to play for the state championship.

Several of our coaches and I decided to make the trip to Gainesville for the December 15 showdown between 14-0 Venice and 13-1 Palm Beach Dwyer. It wasn't even a game. Venice set the all-time scoring record for Florida football state champions in a 77-14 rout.

I cannot begin to describe the sense of possibility that the Venice victory gave our players and our coaches. Sitting in the Swamp that cool December evening, I had two thoughts. The first was: we would have as good a chance as anyone, and a better chance than most, of winning the state championship in 2001. The second and more important thought was: we must honor God in the way we go about our business. If our kids didn't get more than a championship ring on their finger at the conclusion of the next season, then however it ended would be a dismal failure. II Chronicles 16:9 gave me more confidence than the Venice win. My first job was to keep my heart loyal to God.

Four of our players from the 2000 season were listed as honorable mention on the All-State football selections. Senior quarterback Stanley Bryant and senior kicker Bryan Council, along with junior running back Duane Coleman and junior receiver Bruce Gordon, made the list. It was great to see Naples football players getting the attention of folks around the state.

CHAPTER 56

2001

As our coaches headed to the AFCA national convention that January, our first priority was to get video and transcripts of our players into the hands of as many college coaches as we possibly could. Besides our seniors, we finally felt we had enough good underclassmen to start pushing the 2002 and 2003 classes too.

February 7 was National Signing Day for football in 2001. For Naples High football, it was a particularly gratifying time. Four of our 13 seniors would go to college on scholarship. Linebacker Garrette Perrone signed with the University of Dubuque, Stanley Bryant signed with Southern Illinois University, Anthony Denson signed with Elon College, and cornerback Al Green signed with Liberty University. They didn't all play college football, but 11 of our 13 seniors did go on to college. One of the two who didn't go to college would join the Marines, and the other was headed to firefighter school. Our process was working.

Sometime in late January or early February, Susie and I came to a big decision. We were going to take the trip of a lifetime. We were heading to England. Two friends of ours from college, Jill and Rick Wilfert, had been living in England for some time. Both had taken jobs with Lego after graduation, and Jill had accomplished a rather meteoric rise through the company. As a result, two things happened. First, Rick had to quit working for Lego; and second, Jill was stationed near Legoland Windsor, about 25 miles outside of London.

Jill and Rick had invited us to visit several times, but the clock was running out because they had been told they would be moving back stateside in a few months. They assured us that if we could just get there, we could stay with them and would have little or no expense. Jill and Rick had two little boys about the same age as our Courtney and Kelly; we knew the five kids would have a blast just playing together.

Sue Kramer is the most frugal person I know. She is not cheap; she is frugal. Somehow, she was managing our finances on my meager salary. Sue had also been proctoring for the ACT and the SAT. It generated less than $100 each testing day, but the funds from 12 or 13 tests a year for three years added up. Between what Sue had saved from proctoring and what she had somehow scratched out for emergency savings, we had a few thousand dollars.

As I searched for affordable airline fares, I came across a ridiculous deal from Virgin Airlines. The key was that Virgin offered child fares as well as adult fares. It just so happened that our spring break was scheduled the first week of April. I soon found out that April was one of the least expensive months of the year to travel to London.

We would spend Easter in England.

The tickets were going to leave us with little money left over to do much in England. We knew Legoland guest passes would be free, and we figured that we could find other free stuff to do too.

When the tickets arrived in the mail from Virgin Airlines, I noticed immediately that we had not been charged enough. Instead of three child fares, there were five. All of us had been charged as children. I figured that wouldn't fly with the airlines, so I called Virgin immediately to get it fixed.

The lady on the other end of the line had her manager on the phone in short order; I explained the situation. She told me that new tickets would be issued for Susie and me, and that we would not be charged the difference. I could not believe my ears. She assured me the mistake was theirs and that there would be no further charges. What had been a great deal on tickets to London had turned into the deal of the century! I'm not saying it was a miracle, but because of what we saved on the tickets, we could afford every bit of the trip and did not have to put anything on a credit card.

As our time to head to England drew near, Rick emailed me and asked if Susie and I would like to take a side trip to Italy. He said that we could fly really cheap on Ryan Air to Treviso, and then take a short bus ride and a water taxi to Venice for a couple of days. The idea of where to go had been random for Rick. For some reason, Ryan Air had discounted that particular flight, and we could get there round trip for about $60. Another bonus was that Italy was still using lira as currency at the time, and the dollar was ridiculously strong against it. All signs pointed to Venice.

Jill was pretty ambivalent about going, and Sue said she would rather just stay in England and take the kids to Legoland. She really didn't want to travel with 3-year-old Kelly, 6-year-old Courtney, and 8-year-old Katie to anyplace where English was not the official language. Nonetheless, Susie was super-supportive of me going with Rick. This was not the "you go ahead and go, and I will be the martyr" support that some spouses give. Sue genuinely wanted me to go, and she was genuinely happy to hang in England with Jill and the kids. In the end, Rick and I and an expat friend of his named Tom would make the trip. The hotel Rick found for us was the Savoia and Jolanda Hotel, right on the Grand Canal, just around the corner from St. Mark's Square. A really nice room with three separate beds, overlooking the Grand Canal, cost us $25 each per night.

Our whole trip to England was incredible: the castles, the British Museum, the Imperial War Museum, the Tower of London, the pubs, the people, the Tube, Stonehenge, and on and on. The night before us guys left for Italy, Jill and Rick arranged a sitter for the kids. We took a train and then the Tube into London's West End for dinner and a night at the theatre. After a spectacular dinner, we headed to the breathtaking Prince Edward Theatre, where the musical Mamma Mia had debuted in April of 1999. That was a hot ticket, as Mamma Mia was still selling out every show.

While flying over the Alps the next day and looking out the plane window at the indescribable beauty below, it was surreal for me to think that a few hours earlier I had been in London at the theatre, bouncing up and down with the rest of the crowd, belting out ABBA for all I was worth.

Now here I was, looking down on the Alps on my way to Venice, Italy.

I got a lump in my throat as I recalled moving to Naples and the huge financial hit we took. At that time, I thought we would never be able to afford to take our kids to Walt Disney World. Instead, God had allowed our family to go see real castles, and much more.

It reminded me of a story that I heard a preacher tell of a little girl who had a string of plastic pearls. She loved the pearls and wore them constantly. Each night when she went to bed, her daddy would ask her if she would trade the pearls for what he had in his closed hand. Each night, she would decline. She loved those fake pearls. Finally after months of persistence from her daddy, she sadly took off her fake pearls and tearfully gave them to her daddy. She didn't want to trade them, but if he wanted them so badly, she would swap them for whatever it was he had in his hand. Her daddy opened his hand to reveal a strand of exquisite real pearls, much more beautiful and valuable than the fake ones she'd had. The little girl leapt to her daddy's neck in joy, happy to make the trade. Daddy explained that she simply had to learn to trust him; what he wanted to give her was better than what she thought she wanted for herself.

And so it is with our Heavenly Father. He wants to take away the phony cheap stuff that we've grown really attached to and replace it with the really valuable stuff that He has waiting for us. Even so, He will never force it on us. We have to decide to let go of the cheap stuff.

CHAPTER

57

As we headed into spring football for the upcoming 2001 season, we were a confident crew. We had experienced some turnover in coaches from the first spring in 1998, but there was enough overlap and enough of the original crew that we had a good mix of consistency and new energy.

Plus, we had our first real senior class. All but three of our 26 seniors had played with us since they were freshmen; they knew the system, and they knew their way around our weight room.

The coaches who had been with us from day one included: Paul Horne and Sam Dollar, both becoming brilliant coordinators; Ron Byington and Jamie Lemmond, who were proving to be terrific technicians and teachers; and Ryan Krzykowski and

Tony Ortiz, both of whom were young and local, and who really connected with our players in ways that most of us could not.

In addition to being as good an offensive line coach as I had seen anywhere, at any level, Paul Horne was a constant source of inspiration for me. While many of the guys on staff had made sacrifices to be a part of what we were doing, Paul and his wife Shannon had really tightened the purse strings. For much of our first couple of years, Paul had to ride a bike to work. Depending on where they lived at various times, it was quite a haul. Paul did not complain; he did what he had to do.

In the spring of 2001, Paul and Shannon were expecting their third child; 3-year-old Colby and 2-year-old Kirby Lynn were getting ready to welcome their little sister Darby. Even with all that Paul had going on, he was the first of the coaches to have his position players come to his house once a week to eat and hang out after practice. All of the coaches followed suit in short order. Ron Byington opened up his house to the entire defense.

That idea had two sources. In talks with our players, Sam Dollar and I had discovered that many of our guys were not getting enough food, and most of them had terrible eating habits. We tried to educate them on proper nutrition habits, but we also thought it would be great to actually feed the guys a healthy meal — in addition to the pregame meal that some of the moms and wives were helping Sue prepare each week.

Paul Horne and I had an entirely different conversation. Many of our players were from single-parent homes, or families where the dynamic at home was not good. Paul and I thought it would be great for our players to see how an intact, healthy family functions — how a mom and dad under the stress of the season and raising small children can love each other and those around them. Even though Paul was stretched to the limit, he even found time to create a newsletter for former players, so they could stay connected to the program and know we cared for them and counted on them.

Paul's faithfulness in his marriage motivated me. A visit to their house and I would see sticky notes with thank-yous and love notes he had written for Shannon. Besides praying for his wife and kids all the time, Paul would pray that God would give him all he needed to be the husband and father God wanted him to be. Here was a guy that wasn't beating people over the head with a Bible. He was simply doing his best each day to do what God wanted him to do.

With plenty of guys playing football at Naples, we were now fielding all three teams — freshman, junior varsity, and varsity. That meant more coaching positions. Brian Clervoix, Marlin Faulkner, Mike Haddock, Jeff Hanlon, Steve Mirtil, Lamar Moore, Mike Sawchuk, Rich Turner, and Ben Welzbacher all brought an incredible work ethic and can-do mentality. Every guy on our staff was willing to do whatever was asked of him without complaint. The best of the best were the guys who didn't need to be asked.

Our secret weapons were George Bond and PJ Moriarty. Both were part of our original crew, and while neither was an on-field coach anymore, those two were our behind-the-scenes heroes. Helping with anything and everything, from scouting to laundry and from field maintenance to academic support, they never asked for recognition, money, or praise. All that George and PJ ever wanted was a chance to serve.

CHAPTER 58

Spring football in Florida always began on May 1. In 2001, May 1 was a Tuesday. As we approached the date, my prayer each morning was that each coach would make his relationship with God more important than the wins and losses.

I kept a prayer journal for my daily quiet time, and had been writing about a burden I felt for Duane Coleman and Bruce Gordon in particular. Both of those guys were good enough to earn college scholarships, and both came from rough areas. My fear was they would be influenced by those who could suck them down the drain.

As we approached spring football, I was particularly worried about Duane. He was working with us in the weight room and running track, but lately he had become a do-the-minimum kind of guy. Worse yet, he was becoming increasingly distant and uncommunicative with me and the rest of the football staff.

It was in stark contrast to the relationship that Duane and I had always had. Duane Coleman was a rough-cut dude, but he had always been honest with me. He and I had always been real and transparent with each other. Try as I might, I couldn't get through the walls he was building.

The week before spring football began, we issued football equipment to returning varsity players on Thursday and to everyone else on Friday. Players would come with their completed physical and permission slips. By the time Duane showed up, we were almost done issuing equipment. I had been praying about and contemplating what to do with Duane for months, and had come to one conclusion.

Duane Coleman was our best chance to win a state championship in 2001. He was also our best chance to crash and burn if he led our guys in a way that was detrimental to the team. I knew that Duane was our highest-profile player. The problem was, I didn't know which way he would lead us. I needed Duane to get in or get out.

As he walked up to get his stuff, I finished what I was doing and asked the coaches who were there to finish cleaning up, as I needed to talk to Duane. I asked Duane to walk with me, and as we exited the gym, I headed straight to my car. Duane asked what was up, and I explained that he and I were going to take a quick ride.

I told him I had been praying for him and thinking about him for a long time, and that I loved him too much to allow him to wreck his life and our team. For nearly an hour, Duane and

I had a heart-to-heart. It was emotional, it was visceral — and above all, it was honest.

In the end, I made it infinitely clear that Duane's only option — if he wanted to play football at Naples High School — was to be all-in, all the time. Duane made it just as clear that he intended to do just that. On my end, I would do my job, which was to love him — and that included accountability.

Spring football came and went in a flash. We were returning a team with 26 seniors who were motivated and focused. The few juniors who were earning roles were tremendous players and created great competition. Our junior starters, led by Josh Greco, offensive lineman Torey Brenco, safety Jules Montinar, and defensive lineman Andrew Pavel, did not give an inch to our seniors on the practice field.

When Boca Ciega High School showed up for our game in late May, they did not know what hit them. Despite having four of the fastest sprinters in the state of Florida on their team, Boca Ciega was outplayed from start to finish. Our starters didn't break much of a sweat. All of our backups and our backups' backups got plenty of playing time.

CHAPTER

53

As I prayed and thought about the theme for the coaches retreat during the winter, spring, and early summer of 2001, one theme kept coming to mind, and it made me really uncomfortable. In the end, I couldn't shake it. I knew that God wanted me to talk about living a holy life. I also knew I had no idea what that really meant. After lots of prayer and Bible study, I realized I had a flawed concept from the get-go.

In my mind, "holy" had always been synonymous with "perfect"; and that just isn't so. I discovered that holiness is a process. As we spend time in the Bible and with God, we become more like what He wants us to be. We become more like Jesus. The thing is, God meets each of us where we are. None of us is good enough to stand before a Holy God. Every one of us is flawed.

The beautiful part is, God can use me and you, flaws and all. One of the biggest lies we buy into is that we aren't good enough for God to use us. That mentality paralyzed me for years, and it paralyzes lots and lots of people. We want to wait until we get it right ourselves before we step out on faith to impact those around us. All we really have to do is surrender it all to God and allow Him to lead us and work in us. The Bible is clear: if we diligently seek after God, we will find Him.

By the time we headed to FCA camp that summer, the outline of the retreat was pretty solid. What I didn't know was that God was going to hit me between the eyes with something else. Several coaches at the FCA Black Mountain Coaches Camp and one of the guest speakers referenced a book called *The Prayer of Jabez* by Bruce Wilkinson. As I looked into it further, it was life-changing for me. The book is based on the Old Testament passage I Chronicles 4:9-10:

Now Jabez was more honorable than his brothers, and his mother called his name Jabez, saying, "Because I bore him in pain." And Jabez called on the God of Israel saying, "Oh, that You would bless me indeed, and enlarge my territory, that Your hand would be with me, and that You would keep me from evil, that I may not cause pain!" So God granted him what he requested. (NKJV)

As simple as it sounds, the concept of asking God to bless me was foreign to me. Generally, my requests in prayer were for others, or for me to stay the course and keep out of trouble. "Blessing" me did not necessarily mean that God was going to make us win state championships, although the competitor in me really wanted to. To me, blessing and expanding territory would mean expanding my influence and credibility.

The fact is that there are not a lot of folks who are going to buy into a guy or a program that isn't successful. So while I think it would have been pretty unusual for God to miraculously determine the outcome of an athletic contest, I don't think it would have been unusual at all for God to grow me if I implemented and followed a process that honored him.

Here was this Jabez guy, asking God to not only bless him but to expand his territory, and he was asking God to do that despite his own nature. The name Jabez means "pain." His mom's naming him that was her way of saying, "This guy brings pain." At the end of the prayer, Jabez implores God to keep him from evil, so he might not cause pain. So, I could pray for a blessing and also for God to change my very nature. It sounded like part of a life of holiness to me. At the coaches' retreat that late July, we talked about holiness. I gave each coach the book, The Prayer of Jabez.

For camp that summer, we upped the ante a bit. After a Lift-A-Thon weightlifting fundraiser, our players had raised enough money to pay for us to go away to football camp. I really wanted to get our guys away to start the year, so we could separate ourselves from the day-to-day. I wanted to be able to focus on the task before us, evaluate the cost of success, and have our players make real commitments to each other.

Cocoa-Expo was a ramshackle athletic complex just west of I-95 near Cocoa, Florida. The former Houston Astros minor league training facility had seen better days. It was spartan, and it was exactly what we could afford. It was also exactly what we needed. The camp was located inland, not near the beach or the breeze. Evidently it was also located near a breeding ground for some sort of genetically-engineered mosquito. The mosquitoes were everywhere; they were the biggest and most aggressive suckers I had ever seen. When I was quick enough to actually smack one of them as it was feasting on me, it often only made them mad.

When I say it was hot and humid, I mean there was a tropical sun daring you to come outdoors, and air so dense you could cut doughnuts out of it.

I realized during our first practice just how hot and humid it was when I looked up and saw lineman Steve Alajajian with our trainer. Steve was experiencing muscle cramps, which was rare for our guys. What made Steve an extra special case is that he was cramping when we got in our stretching lines at the **beginning** of practice. Cocoa was hard.

I loved it because we were in the middle of nowhere. Our guys had nowhere to go and no way to get there. They had no televisions, no computers, no internet service or cell service, and no video games.

I loved it because our guys had each other and three practices a day. Our guys had all the food they could eat and all the water they could drink, and time enough between practices to talk to each other and build or strengthen relationships. At night, coaches would meet with players individually and in groups, and the whole team worked toward defining what we expected from each member. When we left Cocoa, ours was a tired team. It was also a galvanized group of guys, ready to fight for each other.

CHAPTER

60

The Floridakids.net Gatorade Top 25 preseason poll listed Glades Central as the top team in the state, with a 35-game winning streak; they had 393 points. The poll was a composite that included every classification in the state. It was voted on by the sports editors at the biggest newspapers in Florida. While Naples did not actually appear in the Top 25, we were in the "also receiving votes" listing with a total of 12 points. Watch out, Glades Central.

On August 14, I wrote in my prayer journal that Bruce Gordon had missed two practices with unexcused absences. By our rules, that meant he would have to sit out our first game. It also meant that with one more unexcused absence, Bruce's career at Naples High would be over. I loved Bruce, but I hated that he had put himself in the position he was in; the decision to sit him was easy. I could either follow our policy or be a liar — a pretty simple choice.

On August 20, my prayer journal included two sentences: "Bruce Gordon, in or out? God, please give me wisdom and direction." As talented as he was, I did not want to put a lot of stock in Bruce Gordon if he was too immature, undisciplined, or selfish to keep the commitments he had made to his team and his coaches.

Our first game, the Kickoff Classic, was against LaBelle High School, a small school from a nearby cattle and farming community. The Cowboys were not ready for the Golden Eagles. LaBelle was overmatched in every phase, and we played every guy we could en route to a 55-0 blowout.

Our first game of the regular season would match us up against Lee County powerhouse Estero. Estero had a record of 33-6 over the previous three seasons, and they were our first challenge on one of the toughest schedules — if not **the** toughest schedule — in the state.

Estero opened the game with a well-orchestrated drive. The Naples defense finally held at the Naples 19-yard-line, forcing a 36-yard field goal. Estero's kicker Matt Prater easily made it. For Matt it was a chip shot, and he would prove his consistency later on with a really long and successful NFL career.

Prater's ensuing kickoff didn't quite make the end zone, and 98 yards later, Duane Coleman gave the Golden Eagles a lead they would never relinquish. For Duane, it was a career night. His 303 yards on just 14 carries was breathtaking. In addition, Duane had not one but two kickoff returns for touchdowns. The Naples defense was solid, giving up just 14 points. The final score in the 54-21 drubbing was an Estero 80-yard fumble return for a touchdown. When the media swarmed Duane, he made me proud. To anyone who would listen, Duane made it clear that he would have done none of it without his teammates, especially the guys up front.

CHAPTER

61

Week 2 found us going to Immokalee. The Indians were again loaded, and they were glad to have us at home in Gary Bates Stadium for the second consecutive year. I did not like going there two years in a row, but I had nothing to do with scheduling. I focused on controlling what I could control.

Our work week was terrific. Our players and coaches were upbeat and eager to make amends for the previous year's loss — a game that each of us felt we gave away. The best part of that first week in September was the new and improved Bruce Gordon. For the previous couple of weeks, Bruce had been a great teammate. Although he hadn't caught any balls against Estero, Bruce had been terrific at blocking their defensive backs; several times, it was his block that gave Duane the space to break the long runs.

I was looking forward to beating those Indians at their place and then resting up a bit, as the following week had a scheduled open date. I knew we had a tough regular season schedule ahead, and I was hoping we would have a long playoff run.

Sue Kramer had the pregame meal down to a science. From the shopping and prep work on Thursday to Friday's cooking and cleanup, she was flawless. On game days, just before the dismissal bell, Susie would transport all of the food to the home economics room at the school and finish the cooking and set up. Peggy Sadelfeld was clutch as always, helping Sue get the water boiling for the pasta that was soon to be in the pots on several of the stoves in the home ec kitchens.

Just before 4 p.m., the team lined up outside the home ec door. One of the boys said grace, and then they went in and made their way through the food line. Sue would buzz around, replenishing and making sure everyone had what they needed, and some of the coaches' wives and some moms would serve the boys. After the meal, Sue and her crew would clean up the dishes, kitchens, tables, and room, and then circle up and pray for our guys before heading home to get ready for the game. Katie and Courtney were part of the process. Kelly would be, too, as soon as she was big enough to use the tongs to hold a dinner roll. Years later, our fourth daughter Cassie would follow in her big sisters' footsteps.

On the afternoon of the 2001 Immokalee game, I did what I always did for pregame meals. I came in after all the boys were seated and eating. If the game was at home, I would remind the boys to move their cars from the stadium parking lot to the parking lot at the back of the school. On game nights, the stadium parking lot was managed very efficiently by our ROTC, who used it as a major fundraiser each year. The lot at the back of the school was free.

On this particular afternoon, when I walked in and saw Sue's face, I knew immediately that something was wrong. I gave her a kiss and a hug as always, and asked what was up. Although she smiled and shook her head, I knew something was bothering her. It only took a scan of the team for me to figure it out.

"Have you seen Duane, Pat, or Francesco?" I asked. Sue sadly confirmed that she had not. Sue knew what every player and coach knew was my one rule on game day: There would be no problems on game day. That meant that if any guy was a problem, he would go home, and he would no longer be a problem.

If a player didn't wear a tie to school, even though they had dress shirts and ties provided for them, he would not play or be on our sidelines that night. If a guy was horseplaying in the locker room, he would go home. Music from earphones so loud that it disturbed someone else? See you Monday. And if by chance a player chose to act up in class? That would be bad for all of us, because he would have to go home. We trained year-round for ten regular season games. If a guy was too selfish or unfocused to just be reasonably mature on game day, he was probably going to get us beat anyway.

I walked to the locker room in hopes of finding the three of them in there. I was going to hustle them to the pregame meal and grab some pasta myself, as I was hungry. I entered through the gym's south double doors. As I crossed the gym, I could see out through the double doors on the east side of the gym; both were propped open. I saw Duane, Pat and Fran walking from the parking lot and onto the sidewalk leading to the locker room. That was not good.

I met them entering the locker room, and because there were some players who had finished eating already in there, I asked the three to walk with me to the weight room. There was not a peep as we entered. The good news was, the three were honest with me and immediately gave me the truth, the whole truth, and nothing but the truth.

Earlier in the week the three had been at Fran's house, and somehow the topic of the pregame meal came up. Francesco's mom is a sweet and kind lady; she offered to cook the boys an authentic Italian meal instead. That was it, simple.

The answer from me was just as simple. I walked into the office, grabbed the wireless phone, and told them to call their parents. I told the boys to let their parents know that they might not want to drive all the way to Immokalee that evening, as none of the three would be playing. I reminded them of our one rule on game day.

I also reminded them that the opposite of love is not hate; it is selfishness. What they had just indulged in was pure selfishness.

I was proud of their honesty with me. They told me they knew what they did was wrong. They had actually talked about it beforehand, and the consensus was that I would suspend them for just the first half of the game.

I asked them to imagine if everyone on the team did what they had done. Would it have been OK? I also told them if they had wanted to arrange for the whole team to get an authentic Italian pregame meal, I would have helped them organize it. I said that I was sure that Sue and the moms would have liked a week off.

I quickly went and told the coaches what had happened. I then went through the gym, training room, and locker room, and hustled everyone into the weight room. By the time all were assembled, the guys had already deduced what was going on. Everyone knew those three guys had missed the pregame meal, that I had met with them privately, and that they were leaving. Not a lot left to figure out there. I told the team we just had to treat it as we would an injury or an accident, and move forward. I was convinced that we could win the game without those three.

That was a really hard sell to the team.

Fran was one of the best kickers in Florida. He would go on to a terrific football career and a degree from the University of Miami. Pat was one of the best defensive linemen in Florida. He too would go on to a terrific football career, and a degree from West Virginia University. Duane was one of the best running backs in Florida. He would also go on to a terrific football career, and a degree from Clemson University. The three of them had been stellar all year. Working their tails off and making the guys around them better. I knew that this was a one time thing; I also knew I had to make sure that this was a one time thing ever in my tenure at Naples High School.

There are no problems on game day.

CHAPTER

62

It was a sulky bunch climbing aboard those yellow school buses heading to Immokalee. The first half of the game wound up being a comedy of errors, but no one on our sideline thought it was funny. Naples committed what the newspaper would call "countless penalties and errors," although with enough time, we could have actually counted them all up. We jumped off-sides. We dropped balls. We missed tackles. I had done a terrible job getting our guys ready to play.

Behind the fence that separated our fans from our sideline was a mass of distraction. Our three suspended guys had driven to the game. Wherever the three amigos went, they were surrounded by a mob of people trying to get the straight skinny. There was a loud, if not large, contingent of fans who were letting me have it. They were screaming all kinds of things at me that basically added up to "Let the boys play, you idiot!"

As we went into the locker room at halftime, our coaches realized that as bad as we had played, we were fortunate to only be down 17-0. We could still win the game if we would just do what we were capable of. We didn't need any superhuman performances.

By the time we came out of the locker room at halftime, our players had realized the same thing. Our defense played lights-out, actually scoring our only points of the third quarter with a safety. Our offense, with quarterback Josh Greco, receiver Bruce Gordon, and running back David Lightner, moved the ball effectively. Yards were given up grudgingly by a salty Immokalee defense, but in the fourth quarter we were able to move the chains and score two hard-earned touchdowns. With under a minute to play and the score 17-15, it looked as if we were going to have a Disney movie ending.

After driving the ball with our hurry-up offense, we had come up against a wall. We found ourselves with fourth and long, and the ball on the Immokalee 16-yard-line. Our punter, Scotty Turner, was about to attempt the first field goal of his career. I thought it would be the perfect poetic justice for him to drill it, thus proving once and for all that no one guy, or three guys, are bigger than the team. Perhaps that would shut up the critics who had been fussing at me from the stands all night.

I hated that Scotty was being put in that position. I had not given him any game reps kicking the ball ever, and I had only given an occasional rep in practice. If he missed, it was all on me. Scotty was a tremendous athlete and a tremendous teammate. I prayed silently that he would make it, despite my poor preparation. The snap was good but not great. The hold was good, and as the kick went up, I thought it was good too.

I was wrong. It faded just a tiny bit right as it got to the right upright. Ball game.

I met Scotty coming off the field. As he tried to apologize, I assured him it was my fault, and I would be sure to get him more reps so he would be prepared if he had to be our kicker again. Our team loved Scotty, and everyone felt terrible for him. We all knew Scotty would blame himself. Everyone also knew that the rest of us should never have put him in that position.

After the handshake lines, I gathered the team on the 20-yard-line as I always did and spoke from my heart. I told them that each of us knew the outcome of the game had nothing to do with the suspended guys. If we had controlled the things we could control — our effort and our attitude — we would have won the football game. I implored them not to listen to the negative voices that they would undoubtedly hear. The only voices that mattered as far as Naples football was concerned were the voices from the guys on that field — not the voices from anyone in the stands, at home, or in the media.

When I was finished, we huddled up, broke the huddle as we always did, and headed to the southeast end of the stadium. We had coolers with some sandwiches, and it was going to take a few minutes for the crowd to thin out and our buses to queue up.

A number of Naples fans were letting me have it as we exited the field. Ten or 12 of them had attempted to follow us to the corner of the stadium where we had gathered to collect ourselves, eat, and wait for our buses. The most boisterous of the fans was the uncle of one of our backup wide receivers. He was a former airplane pilot, and I remember thinking that a guy in that line of work should have had the presence and discipline to know better. Ronnie Byington was all over the situation, and had the nearby on-duty sheriff's deputies move the malcontents to the other side of the field fence, where they could not bother us.

We were not there very long when someone came running up and hollered to me that I had better come, because some fans were messing with my wife. Paul Horne was close enough to hear, and knowing that his wife and kids sat with my wife and kids, he joined me immediately in running towards the exit of the stadium.

As we ran, I was flabbergasted. Why would Immokalee fans be messing with my wife? I guessed that perhaps some knucklehead was rubbing it in about beating us, and was saying something ugly about me. I couldn't imagine Sue responding. More than likely, her dad Duke had heard something he didn't like, and had responded. That I could believe, and then maybe Sue did get involved. Duke was not in great health, and Sue was always cognizant of anything that might stress his heart.

Paul and I caught up to the exiting crowd and found our wives and kids with the rest of the coaches' families. Duke and Angel were there, as was Joe Scott, our school resource officer. Sue was holding a teary Katie, and Duke and Angel were holding our other two girls. It was obvious that Joe Scott was herding the group out, hurrying everyone to their cars, picking up police help along the way.

When our fussy fans could not get to us anymore, someone among them figured that they would go and give our wives the message for us. In an effort to get to Sue, one of our fans trampled Katie, who was walking next to Granny Angel just behind Sue. I didn't care if it was an accident. I didn't care if he didn't see her. All I know is that when I got to her, Katie had been stepped on hard enough to break the straps on her sandal and tear it off her foot, and she had a footprint on her leg.

I asked Sue who did it. She wasn't exactly sure, but Uncle Pilot had been in her face and in Mandi Lemmond's face, and he had been the most aggressive. Sue told me it had all happened really fast, and that Joe Scott was there almost immediately. Joe confirmed that he didn't see it happen. He just heard the commotion and came running to get the wives and kids out safely. The guilty guys had taken off just before he got there. As we came close to the cars, I kissed all of my girls and told them I loved them, as Paul did the same with his wife and kids. Then the two of us hit a sprint back to where the rest of the team was.

I don't remember talking to Paul about it, but both of us knew exactly what we were going to do. Paul went straight to whoever had keys to one of the school vans that we used for equipment. I found Sam not far away, and I told him he was going to have to get someone to handle the offense's bus and get the kids back to the school.

Sam didn't ask any questions, and in a blink Paul was driving us back to the school. We were going to find Uncle Pilot, who would have to go back to the school to pick up his nephew, and I was going to hurt him. Paul was going to deal with anyone else who might want to get involved. As far as I was concerned, it was not going to take long. I had nothing to say, and I was not going to listen to anything Uncle Pilot might have to say.

I wish I could tell you that I was prayerful and I was faithful. I was neither.

Uncle Pilot was not at the school. By the time I got home to Susie, she was fast asleep. I checked on the girls as I normally did, gave them all an extra kiss or two, and headed to the shower. I was not going to get much sleep before I had to be in the office to grade the film. The players had Saturday off. The coaches only had to have their video graded and ready to go by Monday after school; other than that, they were off too. With an open week ahead of us, I had plenty of time to deal with Uncle Pilot.

When I got home from work that Saturday, Katie was fine; the bruise on her leg wasn't very bad, and she was playing with her sisters like nothing ever happened. Sue wasn't fussy, but she did let me know in no uncertain terms that she had been worried about me the previous night. I would do none of them any good sitting in jail, she said. She reminded me that she wasn't certain that Uncle Pilot was the one who knocked Katie down or stepped on her, just that he was the first one to approach her and the most aggressive. I told Sue that I understood everything she was saying, and that I was not mad at Uncle Pilot anymore, which was the truth. The rest of the truth, which I didn't tell her, was I had a calm resolve that the next time I saw Uncle Pilot I was going to hurt him like he had hurt Katie.

At some point that weekend Ernie and I talked, and he asked what had happened at the conclusion of the game. When I explained, he was pretty fired up at Uncle Pilot. Nonetheless, he asked me to just leave it alone, and to let it be handled administratively.

Monday morning was business as usual, until Ernie called and asked me to swing by his office as soon as I could. I grabbed one of the coaches to cover my class and headed over. As I sat down, Ernie looked at me with no expression whatsoever and told me that he'd had a call from Uncle Pilot that morning. He said that Uncle Pilot wanted to sit down and meet with both me and Ernie that very afternoon, if possible. Ernie went on to explain that Uncle Pilot told him he was planning on taking out a restraining order against me. No small irony there. You trample my 8-year-old daughter, and then **you** get a restraining order against **me?** Nice. I agreed to the meeting. Ernie pressed me hard that I would control myself during the meeting; I gave him my word.

Ernie was sitting at his desk, and I was seated in one of the two chairs across from him when Uncle Pilot walked in. No one offered a handshake. Uncle Pilot sat down; everything about his demeanor said that he knew he had screwed up. Ernie was awesome. I have been in many parent meetings with Ernie Modugno, and parent meetings may have been the thing he did best. He was always rational, thoughtful, and really smart. The conversation never strayed for more than a moment from whatever Ernie wanted to discuss.

I didn't really speak much; Ernie handled it all. He let Uncle Pilot know that he would no longer be allowed at any sporting events where Naples High was participating, and that he would only be allowed on campus if he was asked to a meeting. He could still pick up and drop off his nephew as long as he stayed in his car.

I wasn't over it.

CHAPTER 63

We didn't practice that Monday afternoon, but we did show the game video. It verified what we had suspected the previous Friday night — we had given one away. It was encouraging to see that our three amigos were apologetic and ready to work. They'd watched the video with everyone else, and each of them felt that he would have been the difference-maker to tip the game in our favor. They were all probably right.

Tuesday practice was going to be a little more chill than usual. We were going to treat it basically like a Monday: go over the scouting report, head out to the field for some position group fundamentals, some special teams work, and some introductory work on our next opponent, Fort Myers. Fort Myers was really well coached. Sam Sirianni was a legend in Florida, and his son

Sammy Jr. was his gifted offensive coordinator. Undefeated Fort Myers was also loaded with talent; they were ranked No. 1 in southwest Florida and in the Top 20 for the entire state.

As I went about my teaching schedule on Tuesday morning, the Fort Myers Green Wave was never far from the front of my mind. The Greenies' defense had not yet allowed a point to be scored on them that year. Those guys were for real. I was walking across the blue gym floor when a girl walked out of the former classroom, near the laundry room, which we had set up as an aerobics room. The room had a few elliptical machines, a couple of stationary bikes, some yoga mats, and a TV. The girl motioned for me to come over, and told me I needed to see what was on television. As we got near the door, another girl who had been using the equipment walked out and told me the same thing. As I entered the room and looked at the TV, I saw one of the twin towers of the World Trade Center in New York with black smoke billowing out of it.

The girls explained that they had been riding the elliptical machines when the show they were watching had been interrupted by a news update. I stared in disbelief as I listened to the newscaster say that a big plane had somehow run into one of the towers, and that the tower was being evacuated. As we stood there and listened, I was trying to explain to the girls how it could have been an accident. What I didn't say is that realistically it would be very difficult for a plane to just accidently fly into that building. I started guessing about the possible cause. Maybe the pilot was having a heart attack. Maybe he wanted to commit suicide. Maybe the plane was hit by some sort of missile or something, and had inadvertently veered into the building.

A few minutes later, at a little after 9 a.m., I — along with millions of other Americans — was watching the live television feed when the second World Trade Center tower was hit. It took me a moment to formulate the thought before I said, to no one in particular, "We are under attack."

I went in to the main gym, where our boys' basketball coach, Ed Starcher, was teaching his phys ed class, and told him to come take a look. Both of us had a hard time wrapping our minds around it. Whatever was going on, this was bad. The day moved forward slowly, and as the horrible events of the day unfolded, I spent a good bit of time praying for the families who were directly affected by the terrorists. The school district canceled all athletic events for the day.

We met with our guys during the weightlifting class and talked about what was happening. We talked about how quickly our lives can change, the importance of loving our friends and family, and how important it is to let them know we love them. It is a sad truth that it sometimes takes a traumatic event to make us pause and get perspective. As I processed my gratitude that our family was intact and healthy, I also processed what had happened at Immokalee. I did not condone what had happened to Katie the previous Friday night, but I no longer had the burning in my belly. It was time for me to forgive Uncle Pilot.

CHAPTER
64

We went through an abbreviated practice schedule that week. Many schools canceled the Friday games, but none of it affected us, as we had a scheduled open week anyway. Throughout the week, I kept having the sense that we could not back down or be afraid of these terrorists or people like them. They were counting on people being paralyzed by fear, and on people giving in based on that fear. I felt strongly that we should be vigilant and prepare to fight them.

Later in that week, I was watching television and a commercial came on, advertising some ridiculous airfares to and from several big cities. It hit me that Sue and I should fly somewhere. I did not want to be afraid to fly. I figured that one of the best things our citizens could do would be to get on a plane as soon as possible.

CHAPTER 64

In the back of my mind, I had Bubba Cunningham's offer to come and take in a Notre Dame football game. I started looking at fares to cities close to South Bend and came across a favorable fare to Chicago. Sue and I could both fly round-trip for under $100 each. I knew that we had a Thursday game in a few weeks; we could fly out on Friday morning after the Thursday night game, and return Sunday morning.

The more I thought about it, the more I wanted to do it. I called and asked Angel if she and Duke would watch the girls; she said that they would love to. I called Bubba and asked if his offer was still good for the November 6 home game against the University of Pittsburgh. I figured it would be doable for Bubba, as high school coaches get a courtesy ticket to pretty much any college game in the country. Head coaches usually get two courtesy tickets.

Bubba was fired up that we were considering a visit, and immediately offered for us to stay with him, his wife Tina, and their four kids. I politely declined; I was sure that I could find a decent hotel somewhere between Chicago Midway Airport and Notre Dame. Bubba was having none of it. He insisted we come and spend the weekend at his home; soon, it was a plan. Sue and I would fly to Midway, pick up a rental car, and drive directly to Notre Dame and Bubba's office. He would take it from there.

In the meantime, I had a really good football team to prepare for. The weeks following 9/11 were somber for all of us. Each day, the news gave a clearer picture of the evil, and the heroism, that happened that day. It was a constant topic of conversation among the coaches and the players. By the time the September 21 game against Fort Myers rolled around, everyone from both communities was ready for it.

CHAPTER

65

There was almost a sense of defiance in the stadium as both teams and both sets of fans packed Staver Field to participate in something that is quintessentially American — high school football. Every bit of that game that night was Americana: the ROTC cadets parking cars, the cheerleaders, the bands, the concession stands, all of it. There was full-throated singing and goosebumps all over that stadium as the Star-Spangled Banner was played. It seemed as though every person was going to be the best fan, or player, or coach, or vendor, or whatever role was theirs that night. We were all Americans; in the chaos of hatred, we were going to be normal. Every player on both teams played like his hair was on fire. While our guys played really well, it seemed as though Fort Myers had all of the lucky charms.

CHAPTER 65

The first score was a halfback pass. A Naples DB was a little too aggressive versus the run, and he allowed a Fort Myers receiver to get open behind him for a touchdown. Later in the first half, the Fort Myers quarterback was hit as he threw a pass; somehow the ball flew sideways, and was tipped into the arms of offensive guard Brent Smith. Normally, an offensive lineman cannot catch a forward pass; not realizing the ball was tipped, our guys relaxed just enough for Brent to rumble 47 yards to the Naples 1-yard-line. The Greenies scored three plays later.

At halftime, the scoreboard read Fort Myers 22, Naples 20. I implored our guys to control what they could control. Our offense had really not been stopped, and the law of averages had to even out for our defense.

The second half found both defenses making terrific halftime adjustments, and the only third-quarter score was a Fort Myers touchdown. Defensive end John Cole picked up a Naples fumble and sprinted into the end zone on a scoop and score.

There was no panic in the Naples High players or coaches. In fact, our guys turned up the heat. As the fourth quarter rolled around, the Greenies' two-way players were starting to slow down just a little. That was all our guys needed. Nineteen unanswered points later, the final score was Naples 39, Fort Myers 29.

Our offense had accumulated 505 yards. The bulk of it belonged to Duane Coleman, as he rushed for 283 yards and four touchdowns. Again, I was proud of Duane for the way he responded to all of the fan and media attention. He constantly and sincerely gave the credit for his success to his teammates; specifically, his offensive line. Rick Martin, Jason Gore, Torey Brenco, Danny Murray, and Chris Jones were the unsung heroes, and Duane wanted people to know it. He also made sure everyone knew that his personal stats meant nothing. The only statistic he cared about was the win column, and he would do whatever he could to help his team win.

Josh Greco was spectacular against the Green Wave too, throwing for 156 yards and a touchdown. David Lightner played a critical role as well — his 64 yards rushing was on just seven carries. He averaged more than 9 yards a carry. I saw David's confidence grow as the game went on.

Our guys were happy, but not satisfied, as we gathered together the next morning to go over game grades and watch the video. As cool as it was to beat Fort Myers the previous night, we were feeling the effects of a really physical football game. Plus, we all knew that the next game, against Bradenton Manatee, would be an even bigger district matchup.

CHAPTER

66

The pollsters that week had undefeated Manatee ranked third in the state with 140 points. After the Fort Myers win, Naples wasn't ranked, but we did appear in the list of other teams getting votes, with 14 points.

Manatee was ranked that high for good reason. They were bigger than we were at every position; in some cases, a lot bigger. I'm talking six or seven inches and 60 or 70 pounds bigger. Regardless, the coaches and I were convinced — and soon the players were as well — that we were stronger and in many cases quicker than they were.

We also believed we were more technical, and we thought that would be the tipping point. I hoped that we were right. Sometimes sheer mass does come into play, and it is a great unequalizer, regardless of the other variables.

Ours was a confident and salty crew that week of practice. This game was the de facto district championship, as we believed that both teams should beat the other district teams remaining on the schedule. A win would mean a home playoff game, something that had not happened at Naples High since before our players were born.

By Wednesday, news reports predicted a tropical depression heading our way. I didn't know how the Manatee folks felt about it, but I did not want to reschedule the game. It didn't take me long as a head coach to figure out that we were going to have whatever weather God wanted us to have on game night. If God wanted us to play in a deluge, then that was what we would do.

The morning of game day, September 28, 2001, was wet. It was overcast and spitting rain most of the morning. The radar showed that a lot of moisture was spooling up out of the gulf, and there would be a 100 percent chance of rain during our game.

I did my best to keep our guys dry during pregame warmups. We stretched in the blue gym, and we did as much warmup inside as we possibly could. On normal game nights we would go back into the locker room 30 minutes before kickoff. But on that night, we went in a few minutes earlier so we could pull the jerseys off our guys and throw them in the dryer.

I had asked our guys earlier in the week to bring extra socks, and most of the team went about changing socks. A bunch of the guys had warmed up in practice shoes, and then changed into game shoes.

Ben Welzbacher made sure he had every towel and dry ball we owned ready to go. We also planned to hustle our guys in at halftime, dry the jerseys again, and give out every pair of dry socks that we had. This contest was most likely going to decide the district champion, and I was not going to leave anything in reserve.

It rained and rained and rained.

During the worst of the squalls, it was difficult to see the opposite sideline clearly.

Manatee opened the scoring in impressive fashion. After driving the ball to the Naples 14, Manatee kicker Wes Thompson booted a rain-soaked 31-yard field goal. With 3:12 left in the first quarter, Manatee had the lead.

Even though we were down by 3 in a pouring rain against a much bigger team, our sideline was confident. Our fear before the game was that the rain would give the advantage to their bigger guys on both the offensive and defensive lines. But we were holding our own, and that was enough for us to win.

Our offense took the ensuing kickoff and moved the ball, albeit in small chunks, just past midfield. As the quarter changed and our guys came to the sideline during the accompanying brief intermission, I asked Ben Welzbacher for a dry ball. I then asked the official on our sidelines to swap it with the one they had left under a towel on the Manatee 49. I guess the rain-soaked towel on top of that ball was supposed to keep it dry.

I figured that it could be our last chance with a guaranteed dry ball before halftime. I called a play-action pass with Cleannord Saintil lined up wide to Josh Greco's right, and Bruce Gordon in the slot halfway between Josh and Cleannord. The play called for

Josh to fake a run to his right; Bruce was to block the guy covering him for an instant, and then release right down the middle
of the field. Cleannord was to block for an instant and then slip
past his guy and run down the right sideline.

After his play-fake, Josh was to take three drop-steps while
reading the safety that lined up over Bruce. If the safety covered
Bruce, Josh would throw it to Cleannord. If the safety ran and
covered Cleannord, then Josh would throw it to Bruce — simple
Boolean logic.

Josh took the snap and with Duane Coleman, gave a great
play-fake. Bruce and Cleannord ran excellent routes, and when
Josh went to read the free safety, there was none. All of the
Bradenton Manatee secondary had bitten on the run-fake. An
instant before he was hit, Josh was able to lob a pass just left of
the middle of the field. Bruce ran it down effortlessly, and in a
blink he was in the end zone.

Josh Greco did not see any of it. He had been hit in the
chest just as he threw the ball. There was so much water on the
field that he slid for 5 yards on his back. But Josh didn't need to
see it to know what happened. He knew from the small, rain-
soaked crowd's reaction that he had completed it, and that Bruce
had scored.

Manatee was not afraid. Theirs was a team of big athletic
competitors, and after a Francesco Zampogna kickoff, the Hurricanes started to drive the ball. Our defense was playing well,
but Manatee was gaining just enough ground to move the chains.
With 5:51 left in the half, and with the ball in Manatee's possession on the Naples 15-yard-line, running back Edrick Hines was

hit hard by a Naples defender. The ball popped out and squirted towards our sideline.

Reggie Carter, the Naples corner who would go on to a terrific football career and a degree from Pitt, made it look really easy in the rain. Reggie came off his coverage and never broke stride. He scooped the ball, and 91 yards later Naples was on the board again.

Manatee was starting to feel the pressure a bit. On their next possession, our outstanding safety LJ Montinar hit their quarterback hard, causing him to fumble the ball. Once again the Dollar defense came up with a critical turnover, this time at the Manatee 29.

Four plays later, Duane Coleman found the end zone. With 4:21 left in the half, Naples was up 21-3.

Manatee had too much pride to give up the ghost, and they managed a drive of their own before the half. As we headed into the gym at halftime for dry socks and jerseys, Naples was in new territory, leading Bradenton Manatee 21-9.

There was not much to change at halftime other than our wet clothes. As we walked through the parking lot separating Staver Field from the locker room, Benjie Welzbacher collected the wet jerseys from our players. Using every moment of halftime, we dried the jerseys and changed socks. Most of our skill guys were able to get into dry pants too.

I am not sure that the dry stuff made much of a physical difference. It was raining hard. It never quit raining hard. Regardless, the psychological effect of the dry clothing was energizing. Our guys just felt better, and that was a big help in and of itself.

After the second-half kickoff, our offense started with the ball on our 20. It was a thing of beauty to watch our guys march methodically down the field, 80 yards in 12 plays, to extend our lead to 28-9. There was no quit in Manatee, and just before the end of the third quarter, their big back — appropriately named — Jordan Biggers scored from 12 yards out. The PAT made it Naples 28 and Manatee 16.

The rain was relentless. Shoes, socks, and footballs were soaked; fingers wrinkled like prunes. Puddles on the sidelines were so deep that I worried about the guys who were face-down in them after being tackled. Both teams played on, giving the few fans willing to endure the storm indelible memories of tremendous effort and focus in some of the worst football weather ever. Duane Coleman definitely did not care about the weather. His fourth-quarter score was the final nail in Manatee's coffin, and as the seconds ticked off the clock, it was 34-16 in favor of the good guys.

I was really thrilled with our guys' demeanor after the game. They didn't jump around like they won the Super Bowl; they maturely congratulated each other and very respectfully shook hands with the Manatee players and coaches. All of us were exhausted and soaked to the bone.

It was great watching the game video the next morning. Our guys had played really well. It was obvious that they sincerely cared about each other and really believed in each other, and in our coaching staff. The 5A poll the following week had us at No. 7, right above No. 8 Manatee. We were in the driver's seat for the district championship.

CHAPTER

67

Our next game would be played on a Thursday night against a struggling 1-3 Sarasota Booker team. Here was the perfect trap game: after two big emotional wins, we would then face a very athletic but struggling team, on a shortened work week due to a Thursday night game. To top it all off, it was homecoming week. Much of the conversation I heard from our players each day was about what girls they were taking to the dance, and what the pre- and post-dance plans were.

I pointed all of those factors out to our players — repeatedly. All of our coaches made a concerted effort to keep our guys focused on the main thing, which was the game — not the dance, the homecoming court, or all of the other really great and distracting stuff that homecoming week brings.

The truth was, I was distracted too. I knew that after the game, I was going to get on an airplane with my girlfriend and fly to watch a Notre Dame football game. That was a big deal. Just spending time alone with Susie was a big deal. It would be the first time in a long time that we would take off, just the two of us.

The perfect trap game was just that. Our guys came out flat and unfocused; rather, they were focused on other things. In contrast, the Booker guys were playing as if they were playing the best team on their schedule — which they were. Unfortunately, we did not play like the best team on anyone's schedule. For the game, Booker had no fumbles and threw no interceptions. Naples had five fumbles — losing two, two interceptions, and two penalties. Fire the coach.

Even with all of that, at 1:36 left in the game, we were able to tie the score on a 2-point conversion that found Duane Coleman with the ball, and with Paul Horne's offensive line willing him into the end zone — running right at the teeth of the Booker defense. The biggest reason we ran at the teeth instead of the perimeter of their defense was because Booker had two monsters playing defensive end. One of them, Baraka Atkins, wound up being a really good player for the Seattle Seahawks and the San Francisco 49ers.

We won the toss in overtime and chose defense. It proved to be a wise choice. Booker scored on its second play, but we were able to block the extra point. Now our offense had only to score and make an extra point, and there you go — a fairy-tale ending.

On third and goal from the 5, Duane Coleman took the option handoff. As he juked past the linebacker at the 2, the safety who had no shot at tackling Duane dove at him from an awkward angle and managed to poke the ball out. A Sarasota Booker player fell on the ball.

Ball game. There was no joy in Mudville.

After the postgame handshakes, we huddled together in the north end zone, not far from the flagpole. I implored our guys not to judge themselves based on whatever they thought just happened in the game. I asked every guy to go home, eat and rest. I reminded them that playing on a Thursday night did not exempt them from being at school on time at 7:05 the next morning. I urged them to wait until they saw the video and got their game grades before they judged themselves. When you spend years studying game video, you realize that a game is never as bad — or as good — as you thought it was right after the game.

CHAPTER

68

I had one goal during our short drive from Chicago to South Bend. I wanted a real, authentic Chicago hot dog.

As we walked through Chicago's Midway airport en route to our bags and rental car, I saw several hot dog stands. I wanted to wait until we had the car, and then eat on our way to South Bend. Besides, I figured that those airport terminal hot dogs were probably not the really authentic Chicago dogs.

For those unfamiliar, a Chicago-style hot dog is topped with yellow mustard, chopped white onions, bright green sweet pickle relish, a dill pickle spear, tomato slices or wedges, pickled sport peppers, and a dash of celery salt. They are delicious.

Sue has a better sense of direction than anyone I know. She had a plan for getting to the interstate and then on to South Bend.

CHAPTER 68

But I talked her into taking a slight detour to try and find an authentic hot dog stand. Good idea, bad execution. I wound up in a really sketchy neighborhood, and figured I'd better cut my losses and get to the interstate. Sue figured out the route quickly, and then just as we got near the interstate, we saw a hot dog stand. It was the same franchise name that we had seen in the airport.

Just to reiterate, Chicago-style hot dogs are delicious. Also, you can get good ones in the airport.

CHAPTER
69

It was a beautiful drive on that crisp, clear October day as we headed almost due east along the southern end of Lake Michigan to South Bend. We followed Bubba's instructions and drove straight to his office. As we neared the campus, I was amazed at the number of tailgaters who were already set up and waiting for the game. It was early afternoon on Friday, and Notre Dame was 0-3 going into the Pittsburgh game.

I soon learned that with fans of the Fighting Irish it wouldn't matter if Notre Dame was 0-100, they still would come to the game. They treat the game like a religious experience, and the campus and stadium are like holy shrines. It was awesome.

Bubba could not have been more gracious and welcoming. After catching up a bit, he encouraged us to take a little time to check out the campus and then meet him back at his office to follow him home at the end of his work day. We had a couple hours to kill, and soon found out it wasn't enough.

I had never really been a Notre Dame fan. I didn't understand their rabid fans, and I did not like that this independent school got so much love from the pollsters. To top it off, the Irish had the gall to secure a really lucrative television contract for their football games. It was the first time that a single school had negotiated with a major network (NBC) to carry football games. It seemed pretty arrogant to me.

However, when I saw the campus and experienced a football weekend there, I realized just how ignorant I had been. Up to that point, Disney World was the prettiest and most well-kept public place I had seen; Mickey kept his green space immaculate. Notre Dame made Mickey's place look like a pig sty.

We basically just tagged along with Bubba and Tina for the weekend. The pep rally on Friday night was like nothing I had ever seen. The place was so full that students were leaning on and sitting on the rafters. Everywhere I looked, there was someone who was trying to cheer louder than their neighbor. The band was all-in, as were the cheerleaders and the rest of the students. It was inspiring. It was a deafening chorus of unwavering support for a team that had begun the season in the Top 20, but had lost three consecutive games and any chance of reaching their lofty goals. And still, the students and fans roared.

The game the next day was everything I had expected and more. The Irish played well against a scrappy Pitt team and pulled out their first win of the season. I was amazed at the attention to detail that ran through every part of Notre Dame. I was also rejuvenated. I realized that the pride and attention to detail that permeated that place was not a result of the excellence and beauty that existed there. The pride and attention to detail came first — and were what caused and maintained the excellence and beauty that is Notre Dame.

I did not arrive there a fan, and on any given day I might not necessarily root for the Irish. But I certainly want to watch. I gained the utmost respect and admiration for what they do and how they do it.

CHAPTER

70

I did not talk about Notre Dame or make comparisons to our program in our preparations the next week. But I did pay a little more attention to detail, and I did coach with a tremendous amount of energy and enthusiasm. Our guys did not need much prodding. The Booker loss had left us chapped, and we had an exceptionally spirited week of practice. One of the problems with an open week was if you lost the week before, you would have to wait two weeks to get that bad taste out of your mouth. Our guys had a really bad taste in their mouths.

Lely and Naples were both 1-0 in the district. Although Lely had a 1-4 record and were down to their third-string quarterback, our players and coaches had just lost to Sarasota Booker's one-win team. We were determined to leave no doubt in our preparation and in our performance. Besides, this was the Coconut Bowl.

The Lely game would be televised on local TV and broadcast on the radio. My friend and former Lely head coach Mark Swanson just so happened to be the color commentator for the radio broadcast. When Mark and I finished taping our on-field pregame interview, he thanked me, took a few steps to walk away, and then turned and said, "Do me a favor, kick their ass, will ya?"

"Yes sir," I assured him. "We will."

I could not imagine us losing the game. Our team was in the best mental, emotional, and physical place we had been all year. Lely was starting their third-string quarterback. There was a reason that, halfway through the season, they were already on their third quarterback. They were not very good at keeping their quarterbacks from getting hit.

My goal before the game was to completely dominate this district game. (Be careful what you wish for.) Lely received the opening kickoff and was stuffed on three consecutive plays by the Naples defense. The ensuing Lely punt was blocked, and Bruce Gordon recovered it in the end zone. 7-0, Naples. The second series of plays was a near duplicate of the first, including the blocked punt. 14-0, Naples.

I asked Fran Zampogna to pooch our next kickoff to the right side of the Lely return team. A Lely player muffed it, and Naples High sophomore running back Danny Dunford grabbed the loose ball and raced into the end zone. With 7:29 left in the first period, the score was Naples 21 and Lely 0. Our offense had not been on the field. Twenty-one points, and we had not snapped the ball.

Lely was able to field the next kickoff cleanly, but that did little to stop the dam from bursting. The Naples D held again, and after a successful — if somewhat short — Lely punt, the Naples offense was finally on the field.

To really grasp what happened next, it is best to watch the game video. Naples scored 42 points in just over five minutes. That is 1 point every 7.3 seconds. Four Josh Greco touchdown passes, one Duane Coleman 25-yard run, and one Mike Whooley fumble-recovery scoop and score later, the score was Naples 63 and Lely 0.

The score was 63-0 at the end of the first quarter.

I didn't know it until a couple weeks later, when I got a letter from the National Federation of High Schools, but we had scored the most first-quarter points ever scored in a high school football game. Of course, it broke the state record too.

Everything that could go right, went right. It was surreal. We played every guy on the bench and had a running clock for the entire second half, and still we scored. During the hour-long first quarter, our fans went from cheering madly as we started out with terrific defense and special-teams play, to barely making a peep as we scored our 63rd point at the end of the quarter.

By the end of the game, our stands were silent; even the crickets were too embarrassed to chirp. Needless to say, the Lely fans were not happy, and neither were their coaches. Nearly all of them saw me as the worst example of good sportsmanship ever on God's green earth — or perhaps I was the best example of the worst sportsmanship ever on God's green earth.

I am the first to admit that at first blush, it looked as though we ran up the score. The fact is, we emptied the bench. Yes, our backups played hard and tried to win every play. That is exactly what they should have done.

The other option would have been to take a knee each play when we were on offense. There are some good people who truly believe that is what we should have done. In my view, that would have been the most disrespectful and offensive thing we could have done. What I did do was take Josh Greco and Duane Coleman out of the game. The problem was that David Lightner, who was our backup quarterback, wasn't banged up a little and was in street clothes on our sideline.

Our third-string quarterback happened to be Duane Coleman, who had practiced lining up in the shotgun and running the ball in the event he had to play quarterback. There was no way I could put him in at quarterback; we would have blown up the scoreboard.

Remembering that our starting senior cornerback Willie Brice had played quarterback his freshman year, I asked him if he would be willing to go in and try to get us through the game. Willie enthusiastically agreed, and immediately went behind our bench and began taking snaps from our center — something he hadn't done for three years.

Not long after Willie got in the game, he turned the wrong way on a handoff; he was met by a Lely defender, who drove him into the ground so hard that I thought we'd lost him for the season. Willie was not badly injured, but he was done for that game. Re-enter Josh Greco, with explicit instructions to just hand it off and finish the game healthy – which he did.

Our only second-half pass completion was to Steve McMullan. Steve was one of the hardest workers and best teammates on the team. He was a senior wide receiver and had not caught a ball all year. If I was a bad guy for making sure that Steve McMullan caught a pass his senior year, then I was a bad guy.

After the game, our staff crammed into the tiny coaches' office. The general topic of discussion was speculation on how much blowback there would be about the game.

There was plenty.

There were letters to the editor, nasty emails, voicemail messages on my home phone that needed to be screened so the girls didn't hear them — and yes, of course, we had another Collier County school district investigation. Sue actually saw a panel truck driving around town with a sign in the back window, depicting me being hung from a goalpost, and the words, "Hang Coach Kramer from the goalpost by his balls."

It took a couple of weeks for most of it to calm down. The City of Naples Police Department was very accommodating; patrolmen would drive by our house as often as they could while on patrol. That helped us sleep better. The good news was that since the criticism was directed at me, it wasn't much of a distraction to the team.

I understand that the school district had to look into it. Enough people were making noise about it that they needed to do something. But it did not make it any more palatable for me. I hate wasting time, and the investigation was definitely a big waste of time for everyone involved.

The investigator this time was Assistant Superintendent Eric Williams. If he knew anything about football, he did a great job of not letting on. Eric was a University of Virginia grad; he was very bright, very professional, and very polite. From the outset, it was obvious he was going to do his job to the best of his ability, and he was absolutely consistent with his demeanor. I didn't know if he thought I was Jack the Ripper or Mother Theresa. I still don't.

The tipping point of the investigation was when Eric, Ernie, and I sat down with the video in our principal's office. We went over the game, play-by-play, with me explaining the play-calling. After that, I didn't hear anything else about the game, unless you counted the occasional grumblings from Lely fans and anyone with an ax to grind against Naples. The vast majority of those who said that Naples ran up the score never even saw the game.

CHAPTER

71

The week after the Coconut Bowl was bound to be a dogfight, as we were headed to Venice again. Ten months removed from the intoxication of a state championship, Venice was still a little hung over. Their 2-4 record camouflaged the fact that they had many starters returning from the most dominating win in Florida championship history. Venice was scoring plenty of points, but their defense was just not getting enough stops. Our staff was hoping that trend would continue.

The game started better than we had hoped. Three long TD plays, including two long runs by Duane Coleman and a Greco to Gordon pass, put us up 22-0 at the end of the first quarter. We all knew that Venice would be really dangerous with their backs against the wall, and dangerous they were.

In typical Venice football fashion, those Indians played with a sense of desperation that was very difficult to match. The only hope that Venice had to make the playoffs was as a wild card, and that made our game a must-win for them. In the end, Coleman, Greco, and Gordon were too much for them, and we headed back home down I-75 with a 43-35 win and a 5-2 record.

Next on tap for the Golden Eagles was Gulf Coast High School. Gulf Coast was 0-8, and they looked like it in the video we watched. As always, I told our guys the truth: we should dominate those guys, and everyone was going to get to play. It was so obvious this time that even Sam Dollar didn't try to sell the possibility of a Gulf Coast win. Practice was very workmanlike. There was not a lot of hype or hoopla. Our guys wanted to get the win and move on down the road.

Both our offensive and defensive staffs worked on put-ins for the upcoming home playoff game. It was nice to have enough breathing room so that we could run our base stuff against Gulf Coast, and use practice time to prepare new stuff for the playoffs.

Naples won the coin toss, and as we generally did, we deferred the choice to the second half. Gulf Coast mustered one first down before losing the first of the two fumbles they would lose that night. Naples took advantage of the turnover, scoring on a 14-yard Greco pass to Cleannord Saintil — the first of two he would catch on the night. Gulf Coast played hard, but they were simply no match, and the halftime score was Naples 35 and Gulf Coast 3.

Going into the locker room at halftime, the starters were pressing me to keep them in the game. The Gulf Coast field goal prevented the running clock from being in force. I let everyone in the locker room know that our starters would play one more series before we put in the twos. Duane Coleman's effortless 75 yard touchdown run on our first offensive series of the second half meant that our twos would be in the game almost immediately. For the game, Duane Coleman had eight carries for 197 yards and three touchdowns; those are gaudy numbers. The final score was Naples 48, Gulf Coast 10.

With the win, Naples sat at a respectable No. 8 in the 5A football poll, three places behind 7-1 Manatee. I guess the sportswriters figured in the fact we had beaten them in a monsoon and had home field advantage. If we both kept winning, we would see Manatee in the playoffs again.

Because the Gulf Coast game had been on a Thursday, it allowed the varsity coaches to join the freshman football team coaches in scouting a future opponent on the next night. We always had at least two sets of scouts out. Their job was to get the physical dimensions of the guys we would be playing and to write down every play that each team ran. The plays were put on cards and then the cards were matched to the game video back at our office, so no detail was missed.

On that particular Friday night, I went with the group that watched Northeast High, out of Pinellas County. Northeast had already clinched their district championship, and I trusted Paul Horne when he told me that both Naples and Northeast would win their first-round playoff games. He believed that we would face Northeast at home in the second round of the playoffs. Paul Horne was really good at predicting playoff scenarios; he used the same statistical and logical expertise that he used week in and week out to pick apart deficiencies in the defenses of our opponents.

CHAPTER

72

The final game of the 2001 regular season returned us to Barron Collier. The last time we had been there was Goalpost-gate. I guessed that would be a theme in the media again. Barron was 5-4, and according to our players, Barron players had been talking smack to our guys throughout the season whenever they had seen each other out and about. Thank you, Barron Collier football players — you really helped me motivate our guys.

Knowing that a home playoff game was on the horizon, practice was fast and focused as we prepared for Barron Collier. Some of the spark in our stride may have been from the cooler weather that the first week of November usually brings to southwest Florida. Whatever it was, our guys came out fired up and completely dominated from start to finish. I don't know who originated the saying, but many times I heard Jamie Lemmond tell our players, "I don't want to hear you say it, I want to see you play it!" Play it we did.

Barron Collier wound up with 135 total yards of offense, only completing one pass for 4 yards. Naples wound up with 467 yards of offense, with Duane Coleman rushing for 304 yards and three touchdowns on just 14 carries. The final score was Naples 49 and BC 0. There were no incidents involving goalposts or anything else after the game.

Were it not for a missed field goal, we would have broken the single-season scoring record again. The previous record had been set in 10 games. Having only nine regular season games in 2001, we missed breaking the record by 2 points. We weren't thinking about that at the time. In fact, the last Naples touchdown was scored on a scoop and score of a Barron fumble by backup defensive lineman Alex Nickel. It was nice to be able to play everyone, still get a shutout, and score a bunch of points.

CHAPTER

73

Our first-round playoff opponent had made the playoffs as a wild card. The St. Petersburg Gibbs Gladiators were 5-5 and had won their last three games. They were led by quarterback Ron Mathis, who had thrown for more than 2,000 yards and 23 touchdowns. The problem for the Gladiators was that they gave up more than 29 points a game.

It would be a televised game, and I asked Sam Dollar if he would like to do the pregame TV interview. I thought it would be a good experience for him. I stood within earshot as the interviewer spoke with the St. Pete coach and then Sam. I was pretty surprised when their head coach said he really didn't know much about Naples. I was also surprised when he had to be prompted to talk about Duane Coleman — the same Duane Coleman who was leading the state of Florida in rushing. That definitely gave me confidence as we headed into the locker room at the end of warmups.

Naples won the toss, and as usual we deferred to the second half. After a Francesco Zampogna touchback, Gibbs started on their 20-yard-line. Gibbs's opening drive was impressive. Ron Mathis was as good as advertised in throwing the ball, and the Gladiators were across midfield in short order. But Mathis was paying a price. On nearly every pass, he was getting hit hard by a Naples defensive player. I knew if that continued, there was no way he would be able to finish the game.

The Dollar defense dug in and forced a Gibbs punt, which was almost blocked by Duane Coleman. Duane was also a standout on special teams, giving tremendous effort every time the ball was snapped. As our returner Willie Brice settled under the punt to field the ball, I saw a flag come out, and I immediately turned to tell the offense to hold up. I was afraid that we had roughed the St. Pete punter, and if so, our defense would have to stay on the field.

The official's call was not roughing the punter, but rather running into the punter, which carries a 5-yard penalty instead of a 15-yard penalty. St. Pete accepted the penalty and lined up to punt again. This time Bruce Gordon stuffed the punt, taking it off the punter's foot exactly as he had practiced hundreds of times. Bruce had the presence and athleticism to find and recover the blocked ball, as well as break a tackle en route to the end zone. Naples 7, Gibbs 0.

Once again Zampogna's kickoff started Gibbs at their own 20, and once again they moved the ball in chunks, riding the arm of Ron Mathis. Mathis was taking a beating, but he was not giving in. The Dollar defense was able to bend but not break, and Gibbs was held to a 27-yard field goal. Naples 7, Gibbs 3.

The Naples offense picked up where it had left off, and Duane Coleman made it 14-3 with a 26-yard touchdown run. Duane was just getting warmed up. I was really proud of the way Paul's offensive line, though clearly undersized, was getting off the ball and creating space for Duane. The line was also doing a good job protecting Josh Greco when we threw the ball. Seniors Rick Martin and Jason Gore were leading a group of guys that simply did not care how big, fast, or strong the opposing defense was. The offensive line believed in Paul Horne and our system, and each guy knew we would not ask him to do something he was not capable of. If every guy did his job, we would win.

I had been a bit concerned about our offensive output coming into the game, as David Lightner, our other starting running back, was nursing a sore ankle. Sophomore Danny Dunford was starting for him. David was dressed out and was available in case of emergency. Fortunately, there was no emergency.

Duane Coleman rushed for 368 yards and five touchdowns. Josh Greco was 10 of 18, passing for 195 yards, with two touchdowns and no interceptions; Bruce Gordon had five catches for 83 yards. Bruce also scored two touchdowns, one being the blocked punt scoop and score. When the dust had cleared, the Naples High offense had accumulated 694 yards of offense. Sophomore Danny Dunford gave a preview of things to come, rushing for more than 10 yards per carry on his nine rushing attempts.

The defense had been nearly as capable against a Gibbs team that could really score points. Pat Liebig dominated the line of scrimmage from his defensive end position, and, with his cohorts, pounded Gibbs quarterback Ron Mathis into submission. On the first Gibbs series of the second half, just 14 seconds after Duane Coleman scored on a 56-yard run, our defensive end Thomas Martucci knocked the ball loose from Mathis. Liebig picked up the fumble and rumbled 8 yards for what is every defensive lineman's dream — a fumble recovery scoop and score.

When Ron Mathis limped off the field early in the third quarter, he had had enough. His backup came in and got pounded too. The final score was Naples 69 and St. Pete Gibbs 22. The only negative from the game was an injury to wide receiver Cleannord Saintil. During the second quarter, Saintil had lined up in the slot, beaten his man coverage on a vertical release, and hauled in a dart from Josh Greco for a nice gain and a first down.

Cleannord wasn't really even tackled; his momentum had brought him to the ground. Although he popped up immediately, he took a few steps and then stooped over, calling for the trainer and pointing to his knee. Our team orthopedic physician, Dr. Mike Havig, evaluated Cleannord on the sideline. He suspected that Cleannord had torn his meniscus and that a small piece was caught in the joint line. Mike Havig is one of the best doctors on the planet; the MRI confirmed exactly what he said.

By the time we were lining up to shake hands, our scouts had called to tell us that Northeast was up 28-0 late in the fourth quarter in their playoff game. We would play Northeast at home in the second round, the next Friday. Paul Horne was right again.

Our fans were jubilant. It had been 19 years since a Naples High School playoff win. Our players were happy, but not satisfied. I could feel their vibe, and I really liked it.

CHAPTER

74

I was glad I had seen Northeast in person. This was a team that fed off a really tough defense. For the year, Northeast had averaged giving up just 118 yards per game and only 10.9 points per game. They were tall, fast, and really athletic. I was banking on us being stronger, fast enough, and more technical.

Practice that second week in November was focused, but not very emotional. I could sense that our coaches and players all had low fuel tanks. I was looking forward to a win at home and then Thanksgiving week. We would still practice during Thanksgiving week; our game would be the Friday after Thanksgiving. At least we would be out of school for a few days, and our guys could all catch up on sleep and recharge a bit. Still, we had to keep first things first, and that meant doing the work to beat a really good Northeast team.

The guys on the Northeast defense who troubled me most were their two defensive ends. On our left, Dominque Bacon stood 6'6", 240 pounds, and he could move. To our right was Martin Teal, 6'5", 195 pounds; athletic enough to play end on defense and wide receiver on offense. I really hoped that Teal would get tired while lining up for their offense. Martin Teal would go on to a stellar career at Troy University, and would be one of the few players in the 2007 NFL draft listed as both a defensive player at linebacker and an offensive player at wide receiver.

The media presence at practice that week picked up noticeably. We were the only Collier team still playing; Lee County was down to just two teams left, with both Estero and Bishop Verot winning the previous week. More noticeable than the media was the spirit at the school. Students, teachers, administrators, custodians — everyone was fired up for the upcoming football game. Their vocal encouragement gave all of our players and coaches a little more in the tank as we went through each school day that week.

By the time Friday night rolled around, our guys had an obvious swagger — and rightly so. We all found confidence by doing the work and preparing in a way that made us feel that we deserved to win. I found tremendous confidence and peace in my morning quiet times with my Bible and my *Prayer of Jabez* devotional book. I was praying the prayer on a regular basis. I was confident that God wanted to bless me and our team, and it didn't necessarily have anything to do with the scoreboard. I would like to say that my study and prayer took all the pressure off, but as my days went on, the pressure to be excellent and to overachieve would build. I can't imagine what it would have been like without that daily quiet time and prayer.

Northeast took the opening kickoff and ran the ball down our throats. They were bigger, faster, and stronger than we had anticipated. On the ensuing kickoff, special teams coach Jamie Lemmond called a play that we had been working on all year and saving for the right moment. Jamie was always cognizant of keeping things as simple as he could for his players. We wanted guys to play fast, and they wouldn't do that if they had to think too much.

Consequently, the name of this particular kickoff return was simply Brucer Reverser. You got it — Bruce Gordon was going to run a reverse on the kickoff. Duane and Bruce were our returners, with Duane fielding most of the kickoffs. Jamie had devised a play where Duane would field the kickoff and run to the left boundary, where Bruce would be waiting to take a handoff. Bruce would then run up the right boundary.

The play worked to perfection. Duane tucked the ball and ran hard. Bruce was patient and gave time for the entire Northeast squad to chase Duane, and when Bruce got the ball, it was sayonara. Eighty-six yards later, the score was tied.

It was the loudest roar I had heard from our crowd to date. The play was slow-developing, and many of our fans had a vantage point to see it as it happened. Once Duane gave the ball to Bruce, it was a long haul across the field and then up the boundary, and the crowd noise grew with every step he took. The crowd never quit. For the rest of the game, the Naples fans were all-in. It was a coach's dream.

Both offenses were moving the ball, but we were not getting as many opportunities to touch the ball as we were accustomed to. Northeast was controlling the ball and the time of possession. The scoreboard at halftime showed a dogfight; Naples 28 and Northeast 28. But the stat sheet at halftime told a different story: it read that Northeast had accumulated 294 yards of offense to Naples' 191.

We were fortunate to be tied. The good news was, at halftime our players and coaches were energetic, communicative, and determined. Sam knew exactly what needed to be done to stem the tide, and everyone on our defense knew they just had to do what he said: "Just do your job."

Duane Coleman was determined to do his. Naples took the second-half kickoff and went straight down the field. Three plays and 57 seconds later, Duane scored from 10 yards out.

On the ensuing Northeast possession, the Dollar defense took control, forcing a three-and-out and a Northeast punt. Naples' special teams were special once again and blocked the punt. Duane Coleman recovered the ball in the end zone, and after Zampogna's PAT, Naples was up by 14.

The Dollar defense spent the rest of the half stuffing the run and making the Northeast quarterback and receivers pay for every completion. The second-half stat sheet was much different than the first-half stat sheet. The Naples High defense held Northeast to minus 30 yards rushing, including a sack for a safety in the fourth quarter. Naples' offense took advantage of the short fields that the defense provided, and when the time clock hit 0:00, the score read Naples 58, Northeast 28.

We were going to get to practice on Thanksgiving.

CHAPTER 75

Naples High School was hopping Monday morning of Thanksgiving week in 2001. The students and staff were buzzing with excitement about the upcoming regional final game. The short school week put us in hurry-up mode to get buses and make travel arrangements for the team, cheerleaders, band, and fans. It would be a two-and-a-half-hour trek to Seminole High School near Tampa. There were eight 5A schools left standing, and Naples would be playing in one of four games that weekend. The Naples faithful were fired up!

I had a few students and teachers wish me well and tell me they would have liked to come to the game, but they had made Thanksgiving plans some time earlier and could not change them. I made a new goal that Thanksgiving games would become something our students and fans planned for every year. What better way to celebrate Thanksgiving?

The media attention intensified a bit more that week, as Naples and Estero were the only southwest Florida teams still playing. Our players and coaches took it all in stride.

The Seminole Warhawks were a salty bunch. They were fast, physical, and well-coached. Every guy on that team played with a chip on his shoulder. Defense was definitely the Seminole team strength. On the season, they had given up just 68 points in 12 games for a 5.7 point-per-game average. We had scored an average of 47.5 points per game. Something had to give. On offense, the Warhawks were patient and deliberate. They ran the ball, ate clock, and waited for their defense to get a turnover or great field position that they could take advantage of. Paul and I were convinced that we would not have many possessions. We would have to take advantage of the ones we had.

On both offense and defense, and on special teams too for that matter, the Seminole Warhawks were led by D'Qwell Jackson. He was their heart and soul, and he jumped off the scouting film as we reviewed it. He looked like a superhero. He played middle linebacker on defense and running back on offense, and he was their punter as well. He dominated the game from every position.

In the media, Seminole players and coaches talked about looking for redemption. The Warhawks had lost to Venice the previous year in the regional finals, and they were bound and determined to learn from history and not repeat it. Seminole was saying it and playing it. The videotape showed that those guys were mauling people. They were **really** physical. I was stating the obvious when I told our guys that there would be no place for the timid on Friday night.

One of the nice things about playing some easier teams earlier in the season was that it gave us a chance to use a very basic game plan while we practiced new and more complex stuff that we would need later. One of the plays that we had worked countless reps with was counter-veer. That play was really hard for a quarterback — mechanically, visually, and mentally. Thankfully, Josh Greco was doing a good job with counter-veer during practice — because we would need it against Seminole.

Counter-veer is most effective against really aggressive downhill linebackers who are well coached and are disciplined at reading their keys. It brings linebackers — who are generally better athletes than the offensive linemen blocking them — closer to the guys who have to block them. It gives the offense just a little bit of leverage on the block.

Practice went really well that week, and thankfully we had David Lightner back. The big back who was also our backup quarterback hadn't played in a couple of weeks, but he was finally at full speed and ready to go.

Thanksgiving break was a blessing when it came to football preparation. School was business as usual on Monday and Tuesday that week, but there was no school Wednesday through Friday. That meant less distractions, less homework, and terrific weather. I wanted to give the guys as much family time as possible, so we practiced Wednesday morning and held our usual walk-through under the lights on Thursday night. That allowed the guys traveling locally to get wherever they were going on Wednesday afternoon, to enjoy Thanksgiving, and then get back in time for practice. All in all, it was a really good work week, and everyone got a chance to catch up on sleep.

The trip to Seminole was uneventful. We stopped for our pregame meal at a restaurant on the way, and as our guys got off the bus, there was a very focused feel to the entire crew. There were definitely no problems on this game day. Our guys were usually quiet and reserved during the pregame meal, and this meal was extra-quiet. They were not afraid or worried; this was simply the calm before the storm.

On game nights at 6 p.m. — an hour and a half before kickoff — I would take our quarterbacks out to warm up. We would normally walk into a mostly empty stadium. On this night, our fans had the visitors' bleachers mostly full. We finished our practice routine at 7 p.m. as usual, and headed into the locker room. I was really pleased with the demeanor and tempo of the warmups. I was also really pleased with our fans. The size and the noise of our crowd confirmed it – we had definitely reached a new level of fandom.

For our fans, it was a two-and-a-half hour drive to an away game on Black Friday, and half an hour before kickoff, our stands were already full. It was definitely not a cocktail hour crowd. This group was rocking and rolling in the stands. Their energy came at us in waves. As we came out of the locker room at 7:20, the lid of the stadium was torn off. When we walked in view of our stands, a roar went up. I was amazed at the size of our crowd. The bleachers were packed like sardines, and lots of people had to stand. Seminole fans had shown up en masse as well. Both sides seemed to be trying to outdo each other in screaming their support for the teams entering the stadium.

Seminole won the toss and chose to defer.

The Warhawks had a terrific kicker in Morgan Riley, who would go on to kick at Murray State. Morgan buried the kickoff, and Naples started on the Seminole 20-yard-line. Our offensive game plan was very specific to the personnel and scheme of the Seminole defense. Josh Greco had been given a lot of responsibility in checking us out of bad plays and into good ones.

On the first play of the game, our call was a short pass. The receiver got open, and the ball bounced about 5 yards in front of him. I chalked it up to nerves. Josh and I made eye contact, I assured Josh that he was OK, and I called the next play, another pass. Our pass protection broke down courtesy of D'Qwell Jackson. Voila, it was third and 10, and we hadn't taken 20 seconds off the clock.

On third and 10, Josh Greco threw a terrific ball to Bruce Gordon, who made the catch for a 30-yard gain and a first down. I was finally able to do two things I had been unable to do since the opening kickoff: exhale... and look Sam Dollar in the eye. Defensive coordinators are not happy campers when the offense gets the ball to start a game, gains zero yards, takes no time off the clock, and punts it back to the opponent.

Our third-down success was a sign of things to come, really good things. Paul and I were right in our assumption that we would not have as many possessions as we were used to, but we made the most of the possessions we had. Seminole was as good as advertised, and D'Qwell Jackson was the best linebacker I had ever seen play high school football. Thankfully, our guys were poised and patient, and while we did not hit any big plays, we did keep the chains moving and had some really long drives.

The first drive of the game wound up going 80 yards in 13 plays with a touchdown. That kind of start to a game is a defensive coordinator's dream.

Converting third downs was the key to the game. For the game, we converted 9 of 13 third downs, and we were 2 for 2 on fourth-down conversions. Josh Greco did a good job of keeping us in the right play, regardless of the distance on third down. All of our guys believed in our game plan, and on several third and longs, we ran the ball for the first down. In fact, 5 of our 9 third-down conversions were accomplished by running the ball, including a David Lightner scamper for 19 yards on a third and 11.

One of our fourth-down conversions was part of another 13-play drive in the first half. On fourth and 11, from our own 34-yard-line, we lined up to punt — and faked it instead. Josh Greco found an open Reggie Carter, who hauled the pass in to keep the drive alive. That particular drive ended in a Francesco Zampogna 27-yard field goal.

The counter-veer was critical to our offensive success. It bought us just enough time to get a little leverage, and after we ran it successfully several times, it slowed the Seminole defense down enough that they couldn't just tee off on us. Our defense played lights-out. By the end of Seminole's second series, Sam Dollar was confident enough that when I asked him what he thought, he simply replied, "I got 'em."

His confidence made the fake punt from our own 34 much easier to call. Our defense dominated the third downs and held the Warhawks on both of their fourth-down conversion attempts. For the game, Seminole had 98 yards rushing and 127 yards of total offense. By contrast, Naples had 265 yards rushing and 429 yards of total offense.

The final score of 30-0 disguised how hard-fought the game was. The Seminole players fought tooth and nail for every inch of ground, and so did Naples. The bus ride home found me with nothing but respect for the Seminole program, and with gratitude for the folks associated with the Naples program. It also began to sink in that there were only four teams left in Florida. We were in the state semifinals.

CHAPTER 76

Our video session on Saturday morning showed two things. First, we saw that Naples High football players were not making many mistakes. Our guys were fast, strong, and technical, which was helping us win against the decided size advantage that our opponents had just about every week. The second thing we saw was that Delray Beach-Atlantic was, as usual, loaded with big, fast players.

They had a great quarterback in 6'4", 205-pound Omar Jacobs. Omar would go on to a terrific career at Bowling Green, where he would opt for an early exit due to his NFL draft selection in the fifth round by the Pittsburgh Steelers. The Atlantic offense also had wide receiver David Clowney, who would go on to a stellar career at Virginia Tech and then be drafted in the fifth round by the Green Bay Packers. The other starting wide receiver for Delray Beach-Atlantic was no slouch, either; Jamoga Ramsey would later accept a scholarship to Auburn. As expected, the War Eagles of Delray Beach-Atlantic had a massive offensive line. By now our guys were pretty used to the size differential. At this point in the season we knew we could beat, or be beaten by, anyone.

On defense, the War Eagles were really big and fast too. Cornerback Brandon Flowers was a lockdown corner. He could erase just about any receiver he lined up across from. He would go on to an NFL career with the Chiefs and the Chargers that included a Pro Bowl appearance. Atlantic's 6'2", 200-pound safety, Brandon Owens, was perhaps the best player for their defense. His career was cut short when playing for the Minnesota Golden Gophers; he took an awkward hit and sustained nerve damage to his right arm, which ended his football playing days. The 6', 280-pound defensive lineman, Dejuan Guillory, led a stout defensive front that once again dwarfed our offensive line.

The thing that our coaching staff noticed when scouting those guys was that not every guy on the Atlantic team played hard on every play. We could see guys taking plays off on occasion, and that was the chink in their armor. The other thing Paul and I soon saw was that Atlantic defenders would miss tackles. They were so aggressive that they would often be out of control. If our guys stayed in control and finished every play, we would be able to move the ball.

Three things happened that week before the Delray Beach-Atlantic game that I was not prepared for.

First, I had lots of new friends. They became a distraction; they would call my home or work, or just show up to one place or the other. My new friends usually wished me luck or stroked my ego, and then asked if I could get them game tickets. Second, the travel preparation for the potential state championship game 435 miles away at Doak Campbell Stadium on the Florida State University campus became a distraction. I was responsible for every detail of the trip, and there were countless details. Third, the media coverage became a distraction. I had no plan for the increased media demands. I was taking several crash courses at once.

Church on the Sunday after Thanksgiving was full of well-wishers. I even got a shout-out from the pulpit as our pastor offered encouragement for the game the next Friday. After church, I got a call from Ernie. He asked if I could swing by his office the next morning and talk about the state championship game the following week.

Coach Dollar covered my first period class on Monday morning, and I headed to Ernie's office. He told me about the required conference call we would have later that week with the Florida High School Athletic Association and our opponents. We then dug into the details involved in getting our crew to and from Tallahassee, hopefully with a win in the middle.

With players, trainers, and coaches, our entourage was 83 people. We had to get everyone and all of our equipment up and back safely, feeding the crew a bunch of times along the way, while providing three uneventful and restful hotel nights. We also needed a place to practice, and I was hoping to raise the money for some sweats or some kind of cold-weather gear, which would need to be ordered, delivered, and screen-printed with our brand on it in about 10 days.

Our regular work week did not afford any extra time for the stuff that had to be done. Teaching a full load of classes, then practicing, grading practice video, game planning, having the players come eat at the house, and putting out the fires that showed up each day made it impossible.

Thankfully, God had given us a new guidance secretary at the school named Terri Dickerson. Two of Terri's boys played on the team; Luke and Jason "Spud" Dickerson were terrific football players and even better wrestlers. Terri was sweet, smart, and hard-working. She was also a wonderful Christian woman — she didn't beat people over the head with her Bible; rather, she served and loved those around her. Terri offered to do all she could to help with preparations, even offering to travel in advance of the team to make sure that we were ready wherever we went.

Of course Sue was all-in, too. I knew that with the help of these two smart and energetic women, it would be hard for me to screw it up. Mr. Brown was also helpful. He allowed me to use a substitute teacher for a few of my classes so I could work with Susie and Terri to create and implement our travel plan. We needed to get everyone up and back safely, while keeping the main focus on winning the football game.

I really liked the local sports reporters, and I thought the *Naples Daily News's* Tom Rife was the best hometown sports editor in the state. The other area paper was the *Fort Myers News-Press,* and those guys did a great job too. The thing is, they were bound to write as much as they could about the history we were making, so that included lots of interviews with as many players and coaches as possible.

As we went through the week of preparation, I learned that I would need to have a media plan in place in the future, one which would give reporters access at very specific times for very specific amounts of time. The media distraction was my own rookie fault. My philosophy of "all access, any time" was great when nobody wanted access, ever. Now my philosophy was becoming unmanageable.

Each year, the Florida High School Athletic Association sends out a participant manual to the schools playing in the state finals. It covers everything, from possible places to stay, to where the wives will park, to how many championship medals they provide. Every detail concerning the game is covered, from coaches' sideline communication, to credentials, to what would be allowed in the stadium or locker room. In December 2001, with 9-11 still fresh in our minds, security and procedures for this particular state championship game would be the most stringent to date.

The participant manual had a list of preferred hotels with decent rates, and as I started at the top of the list and began calling hotels to make the team reservation, I realized that we were a bit late. The national brand hotels with names I recognized were booked solid. Teams that thought they might make it to Doak Campbell Stadium in Tallahassee had reserved their rooms at least a week prior. My late hotel booking absolutely confirmed that I was a state finals rookie. Eventually, we settled on the only hotel on the list of 17 that was not already booked — the Collegiate Village Inn. The good news was, it was the cheapest hotel on the list. The bad news was, there was a reason it was the cheapest hotel on the list.

I often reminded my players to keep the main thing the main thing. It was really important for me to do that. All those preparations for a trip to the state championship game were necessary. They would also be irrelevant if we did not win the semifinal game on Friday night.

On Monday, Ernie announced that reserved seats for Friday night's game would go on sale the following day; we would sell first to season ticket holders and faculty and staff, and then to the general public.

Reserved seating sold out in one hour and 45 minutes.

Beginning Tuesday afternoon, the number of well-wishing, ticket-wanting folks began to grow. There were even guys who came by the gym during school, or to the practice field after school, hoping to score some reserved seats or maybe even a sideline pass.

I was glad for the support and interest; I didn't want to alienate anyone, but the fact was that I couldn't even help my own coaches who had requests for extra tickets from family and friends. For the coaches, the best we could do was buy them general admission tickets. For anyone else, they would have to buy their own general admission ticket. And by the way, a general admission ticket to Naples' Staver Field did not guarantee a seat.

I received several phone calls that week from various people asking if they could come and speak to the team and give them a pep talk. I tried not to offend as I politely declined each offer. I wondered to myself, *Where were these guys when we were 3-2?*

Besides being the date of the biggest game in the history of Naples High football, Friday, November 30, 2001, was also Katie Kramer's 9th birthday. I knew that if we did not win the game, all of my girls would be devastated. I was really hoping for a happy birthday for Katie and only tears of joy for my girls. With all of the pressure, I still had peace. Much of the peace I felt stemmed from the *Prayer of Jabez* and the newfound grace I found in asking for God's blessing. It was OK to ask for clarity and wisdom and confidence and energy. All of the coaches and I were focused on the process. We were trusting God for the outcome, and that was liberating.

CHAPTER

77

An hour before kickoff, the football stadium at Naples High was full.

The crowd picked up where it had left off the previous week at Seminole. Our folks were cheering and chanting and stomping their feet, and we were still just warming up. The Delray Beach-Atlantic War Eagles traveled well; they packed the visitors' stands and were doing their level best to out-cheer our home crowd. The effect was exhilarating; the atmosphere was electric. However it would go, I was grateful to be in that place at that time.

Atlantic had the ball first, and the Dollar defense performed as well as we could have hoped, forcing a punt on the opening series. Naples punt returner Stevie Weigle settled under the punt, and as his fingers touched the ball, he was drilled by an Atlantic player. The ball was loose and the War Eagles came up with it. The hit could have easily been flagged for not giving Stevie room to catch the ball, but in the end, the officials ruled that the hit was legal. There was nothing for us to do but win the next play.

Atlantic was too talented to give second chances. A few plays later, Omar Jacobs hit A.J. Bennett for an 8-yard touchdown; the PAT gave Atlantic a 7-point lead. The Naples offense responded, although the going was a bit tougher than we expected. The Atlantic pass rush was brutal, and the Atlantic corners were better than we had imagined. The corners were so aggressive that they overplayed every short route, and we were able to shake Bruce Gordon loose on a pump and go. The result was a 23-yard touchdown pass from Josh Greco.

Atlantic put on a show the next series, mixing up the run and pass. At one point in the drive, Omar Jacobs completed seven straight passes. But he was getting hit, and even though his 19-yard touchdown pass to David Clowney put Atlantic up 14-7, our players and coaches were still full of confidence. We knew that our problems were more mental than physical.

Early in the second quarter, we managed to move the ball close enough for Francesco Zampogna's 25-yard field goal. That cut the Atlantic lead back to 4. As the second quarter unfolded, the Dollar defense began to put the brakes on the Atlantic offense. Omar completed just 2 of the next 8 passes he attempted.

With less than four minutes left in the half, Reggie Carter blocked a punt, which LJ Montinar recovered on the Atlantic 10-yard-line. Two plays later, Duane Coleman's 9-yard run and a Zampogna PAT put Naples up 17-14.

In all of their previous games, Atlantic loved to throw the ball at the end of the first half. If Sam Dollar knew that an offense was going to throw the ball, it was usually very bad for that offense.

The final defensive stop of the first half gave us the ball at our own 39-yard line with 51 seconds remaining in the half. We had worked on a play all season that was simply called "double pass." As the name implied, we were going to throw the ball twice. The play called for running back David Lightner to line up in the slot on the left side of the formation. David, a lefty, also happened to be our backup quarterback; he had a cannon for an arm. Josh Greco would throw a lateral to David, who would then throw the ball downfield to one of two receivers, depending on the coverage.

Greco's pass to Lightner was perfect, and David got the ball out right on time. Bruce Gordon came down with it, and just like that it was first and 10, Naples, from the Atlantic 11. Two Duane Coleman runs later, Naples was up 24 -14.

On the ensuing kickoff, the Golden Eagle kickoff coverage ran down the field with their hair on fire and knocked the ball loose from the Atlantic return man. We had just enough time for Francesco Zampogna to nail a 43-yard field goal, his longest of the year. Naples was up 27-14 heading into the locker room. The last four minutes of the half had been a whirlwind, and that wind had blown in Naples' favor.

The third quarter was all Naples. The Dollar defense was able to bend but not break, and Atlantic was unable to put up any points. On offense, we were able to run the ball and eat clock, which was a good thing because our passing game was nearly completely shut down. Duane scored his third and final touchdown of the game, and Josh Greco's 2-point conversion run made it Naples 35 and Atlantic 14 to start the fourth quarter.

Omar Jacobs was hit repeatedly and forced to try and make perfect throws with Naples defenders hanging all over him. Omar had no quit in him; his mental and physical toughness was impressive. A fourth quarter 1-yard touchdown run by Kerry Sanders helped the Atlantic faithful find their voice, but Bruce Gordon's return past midfield on the ensuing kickoff silenced them. A few plays later, Josh Greco's 2-yard touchdown run made it 41-21, Naples.

The Dollar defense went back to slowing down Atlantic, and the final Atlantic touchdown was way too little, way too late to be meaningful. As the scoreboard counted down to zero, the final score read Naples 41, Atlantic 28. The stats showed that Omar Jacobs had given a superstar performance, completing 29 of 38 passes for 318 yards.

After the handshakes and a quick word to the team, I turned our guys loose to celebrate with their friends, families, and fans. Staver Field was overrun with giddy people hugging and cheering, slapping backs, and giving high-fives.

As she did at every playoff game, Sue had used stencils, cut out letters, and made posters that were perfect for the occasion. Each sign, colored in the navy and gold of Naples High, was really big, and looked professionally done. Sue and the girls hid the signs in trash bags in the stands and didn't get them out until the game clock said zero. It was a beautiful sight to see my girls heading onto the field with those playoff signs in their hands. Sue Kramer really is something special.

The players and coaches spent a lot of time taking pictures with friends and family, holding posters which read "2001 Florida Football Finalists," "2001 5A Semi-Final Champions," "Four Down and One to Go," etc., etc.

When the media was finally done and the frenzy had calmed, we herded the players into two lines for the 100-yard walk out of the stadium and back to the locker room. I was amazed to see that as full as the field was with fans, there were as many still waiting in the stands and lining the way out of the stadium. We made our way off the field to the thunder of a heartfelt standing ovation.

I don't think that God supernaturally determined the outcome of the game, but I am sure that we had no business beating that team. Somehow, even though Atlantic outgained us 431 offensive yards to our 336 offensive yards, Naples High would be playing in the state finals. Once again, we had confirmation that we did not need to have the best athletes; we needed to have the best team.

CHAPTER

78

As the Naples coaches walked into that tiny football office, our preparation for the 2001 5A Football Championship began in earnest. We had done all that could be done up to that point, but knowing that did nothing to stop the realization that there was a mountain of work that was just plopped down on us.

Our scouts had gone to Rutherford High School by Panama City in Florida's panhandle to watch the other semifinal game. They watched as Chamberlain High School from Tampa beat Rutherford, 23-17, to set up a title game with us.

I thought it ironic that two teams that were located less than three hours apart would have to travel so far to play each other. In fact, Tampa was right on our way to Tallahassee! As we passed the exit to Chamberlain High, we would have to settle in for another four hours on our charter buses heading to Tallahassee.

I had made contact with the head coaches from Rutherford and Chamberlain the previous week. Per our agreement, our scouts would exchange some video that night, and then one of our coaches would drive halfway to Tampa and meet a Chamberlain coach to trade the video of the semifinal game.

As our coaches worked feverishly to get our video ready for our 7 a.m. meeting the next morning, I walked through the locker room and training room as I normally did after a game. It was all good news. We had no injuries during the game. I was very grateful for that. Once again, I had confirmation that God was blessing us. We were experiencing God's grace. Jamie Lemmond reminded me regularly that a good definition for grace is "unmerited favor."

Whenever I hear a coach being praised for a great season, or a coach being denigrated for a bad season, I think of the things that a coach cannot control. Those things have as much to do with success as all the preparation in the world.

Injuries are one of those things. It doesn't matter what the sport is; injuries are very often the difference between winning and losing. In high school football, the drop in ability from a starting player to his backup can be dramatic.

We had been very fortunate so far. The only significant injury we had was the loss of wide receiver Cleannord Saintil, and Steve McMullan was filling in nicely.

Coaches have no control if family circumstances move an athlete into a different district or if an athlete does something dumb that prohibits him or her from playing. Coaches also cannot control all of the interpersonal stuff that goes on in the locker room, at home, or in the community that can significantly change the course of a season. In the end, like their athletes, all any coach can control is his personal effort and attitude. "Great Day... Today!" is up to me.

Seven a.m. came early, and I was grateful for the extra-large Dunkin Donuts coffee with extra cream and extra sugar that Coach Benjie Welzbacher had waiting for me as I walked into the office. Benjie demonstrated his servant's heart by staying after games and stain-removing, washing, drying, and putting away the game uniforms from the night before. I didn't ask Benjie to do that; he came and asked if he could. With one washer and one dryer, the task took several hours. Benjie was a sterling example of servant-leadership.

Our coaches got to work on grading the Atlantic game, and the video showed a Naples team that was playing its heart out on offense, defense, and special teams. What our guys lacked in size or athleticism, they made up for with strength and technique. Now our staff had to come up with one more game plan to beat a much bigger and more talented Tampa Chamberlain team. The Chamberlain offensive line outsized the Naples defensive line by an average of three inches and 50 pounds. Likewise, the Chamberlain defensive line dwarfed the Naples offensive line — and the Chamberlain guys could move.

In addition to their massive linemen, the Chamberlain offense had wide receivers Brian Clark, who eventually played for North Carolina State; and Greg Lee, who played for the University of Pittsburgh and went on to the NFL with the Phoenix Cardinals and Detroit Lions. Thankfully, Greg played on defense in the Tampa Chamberlain secondary, so he took a breather on offense.

His backup was Brandon Williams, who would play college ball at Akron.

Their running backs were formidable as well. They were a three-headed monster, which made Chamberlain really tough to prepare for. Eddie Lee Ivery was following in his dad's footsteps. Eddie Sr. had played 10 years for the Green Bay Packers, and Eddie Jr. was heading to Georgia Tech. He might have made it to the NFL too, had it not been for career-ending knee injuries in college. Mike Ross was a terrific 11th-grader who would garner scholarship offers from North Carolina State and Iowa State. But the best back of the three was sophomore Donnie Davis. Donnie had been scorching defenses throughout the playoffs, and had emerged as the Chiefs' hottest back entering the championship game.

The defense for Chamberlain was as scary as the offense. The secondary had the aforementioned Greg Lee. He was joined by Sean Dixon, a 6'0", 190-pound corner, who would go on to play for Vanderbilt. Jared Baxley, a 6'0", 190-pound outside linebacker, would play at the Air Force Academy. Jared had the genetics; his father Ed had played linebacker for South Carolina, spent two years in the USFL, and played briefly for the Kansas City Chiefs.

Joe Clermond was a 6'2", 205-pound linebacker who would go on to a stellar career at Pitt and then play for a year for the Chicago Bears. Another linebacker, Oliver Hoyt, was absolutely dominating on video; talk about a freak show. He would be a standout at N.C. State, and would play professionally for both the Dallas Cowboys and the Kansas City Chiefs.

The 6'4", 260-pound Brodrick Bunkley was a terror on the field. If the Chamberlain Chiefs were men among boys, Brodrick was a man among those men. Bunkley would attend Florida State, where he would be an All-American; he would then be selected in the first round of the NFL draft by the Philadelphia Eagles. Bunkley made the Pro Bowl while in the NFL.

As great as all of those players were, the more we watched the video, the more convinced we were that defensive lineman Al Mack was the best player on the field. Al Mack was 6'3", 255 pounds. Paul and I agreed that he was the most disruptive player on the defense. I do not know if Al Mack played college football; perhaps grades or injuries prevented it, but in my view he was the best player on the best defense I had seen in high school football.

The Chamberlain defense had given up just over 13 points a game during the season; the Naples defense had averaged yielding just under 18 points a game. The Naples offense's scoring average was 46 points a game, and the Chamberlain offense had averaged 31 points a game. The biggest disparity between the two teams was on special teams. Naples' kicking game was obviously better than Chamberlain's, and the Naples punt block team had blocked 14 punts in 2001, and forced at least as many shanks.

On paper, they had the players. We had to be the better team.

If intangibles were thrown in, the scale probably swung to Tampa Chamberlain. Billy Turner had been a head coach since 1969, and the head coach at Chamberlain since 1979. That is 33 years as a head coach and 22 years at the same high school — absolutely unheard of. Billy had taken advantage of a retirement offer and was scheduled to retire at the end of the school year. Every player knew that this state championship game would be Coach Turner's last shot. You can also bet that every Chamberlain player, coach, and fan knew that Coach Turner's win-loss record stood at 199-122. One more win would put him in the elite 200-win club.

As our offensive staff watched the video, we realized that this was the biggest, strongest, and fastest defense we had seen all year. These guys were super aggressive, and once again we thought we could use that to our advantage.

As Paul charted their defensive play-calling, it became pretty clear that Chamberlain's defense was somewhat predictable. The best defenses often are. The best defenses often line up in a base front and coverage, and keep it simple. That prevents stupid mistakes and allows players to play fast and physical. Tampa Chamberlain's defense did just that.

Again, Paul and I saw an opportunity. We figured that we could script the game and find success early. We thought we would be able to predict how they would line up and try to stop various formations and motions. After reviewing a few hours of video, we knew that if we called our lead draw on an early down, it might score. Paul schemed it so we could account for all but the linebacker lined up over our right tackle. Duane would have to make that linebacker miss. We both knew that if Duane knew in advance, there was a really good chance he would make him miss.

Our defensive staff was impressed with the Chamberlain offense, but felt like they were somewhat predictable too. And while their offensive line would dwarf our guys, our defensive coaches left the building on Saturday feeling confident about the game plan they put together. As we broke down their kicking game and studied it, it was evident to everyone that we had a decided advantage in that phase of the game. All in all, if Chamberlain didn't just outright dominate us with size, strength, and speed, we would have a fighting chance.

CHAPTER

79

As on every other Monday, we began practice with the entire team meeting in the weight room. I gave out the awards for the outstanding players of the previous game, and presented an overview of our opponent and the plan for the week. After that, our special teams coaches went over the special teams game plans, and then we divided up into offense and defense to go over our respective game plans and scouting reports.

When we put the special teams video on that last Monday practice, the room was quiet and focused. There were a bunch of really big, really fast guys on the field for Chamberlain. Most of our players had come by the school over the weekend to watch video and get an early jump on the VHS scout tapes that our staff made for them. So for most of our guys, the size and speed was not a surprise. For the guys who had not seen the video yet, it was an eye-opener. After the special teams video, the defense settled into the weight room, which is where they watched video and studied the scouting report each week. The offense headed to the school auditorium, where we did the same.

We went over the scouting report and then the script for the game. Paul and I had specifically scripted the first 20 plays, taking field position and possible outcomes of previous plays into account. We were not bound to the script, but at the very least it showed us our preferred play calls, based on down and distance and field position.

The plan for the week was to keep it business as usual, and we as coaches did all we could to keep it that way. The truth was, the week of the 2001 state football championship was anything but usual. The media seemed to be everywhere all the time, and absurdity reached its zenith when one of the TV news crews actually did an on-air interview with the barber that both Coach Dollar and I used. Ridiculous.

Another unusual event was Tuesday's pep rally. Jamie Lemmond and Marlin Faulkner had both been program directors for Kannakuk youth leadership camps. Both of them were experts at organizing and engaging large groups of high school students. During their tenure at Naples High, pep rallies were marvels.

As a rule, I did not like pep rallies. I didn't like them as a player, and I didn't like them as a coach. They tended to be really distracting to the players, and distractions will get you beat. I always willed myself to participate in them wholeheartedly, but I really had to control my effort and attitude each time. Pep rallies done right can generate excitement and put fans in the stands on game night, and that gives them value.

The pep rally that Wednesday was the best. Jamie Lemmond had found the time to make video highlights for each of our starters. This was 2001, before computer software made that easy. In Jamie's case, he had to play and record manually from VHS game tapes to a highlight master tape, to which he also added music.

Jamie and Marlin hung a bunch of sheets on the west end of the massive gym wall, which they used as a projector screen. Since there was no projector in the gym, they had to figure a way to make that work too. And work it did, although we broke a cardinal rule that applies to any gathering of high school students.

We turned off the lights. You never, ever turn off the lights.

With the bulk of our team already in the gym, Jamie and Marlin staged our starting players outside the gym doors... and then the lights went off. So did the student body. Crammed into every nook and cranny of that gym, the roar of the crowd was startling. Thankfully, the emergency lights provided enough light for teachers and administrators to monitor the students; fortunately, the student body behaved exactly as they should have.

As each player was introduced, he would enter the gym through a cloud of smoke. Jamie and Marlin created the smoky haze with a dry ice smoke blower that they had somehow procured. Upon entering the gym, each player's highlight video was projected onto the sheets on the wall. Talk about way larger than life; our guys were 20 feet tall. The smoke and the billowy sheets created a dramatic effect. Each time a player walked in, the roar of the crowd gave me goosebumps.

Wednesday's practice — our final practice in full pads that season — was as normal as possible. That is, we followed our typical Wednesday schedule. But I wasn't sure that, after that pep rally, a practice could be considered normal. Add the fact that our field was busy with all sorts of media and other folks who just wanted to come and watch the last practice, and for sure Wednesday's practice was not normal. Thankfully, our players and coaches were focused and intent on keeping the main thing the main thing. We were going to Tallahassee to earn a ring.

After practice, we went to shower and pack our travel bags. Fortunately, we had state finals gear for our guys to pack. A number of alumni and parents had stepped forward to provide team sweats and polos for the boys. We would look great on the road.

When everyone was showered and travel bags were packed, we headed to the cafeteria, where our families were waiting. Alumni and parents had also sprung for a steak dinner; they wanted to send us off in style. Former Naples High players Jim and Tom Kalvin had hauled in their massive grills, and had the steaks ready as the boys walked into the cafeteria. It was a wonderful time to visit and enjoy time together as a football family.

As I sat next to my girls and surveyed the room, I was struck with profound gratitude. I was with my wife and kids and surrounded by a group of people that had one heartbeat. I knew that God did not love me any more than any other person on the planet, and I knew I did not deserve to be heading to the state finals. God's grace, once again.

When I glanced around the cafeteria at all of those excited faces, one guy in particular stood out to me. On August 14, nearly four months earlier, I had written in my prayer journal that Bruce Gordon had his second unexcused absence from practice the previous day.

Bruce never got to three.

CHAPTER
80

When we finished eating, the boys said their goodbyes and loaded into two charter buses; as always, offense in the front bus and defense in the second bus. As each boy got on the bus, they were handed a goody bag with drinks and snacks for the road. Sue Kramer and Terri Dickerson had our plan in full swing.

The buses pulled out at 7 p.m. sharp. We would drive to Ocala that night, pulling into the Courtyard Marriott at 11:00 p.m. Staying on time was pretty easy, as Sheriff Don Hunter had provided deputies in patrol cars to escort us up and back. Joe Scott, one of the best of the best, was heading up the detail, and I knew we could not be in better hands.

The next morning, Thursday, December 6, we got up, ate breakfast, loaded the buses at 9 a.m. and headed to Tallahassee.

We planned to eat lunch at Ryan's Steakhouse, and then would head over to Collegiate Village Inn to check in.

The trip to Tallahassee could not have been better. The keys were ready with names on them at each hotel; the dining areas were set with water filled and food ready to go; and at every stop, the boys had access to healthy snacks and Gatorade. Sue and Terri did it all with grace and sweet kindness. If they were stressed, it was impossible to tell. And somehow, our three little girls — who Sue had in tow — were always cute and well-behaved.

From the first few minutes on the bus, it was obvious that the trip was a chance for players and coaches to catch up on sleep. Both buses had video monitors, and we played Chamberlain scout tapes during the entire trip. I am not sure how much those tapes were watched; all of us were exhausted from the long season. Whenever I looked back at the players on the offense bus, the vast majority were knocked out cold.

I did what I had done on every football road trip since college. I grabbed my Walkman, now upgraded to a CD player from the cassette tape-playing Walkman I had in college, and I pushed play on the soundtrack from the movie *St. Elmo's Fire*. I too was out for much of the trip.

I hid my disappointment as we pulled into the Collegiate Village Inn. The place was tired, and every room had outside doors with access to the parking lot. Monitoring would be difficult. I wasn't worried about our guys trying to get out; I was worried about fans and families trying to get in. Thankfully, Joe Scott and the other deputies were already planning on sleeping during the day and staying up all night to keep watch over all of us.

The subtle glance Sue gave me as she handed me my room key told me that she had the same concerns I had; she was well aware of the logistics involved with monitoring our guys before and after the game. After checking in at the hotel, we changed into our practice gear and headed to our walk-through practice at Tallahassee's Godby High School. Shelton Crews was the head coach at Godby, and he was extremely accommodating to us.

Our walk-through was focused and loose. My "Great Day Today!" was especially easy, and was greeted with agreement by hoots and hollers as our guys stretched. The Naples football players and coaches on Godby's practice field that crisp December day were energetic and focused — a great combination.

The plan for the rest of Thursday evening looked like this:

3:20	Return to Hotel
4:30	Load for Dinner
4:45	Eat at Golden Corral
5:45	Return to Hotel
6:15	Leave for Doak Campbell
	(4A State Championship Game)
10:00	Return to Hotel
10:30	Team Meeting (Pizza and Gatorade)
12:00	Lights Out

Our buses pulled up to Golden Corral precisely on time. It is amazing how a schedule can be kept with a police escort. As the guys headed to the buffet, Susie brought the girls to me, and they gave their dear old dad hugs and kisses. Sue then pulled me to the side; and, in a hushed and slightly stressed tone, told me that the Chamberlain team had been there already — and their guys were HUGE. She said that many of them looked like full-grown adult men.

Sue Kramer has been to a lot of football games. She went to every one of my college games when we dated in college, and she went to every one of the high school games I coached in. I had never heard or seen Susie Kramer like this. If she wasn't exactly scared for our guys, she wasn't far from it.

Susie also told me with great empathy that Billy Turner, the head coach from Chamberlain, had been there with his grand-daughter, who obviously had special needs. She said that Billy's granddaughter was so sweet and so cute. Sue also said the inter-action between that little girl and her grandpa, as well as with the Chamberlain football players, was incredibly touching. It was obvious from Susie's tone and demeanor that, in any other cir-cumstance, she would be rooting for the Chamberlain Chiefs' head coach and his sweet little granddaughter.

On the bus ride back to the hotel after dinner, I thought about that opponent, who physically outmatched us at just about every position. I thought about that grandpa, one win from 200 with his sweet granddaughter rooting for him. If our season ended in what would be a heartbreaking loss, I would nonetheless be happy for Billy Turner and his crew.

In the meantime, I had a team to lead and a game to win, and I was going to do all I could to control what I could to make that happen. The only thing any of us can really control is our individual effort and attitude.

CHAPTER
81

Doak Campbell Stadium on the campus of Florida State University was the largest continuous brick structure in the United States and the second largest in the world, next to the Great Wall of China. The sight of it, lights glowing, took my breath away.

The murmur among our players told me they were as awestruck as I was. If any one of us had not yet realized that we were really "here," and that "here" was the big time, that changed when we entered the stadium and took in the view of that magnificent structure and the field below.

When planning the trip, I thought it would be important for our entourage to go to Thursday night's 4A championship game. I wanted to erase as much of the WOW factor as I could. There was no way to erase it completely, but I was hoping to downgrade it from WOW to COOL.

Every bit of the experience was cool. Entering through the gate that was reserved for those playing in a championship was cool. Going through the extra security was even somehow cool. It was also a poignant reminder of the privilege we were graced with. Seeing the T-shirts that the vendors were selling with "Naples High" on them was cool. Hanging with our team in our own section of the stadium and watching the 4A championship game together was exceptionally cool.

At one point, some of the Chamberlain players — who were in another section on the opposite side of the stadium — wandered over to us and asked guys sitting near me if our varsity team was coming to the game too. These Chamberlain guys were backup players and did not seem so scary. The big boys had sent them over to scout us out. When they saw our guys, they figured that we brought our JV and freshman guys to come watch the game.

Nope.

I am sure that when they returned to the big boys and gave their report, the big boys did not believe them.

Unlike the trip to Tallahassee, no one was sleeping on the bus ride back to the hotel. We were all wide awake. Terri Dickerson and Sue Kramer had the pizza hot and waiting when we arrived. We had a pizza feast and a guest speaker scheduled before we would head off to bed.

A couple weeks before, I had called Jim Gladden, the assistant head coach at FSU. Years earlier at a Carson-Newman coaching clinic, Ken Sparks had introduced me to Coach Gladden. Jim Gladden is a great coach and an even better man. He is humble and smart and kind and hard-working. The kind of man I want to emulate. I had asked Jim if he could help me arrange for someone from up that way to speak to our players and coaches the night before the state championship game. Jim put me in contact with Clint Purvis, the FSU team chaplain/character coach. As part of his duties, Clint facilitated community service and speaking engagements for the players.

One of the players Clint brought with him was Michael Boulware. Michael was a standout for the Seminoles, following in the footsteps of his older brother Peter. Peter was an All-American at FSU, who in 1997 had been drafted in the first round of the NFL draft by the Baltimore Ravens.

With the pizza mostly gone, we gathered together to listen to what Michael Boulware had to say. In 2001, cell phones were common but not ubiquitous yet. I had borrowed my father-in-law Duke's cell phone for the trip, as I could not afford my own phone or the service plan that went with it.

Duke's phone was in case of emergency for me, and to stay in touch with our advance team and police escorts as we went from place to place. Some of our players and coaches also had cell phones, and I took a moment before I introduced Michael to remind them to please mute those cell phones. I wanted zero distractions as Michael spoke. I had spoken enough with Michael to recognize that he was smart and articulate, and I knew he was in a position to connect with our guys in a way that I or our staff might not.

I said a few words to the team, and as I began to introduce Michael Boulware, I heard a cell phone ring. I stopped talking and waited for the owner to hit the mute button. And then it rang again, and again. The tension in the room was stifling and no one moved. In a terse voice, I said, "Please turn the phone off."

And again it rang.

I was furious. One of the players near me leaned in, and in a hushed tone said, "I think it's you, Coach." And so it was. The phone in my pocket was on low, not mute. I was so new to using a cell phone that I didn't recognize the ringer on the one going off in my pocket. My face flushed. The guys were mostly relieved — and I was mostly embarrassed — as I reached in my pocket and hit the volume button on the phone. Everyone in the room was kind enough to keep the laughter to a minimum.

As Michael began his talk, my mind was racing. I was shocked at myself. I had gone from zero to boiling in a very short period of time, and that surprised me. I had been faithful and prayerful as I went through each part of my week. I had recovered much of the sleep I had lost; yet the evidence showed that I was still very stressed and did not even know it. I was grateful for the phone incident. I gained perspective, which gave me both clarity and caution, as the biggest game of our lives loomed on the horizon.

For his part, Michael Boulware was terrific. He did not talk about his football resume. He didn't have to. All of our guys knew who he was. What he did talk about was embracing the moment and cherishing the time. He talked about the blessing our team had been given, as we had a chance to play the game we loved with the guys we loved. He challenged our guys to consider their Creator and behave in a way that would honor Him.

He said exactly what our guys needed to hear. It was not a rah-rah, "beat the door down, and then beat your opponent down" rant. It was a quiet call for our players to love and serve those around them, much like the call that Jesus gave us in the New Testament. Great stuff.

CHAPTER
82

The schedule for game day looked like this:

Friday, December 7, 2001

9:00	Wake Up
9:30	Leave for Brunch (Shoney's on Monroe)
10:30	Return to Hotel
10:45	Walk-Through at Godby High School
12:00	Return to Hotel
2:00	Meetings (Video)
2:45	Leave for Golden Corral
3:00	Pregame Meal
3:45	Return to Hotel
4:15	Load for Doak Campbell

5:00	Enter Locker Room
5:30	Kickers/Snappers/Holders/QBs/WRs/RBs to Field
5:45	Team Out (Stretch and Warm Up)
6:25	Back to Locker Room
7:00	Beat Chamberlain

As we gathered to load the buses for brunch, I walked through the clusters of players talking among themselves and checked on them, making sure they had slept OK and reminding them to hydrate. When I came upon Duane Coleman, he told me that I would not believe the dream he had the night before; in it, he scored a touchdown on the very first play of the game. He didn't remember exactly what play it was, but that was fine with me. I had a good idea of how to get Duane the ball on the very first play of the game and see if his dream could come true.

The day went according to plan. All of our guys were on time and on point. There is an old saying in sports, "Act like you've been there," and our guys were definitely acting the part. We actually wound up with a little extra time before we were to load the buses to leave for our game. It was a terrific opportunity for coaches and players alike to grab a quick nap before the biggest game of our lives. I put on my earphones, pushed play on my *St. Elmo's Fire* soundtrack, and was out like a light.

CHAPTER
63

Pulling up to Doak Campbell was slightly less intimidating the second time. I chalked it up to having been there the previous night and the fact that the sun was still shining, so the lights did not give as dramatic an effect. Our players and coaches were a quiet, confident bunch. Often in tense situations, high school coaches hear nervous chatter or distracted silliness from their players. We had none of either.

Every part of a state championship pregame is dictated by the state, and the first part of the plan called for us to go through the security checkpoint and head into our locker room. I knew that security would be more intense since 9-11, but I did not expect to see the countless police officers. I also did not expect every player and every bag to be searched. The team entrance was fenced off in a way that only those being searched could get on the inside of the security fence. The rest had to stay outside until called up. The process took much more time than I had anticipated, and we had to quickly rearrange the line of players so the guys who had to get on the field first to warm up were at the front.

I waited with our players who were outside the fence. The rest of our coaches went as quickly as possible through the line in order to get the locker room and field set up. As I stood outside the fence, I heard someone calling to me from the secure side of the fence.

I looked and saw Clint Purvis. He had a small brown paper bag in his hand just like kids used for bag lunch when I was in elementary school. He told me he had something for me and my coaches, and shoved the bag through the bars separating us.

I took the brown bag from Clint, thanked him, and was immediately distracted by one of our escort officers, who had mustered more help or a better process and was now hustling our remaining guys and me through security. In a few moments, I entered what would normally be the visitors' locker room when a college team came to play FSU.

Everything was in place as it normally would be. Players were in various stages of dress — some were getting taped, others were sitting at lockers with their headphones on. The warmup schedule was up on the board where it always was. There was even a table with Gatorade, water, fruit, and energy bars; a nice special touch for the state championship game.

I could see through a door to some of our coaches in what was obviously the visiting coaches' locker room. All of a sudden, the moment was big. I imagined all of the great teams, players, and coaches who had stood right where I was standing, and I had the sickening realization that I did not belong. I felt that I was not nearly the level of athlete or coach as those who did belong there.

In that moment, I was scared little Billy Kramer, a tiny stuttering kid who had never met his real dad and had just barely survived his stepdad.

MOVE! If you don't feel it, fake it!

Heading towards the cover of the coaches' dressing room, I reached into the open zipper of my travel bag and felt the small brown paper bag that Clint had given me. I felt inside the brown paper bag, and it was full of coins, each about the size of a silver dollar or a poker chip. I read the coin in my hand and had instant peace and confidence. On one side of the coin, it was printed: "The Prayer of Jabez / I Chronicles 4:10."

The other side had the actual prayer: "Oh, that You would bless me indeed, and enlarge my territory, that Your hand would be with me, and that You would keep me from evil, that I may not cause pain!"

It was instant confirmation that I was right where God wanted me to be, doing exactly what he wanted me to do. I found Paul Horne. The first thing I blurted out was, "We don't have anything to worry about." He looked at me sideways; I too was surprised that those words had come out. I knew that I had not said anything to Clint Purvis about our coaches' retreat, or our focus on the *Prayer of Jabez* that year. I asked Paul if he had said anything to Clint about the *Prayer of Jabez*. Paul was in full pregame focus, and this question was out of left field. Paul's confused look was the only response I got. I asked again.

As he said, "No," I handed him a coin and told him I hadn't either, and that Clint had just handed me the bag of coins. Paul's smile said it all. Voila, peace and confidence.

I asked the rest of the coaches in the room if any of them had said anything to Clint Purvis about the *Prayer of Jabez*. Evidently, no one had been thinking about the *Prayer of Jabez*. I explained to the coaches in the room that I had not said anything to Clint either, and then I gave each of them a coin. The look on each face said it all... peace and confidence.

I made my way, coins in hand, to the coaches out setting up the field. Each conversation was the same as the one previous, and each reaction was the same. I found out later from Clint that he had just felt led to give us those coins. Thank you, Clint Purvis, for your sensitivity and obedience.

The coins were not some magic beans that were going to guarantee us victory. Rather, the coins were a reminder of what our focus was to start the year, and of what it should be as we finished it. I loved the first part of the prayer, because it freed me up to ask God to bless me. But my favorite was the second part, where Jabez asks God to keep him from evil so that he will not cause pain.

The Hebrew word Jabez means pain. Here was a guy who understood his nature and was honest with himself. *I get it, Jabez. Left to my own devices, when I take God out of the equation, I am going to wind up chasing empty stuff and causing pain to those around me in the process.* The greatest revelation that the coin gave me was the importance of me coaching the game in a way that, win or lose, I would not cause pain to my players or coaches.

The people I was with were more important than the scoreboard or the outcome.

Thanks, Jabez — and once again, thanks, Clint.

CHAPTER

84

I took it in… all of it. The smell of the grass, the sounds of both sets of fans as they settled in and began the din, the graphics on the Jumbotrons — every bit of it was just right. Half an hour before game time, both teams left the playing surface, and the head coach and captain for each team was asked to meet with the game officials in the home locker room for the official coin toss.

I, along with our four captains — Duane Coleman, Pat Liebig, Rick Martin, and Big Jules Montinar — had no idea what we were walking into when we opened the doors which led to the FSU home locker room. Whatever your mind conjures up when I say locker room, forget it. Keep that thought for the FSU visitors' locker room that we were using. But the FSU home locker room?

Insanity! The good kind of insanity. Actually, we were meeting in the vestibule of the home and officials' locker room.

I wish I had video of our faces as we entered the room. It was velvet and crystal and carved wood and gilded. The door we walked through transported us to some kind of medieval jewel display or some sort of museum.

Beautiful trophies filled the cases of the custom wood cabinets. There were all kinds. There were conference and bowl championship trophies; All-Conference and All-American awards. We were not in a position to explore much, as the officials were standing there waiting for us, but my guess is that there were a couple national championship trophies or Heisman trophies in there too.

One thing that sticks out clearly in my memory: right next to a massive overstuffed leather couch was a clear case like they have in a jewelry store. This display case was clear glass on all sides and had that jewelry store lighting. It was stuffed full of really big, extra-ornate championship rings. If someone had told me that they had been borrowed from the Queen's collection that we had seen the previous spring at the Tower of London, I would not have been surprised.

As Chamberlain's Billy Turner walked in, we got a glimpse of the FSU locker room through the big double doors behind him. It was a continuation of the vestibule/museum. Their dressing room was huge, and the custom lockers were massive and immaculate in FSU garnet and gold. On top of the lockers were nearly life-sized action poses of the best players in FSU history. That brief glimpse into the locker room had me looking up at Warrick Dunn, and the custom up-lighting had him looking invincible.

I stood facing the door to the Chamberlain locker room; a few yards to my right was the officials' locker room. Billy Turner was standing in front of me. Immediately to my right and in a straight line, Rick, Pat, Duane, and Jules were facing the Chamberlain locker room door, just as I was. As Billy and I shook hands, three Chamberlain players came and stood in front of my guys. It was difficult for me to concentrate on pleasantries with Billy, as all three of his guys dwarfed my guys. The one with his shirt off was extra huge. He was not just tall, he was the most chiseled, muscle-bound, sinewy high school athlete I had ever seen.

I knew in a moment that he must be Brodrick Bunkley, and that all the hype was true. This guy was an absolute genetic freak. I tried not to stare. If this was Brodrick Bunkley, what did Al Mack look like? As the players began to shake hands, one of the officials asked Billy Turner if there was one more; we were both allowed four captains. Coach Turner spun and yelled, "Brodrick?!" over his shoulder as both double doors boomed open at us. All at once it occurred to me that the guy I thought was Brodrick Bunkley was actually linebacker Oliver Hoyt. If Ollie Hoyt was a genetic freak, which he was, then Brodrick Bunkley was an **alien** genetic freak. Brodrick was also shirtless, and had not tied the strings on the front of his game pants. Every part of him was striated muscle fiber. Again, I did my level best not to stare.

It helped that the referee started talking. In a football game, the referee is the only official in a white hat, and he is the boss. Our referee was a well-respected official from the Central Orlando Officials Association named Cary R. Fields. Mr. Fields went through the usual pregame talk, and explained that because the game was being broadcast live, the coin toss was done in advance so the TV folks could have the appropriate graphics for the starting offense and defense loaded and ready to go.

Mr. Fields went on to say that we would still do a coin toss on the field for the crowd and for TV, but the result would remain whatever we predetermined right there and then. I found it hard to focus on what our referee was saying. As I looked to my right at the officials, I had to look past my four captains. My thoughts kept wandering to our guys, especially Ricky Martin.

Rick Martin, our left offensive guard, was standing next to me. Rick was listed in the newspaper's game preview at 5'11" and 205 pounds. I do not know where that came from. The truth is that Rick Martin was maybe 5'10" and weighed in on that day at about 180 pounds. As the official continued speaking, I watched Rick as he would look up at Brodrick, the player he would very often be asked to block, and then stare down at the floor. As his eyes came up again he would look at Oliver Hoyt, the player he would be blocking when taking a Brodrick break, and then stare down at the floor. That pattern continued as long as the official spoke.

Chamberlain wound up winning the locker room coin toss and elected to receive the kickoff. Everyone shook hands, even if their eyes did not meet. Rick and Duane were quiet as we headed the length of the field to our locker room. Jules and Pat were both talking about the physical specimens we had just seen and how grateful they were that they did not have to line up against those two guys on every play.

Our sideline was mostly empty as we walked back to our locker room. When our fans saw the five of us a roar went up. It was really cool and really loud, but it did not prevent me from hearing Rick Martin tell his two pals in no uncertain terms to shut up about the beasts he would have to block.

With a few minutes left before kickoff, our locker room was poised and confident. I followed our typical routine, gathering with some of our coaches for a pregame prayer. Part of the state finals prescribed pregame procedure that night was for the starters for each team to line up in the end zone and be announced. The rest of the team ran out as a group. I didn't like separating the team like that, as ours was a team of equally invested people. Plus, it is a really cool thing to be announced, hear your fans, and look up and see yourself on the Jumbotron. I wished that all of our guys could have experienced that.

CHAPTER 85

As Francesco Zampogna lined up for the opening kickoff of the 2001 Florida 5A State Championship Game, I was not a bit nervous. I was grateful to be there, and I was fired up to see the band of brothers from Naples High give their very best.

Francesco drove the kick out of the end zone, starting the Chiefs on their own 20. The first few plays of the game were all Chamberlain. As was often the case, our defense had to figure out the leverage against a much bigger opponent. Sam dialed up some good stuff, and soon Chamberlain found itself facing third down and 12 from their own 38-yard line.

The Chiefs hit a short pass to Donnie Davis out of the back-field, and after he was forced out of bounds, the tail of the ball was placed on the 50-yard line. It was fourth and inches. It wasn't a very tough decision for the Chamberlain coaches. The odds were pretty good for the massive Chamberlain offensive line to push our D-line back 6 inches.

And so they did. First down, Chamberlain.

The Chiefs continued to move the ball, and it took a spectacular play by our corner, Reggie Carter, to prevent a touchdown on a perfectly thrown ball from Chamberlain quarterback Sidney Bryant to receiver Brian Clark. Nine times out of 10, that play would have been a touchdown. Thank you, Reggie Carter.

On third and medium from our 30-yard line, the Dollar defense sacked Sidney Bryant, and the Chiefs were in their second fourth-down situation of the game. It was fourth and 9 from just inside our 35-yard-line. Chamberlain did not hesitate, and lined up to go for it instead of punting. As the teams lined up and the quarterback began his cadence, one of the Chamberlain offensive linemen jumped offside. Now it was fourth and 14, from just inside our 40-yard-line. This time, the Chiefs opted to punt.

Special teams at Naples High were just that — special. We loaded them with our very best offensive and defensive players, and we trained really hard to be excellent in every phase, at every position. Our punt block team was elite. Jamie Lemmond had raised blocking punts to an art form, and on any given play, any player on the punt block team could come free and block the punt. In this case, it was LJ Montinar who came free and blocked the punt; it would be our 15th blocked punt of the year.

Our guys fought over the ball, and when the dust cleared, it was Naples' ball — first and 10 on the Chamberlain 37-yard-line. By that time, every guy on our offense knew what our first play was going to be. The play call was Left Red 30 Draw.

37 yards later, Duane Coleman was in the end zone. Duane Coleman's dream and Paul Horne's game plan had both been prophetic. Chamberlain had an 11-play drive with 0 points, and Naples had scored in one play.

Chamberlain's alignment on the kickoff return dictated that we attempt an onside kick. We had done that with regularity throughout the years. When it was successful, our fans thought Kramer was a genius with nerves of steel. When we did not recover an onside kick, Kramer was a dolt.

In this case, Kramer was a dolt.

Thankfully, our defense was stellar and forced a three-and-out. I was disappointed in our punt returner on the ensuing punt; instead of fielding the ball out around the 20, he let it bounce. At Naples High, our punt returners had one job: don't let the ball touch the ground. This one did, and it bounced in Chamberlain's favor. It was first and 10, Naples, but we were backed up inside our own 5.

We managed to move the ball, both running and passing, but after a questionable illegal block call brought back a big run, we wound up having to punt. On their next possession, our defense was able to bend and not break against the goliath Chiefs. We kept them out of the end zone. With 11:11 left in the second quarter, Trey Seaholm hit a 28-yard, line drive, knuckle ball field goal that cleared the uprights by about an inch. There are no points for aesthetics. Naples 7, Chamberlain 3.

Duane Coleman was waiting for the ensuing Chamberlain kickoff at his own 5-yard-line; after his 32-yard return, it was first and 10 Naples, from our own 37-yard-line. Josh Greco did a great job reading our triple-option veer play and throwing the ball in our three-step passing game. In four plays, we were well inside Chamberlain territory. A Chamberlain personal foul penalty helped our drive, making it first and 10 Naples, at the Chamberlain 33-yard-line. We called a play action pass, where we would fake a run to Duane on our right side and then throw back to David Lightner swinging out to our left. It worked like a charm, and David was forced out of bounds at the Chamberlain 6-yard-line.

Three plays later, we found ourselves at third and goal from the 1-yard-line. Our offensive line gave a great effort, and Josh Greco was able to follow and gain just enough ground to get the ball into the end zone. With 8:13 left in the half, the Zampogna point-after made it 14-3, Naples.

Our offensive line was holding its own — barely. It was obvious that Chamberlain had really big, fast guys. Our triple-option was slowing down their defense, making them think just enough to give our guys a fighting chance. Our song remained the same: do what you are coached to do, and you have a chance to win; do anything else, and you have absolutely no chance.

Both crowds and bands were going off during the entire game. Neither school had been in this situation before, and neither school was going to waste it. Odds were that it would never happen again.

Francesco Zampogna's kickoff boomed out of the end zone, and once again Chamberlain was forced to start from its own 20. On the first several plays of the drive, Chamberlain ran the ball with effect. The few passes they chose to mix in were well defended by the Naples secondary. So far, Jamie Lemmond's defensive backs were playing lights-out.

The Dollar defense was giving ground only grudgingly. With just over four minutes left in the half, the Chiefs were faced with a fourth and 7, which they decided to go for. As the play developed, the entire stadium saw 6'3", 235-pound tight end Maurice Howard running with no coverage down the middle of the field. When Chamberlain QB Sidney Bryant released the ball, Howard inexplicably slipped and fell. It was as if the ground just gave way beneath him. Crisis averted, the Naples defense hustled off the field — they had provided another crucial stop.

As the second quarter began to draw to a close, Naples High found itself with first and 10 from its own 40-yard line. The play call was a run; a weak-side veer to our left side. Josh Greco read it perfectly, kept the ball, and gained 15 yards. On second and 10 from the Chamberlain 45-yard-line, Paul and I played the odds. We knew from video study that Chamberlain liked to blitz in that situation. The play call, Left Bone 224 Y-Throwback, worked best versus a strong side blitz. Josh Greco faked weak-side veer and threw a strike to our tight end Joe Wise, who was running without coverage down the field. The guy who would normally have covered him had blitzed from our strong side. With 3:46 left in the first half, the Zampogna extra point made it 21-3, Naples.

We had scored in two plays.

Again, Zampogna's kickoff forced Chamberlain to start on their own 20, and again the Naples defense played great. With just over two minutes left in the half, Chamberlain was forced to punt. Our final possession of the first half began on our own 40-yard-line. The buzz in my headset was: we had enough time to score. We stuck with our script and ran the ball effectively, busting off chunks of yardage and even getting out of bounds to stop the clock. On fourth and short at the Chamberlain 37-yard-line, we took a timeout to talk about it.

After very little deliberation we decided to go for it, and we called our base play. Greco read it perfectly, kept the ball, and seemingly had the first down with yards to spare... when Brodrick Bunkley came out of nowhere and stripped the ball from Josh. The video would later show that Josh was holding the ball with excellent ball security. Brodrick Bunkley was just so big, strong, and fast that he was able to knock it loose.

With 1:11 left in the half, Chamberlain had the ball; first and 10 on the Naples 35-yard-line. Naples' defense was in good form. We thought we had forced a long fourth down and a punt from Chamberlain, but out of nowhere a flag landed on our sideline. Coach Dollar had been flagged for bumping into the official working our sideline.

Sam was not on the field of play, but he may have been just beyond our get-back line. The official working our sideline was not on the field as he normally would be, once the play started; rather, he was out of bounds just beyond our get-back line. He had bumped Coach Dollar with his shoulder as he ran down our sideline following the play. What could have been a sideline warning wound up being a 15-yard penalty. The Chiefs had first and 10 from the Naples 46-yard-line with 16 seconds left. It didn't matter. The Chiefs did not move the ball, and we jogged into the locker room up 21-3.

The halftime statistics showed that Chamberlain led in time of possession, 16:13 to 7:47, and in plays run, 42-21. Naples led in rushing yards, 114-106, and in passing yards, 116-49. Naples also led in the most important stat of all — the score.

CHAPTER
86

You might think that a second-half lead like we had would lend itself to overconfidence or at least a sense of relief. That was not the case for Naples that night. Every player and coach knew that we had nearly flawlessly executed an excellent game plan, and that gave us great confidence.

Every guy in that room also knew that our margin of error was so slim against this ridiculously talented Chamberlain team that we all felt slightly uncomfortable. The best news at halftime was that we had no injuries, even though we were pretty beat up. The Chamberlain guys were big, fast, strong, and physical, but we had all of our guys, which was exceedingly fortunate.

We ran the Brucer Reverser to start the second half and wound up first and 10 from our own 30-yard-line. We ran the veer on first down for a short gain, and threw a short hitch to Bruce on second down for a short gain.

Those first two plays sounded different. Chamberlain's defense was firing off the ball with a different energy. I was hoping they would either get tired or we would find the reservoir of determination to match that effort. On third and short we ran the veer, and our offense was simply overwhelmed. Josh Greco was tackled as he pitched the ball, and it wound up on the ground. Chamberlain recovered.

Our defense was in a tough spot, as the Chiefs' first possession of the half began on the Naples 20-yard-line. Our defense fought its tail off. After 15 yards on first down, it took four plays for Chamberlain to score. For those who believe in mojo, Chamberlain was bathing in it. The ensuing kickoff did not go our way. The Chamberlain kicker missed the ball just enough to hit the perfect low Texas leaguer between the up backs on our return team. The ball hit the ground, took a funky bounce, and when Coleman tracked it down he was buried on our 9-yard-line.

Our offense stuck to the plan, albeit with a greater sense of urgency, and managed a 10-play drive. On fourth and 10, we executed a fake punt play that we had worked on for some time. The play called for our corner, Reggie Carter, to hustle on to the field and then come sprinting towards our boundary as the play clock wound down. Football fans see that in most every game as a player realizes he is being substituted for; he is supposed to get off the field. In this instance, instead of running off, Reggie would stop near our sidelines and get set before the ball was snapped. If a defender ran with Reggie, he would be covered, and we would punt the ball as normal. If no defenders went with Reggie, our personal protector — the guy standing closest to the punter on the punt team — would throw the ball to him.

In the pregame talk, the referee and umpire always ask the head coach if they might call any trick plays. That's done to prevent one of the officiating crew blowing a whistle too soon or improperly flagging a legal play. I'd told the officials about this fake punt play before the game, and I was confident we were good to go.

Our personal protector was Josh Greco, and he threw a strike to Reggie Carter. Reggie caught the pass and ran it deep into Chamberlain territory. We were in business. Unfortunately, the same official who had run into Sam on the sideline wound up throwing a flag for illegal substitution. He thought Reggie had left the field and re-entered it inappropriately.

It was a serious buzz kill; the video would later show that it was a bad call.

After the penalty was marked off, we punted the ball, and the explosive Donnie Davis burst down the field to the Naples 46-yard-line. Donnie may have been tackled around his own 20 if he hadn't been aided by an obvious block in the back (which the officials missed and the video later verified). That's just how it goes sometimes.

Regardless, with about four minutes left in the third quarter, the Chamberlain Chiefs were down by 11 with the ball and a first down on the Naples 46-yard-line. Chamberlain was now drowning in mojo.

The Chiefs pounded the ball, running it for eight consecutive downs. As the third quarter came to an end, Chamberlain had the ball — third and 1 at the Naples 13. Both teams were fighting tooth and nail, giving every single ounce of energy they had. Every man was all-in.

The first play of the fourth quarter found Sidney Bryant converting his third successful fourth down via a quarterback sneak. The mass of the Chamberlain offensive line pretty much guaranteed a 1-yard gain. Two plays later Chamberlain scored, and with 10:57 left in the game, the score was 21-17 Naples.

Our offense had to get it going. Paul and I both knew that the space was getting small out there. We both also knew that if we would just follow our plan and do what we knew how to do, we could drive the ball and score. After a Chamberlain kick into the end zone, we had a long field; we started on our own 20. On first down, Duane Coleman made an incredible run. He ping-ponged through the Chamberlain defense, gaining 9 yards.

On second down, one of our offensive lineman jumped offsides, and back 5 yards we went. Second down found Coleman pounding out a really hard 4-yard gain; then on third down, he took 30 Draw — the same play we used to start the game — to the Naples 47. First down.

Every play was ending in a train wreck for whoever was carrying the ball, and that ball carrier was usually Duane. During the next nine plays, Josh Greco found Bruce Gordon on a critical third-down pass completion to get a first down; he also ran the ball himself twice. The rest was Coleman, the human pinball.

On third and 5 from the 8-yard-line, we ran a play action pass to tight end Joe Wise. Joey found space in the back of the end zone, but the relentless Chamberlain pressure forced Josh Greco into an errant throw. The ball sailed out of bounds, out of Joey's reach. We trotted the field goal team out on the field for the chip shot field goal. Francesco Zampogna could have made that field goal with his eyes closed, and he was a competitor who wanted to be in that moment.

Somehow the one in a million happened, and the ball sailed just outside of the left upright.

There was 3:37 left in the game. The Naples offense had gone on a 72-yard drive that took seven minutes and 20 seconds off the clock in the fourth quarter, but we had come away with no points. The pressure was now on the defense.

The good news was that even though it did not feel like it, we were winning the game. In fact, we were winning by 4 points. A field goal would not help Chamberlain; they had to score a touchdown to win.

On first down from the Chamberlain 20, Donnie Davis slipped and fell as he tried to turn the right corner, bringing it to second and 8. A swing pass on second down resulted in no gain. On third down, Sam Dollar dialed up the pressure and the play resulted in a 14-yard loss for Chamberlain. The Dollar defense had done its job.

Tampa Chamberlain got off their best punt of the night, and with 1:56 left in the game we had the ball to start the series from our own 44-yard-line. While the chains were being moved and our offense took the field, Jamie Lemmond calmly came to me and said that Reggie Carter had just strained his hamstring. He was done for the night. Jamie then told me what I already knew: "You can't give the ball back." We now had no one on our defense that could cover Brian Clark.

The Chiefs had two timeouts left with the 1:56 on the clock. The math said that if we ran the ball, stayed in bounds, and ran the clock down on each play, we would need one first down to win a ring. Paul Horne did the math on that kind of situation each week, and he was all over it as always.

Duane Coleman was obviously exhausted. He was also one of the most competitive players I have ever coached. Duane wanted the ball; everyone in the stadium and watching on TV knew exactly who was going to get that ball.

On first down, we handed the ball to Duane, running to the right. He was stopped cold for no gain. Chamberlain immediately called a timeout.

On second and 10 with 1:51 left in the game, we again handed the ball to Duane — running to the left this time. A great lead block by David Lightner sprung Duane for a 12-yard gain. It was first down with 1:48 left, and Chamberlain had one timeout left. Chamberlain chose not to use their last timeout. The math now said that we needed one more first down before we could just take a knee and end the game.

The ball was snapped with 1:23 left in the game; Coleman took the handoff and strained for another 9 yards. Chamberlain took their final timeout with 1:03 left in the game and Naples facing second and one from the Chiefs 35 yard line.

The suspense would not last long. On the next play, Duane Coleman fought through the Chamberlain defense for 4 yards and another first down.

Ball game.

I was surprised when I realized I felt instant relief. I didn't even know I needed relief. But there it was, instant relief! We stayed in the huddle and let the clock run down. On the sidelines, players and coaches were hugging, and in the stands, our fans were hugging too. I had especially big hugs for Sam Dollar and Paul Horne. Each of those guys are brilliant men, and both had been relentlessly loyal to me since day one. Words could not, and cannot, express my gratitude for them and to them.

Josh Greco took a knee, and as the ball was marked and the game clock ran below 25 seconds, our sidelines erupted. Some of our guys on the field took off their helmets and threw them as high as they could, and the guys on the bench ran onto the field to celebrate with their teammates. It was pure joy and exultation and bedlam.

From out of nowhere, a whistle blew and flags flew. Even though every football fan has seen that end-of-game scenario play out countless times, I suppose that — technically — players are not supposed to remove their helmets and aren't supposed to enter the field. As the officials marked off the unsportsmanlike penalty, we cleared the field, and picked up the helmet insides that had exploded everywhere and snapped them back in place.

The official marked the ball. The clock wound down the last few seconds; then, the unadulterated joy began in earnest. As the clock struck zero, I turned my eyes to find the love of my life in the stands. Susie was up there with our girls, her parents, my mom, my sister Lynette, and the other coaches' wives. I jogged towards Susie, gave her a wave and a thumbs-up, and then I went to shake hands with Billy Turner.

A local reporter caught me on the way, shook my hand, and the first question out of his mouth was something about how good I thought our team would be next year after losing all the seniors. I could not believe it. I have no idea what I said to him.

Billy was gracious and kind. I felt bad for him. He had a team full of hurting kids, and many of them were obviously distraught over the loss. As both teams lined up at midfield and shook hands, the respect among the players and coaches was obvious. No one on that field deserved to lose that night, but one of the beautiful things about the sport of football is there are no ties.

Just after Naples won the 2001 Florida 5A State Football Championship; Duane Coleman is in the foreground with his jersey off.

CHAPTER 87

By the time we finished shaking hands, Sue and some of the other wives had made their way down to the field. We gave each other a big hug and a serious kiss. We then followed the instructions of the game managers hollering at us, and made our way towards the medal stand for the presenting of the trophies.

One of my fondest memories is an exhausted Duane Coleman sitting near our sidelines in a crouch just taking it all in. I had never seen him smile that long or that big. That moment is frozen in my mind forever.

The awards ceremony at the state finals was very structured. After the prescribed time to compose ourselves, the athletes and coaches lined up next to the awards platform. As each name was read, that person walked up on the platform, and the principal from their school took a medallion from one of the FHSAA honchos and put it over the head of the recipient.

Our guys all stood in respect as the Chamberlain players and coaches received the runner-up medallions and finally the runner-up trophy. There were a lot of heartbroken kids in that crew. As I stood there, I was hopeful that in the near future those guys would recognize what a rare and wonderful experience it was to play in that game. Most coaches and players coach or play their whole careers and never come close to a state championship.

Standing there during the ceremony gave me a little time to reflect on the night and the season. Above all, I had an overwhelming sense of gratitude. I was thankful for my beautiful loving family, thankful for our faithful coaches and players, thankful for Gary and Ernie and the faithful friends they had become, thankful for the greatest team sport ever invented by man, and thankful for a Creator who loved me unconditionally.

The head coach is the first team member called to the awards stand. As my name was called and I made my way there, a roar went up from the Naples faithful. I hadn't noticed until that moment that our fans had stayed to watch us get the trophy. Near the awards stand stood Ernie and Gary; both had looks of combined joy and disbelief. This was a once-in-a-lifetime moment, and all of us knew it.

*Sue and me with the girls. Kelly has the pompom,
Courtney wears the state championship medal, and
Katie holds the championship trophy.*

CHAPTER 88

Our trip back to Naples High the next day should have taken a little over six hours. As we got to the Collier County line, it got longer. Six patrol cars and some motorcycles joined the couple of deputies already escorting us, giving us four cars in front and four cars behind our entourage. In addition, our guys were straining their necks to look out the bus windows to see the sheriff's department helicopter we could hear from above.

I realized what was happening just before our bus driver turned to tell me that the patrol cars were slowing us down. In fact, we had slowed to a little over 50 mph. I had no idea why they would slow us down. This was I-75, which connects Tampa to Naples, and it connects both of those cities to Fort Lauderdale and Miami. It was the evening of Saturday, December 8, a very busy time on the roads in southwest Florida.

I grabbed the mic that was hanging near the driver to encourage our guys to get pictures if they liked. But I also wanted to remind them that even though we were getting a hero's welcome, we were not heroes. None of us were returning from war. I also reminded them that whatever the fans and media were doing, we needed to remain humble and grateful.

We took the Pine Ridge Road exit, which would get us off the interstate and head us toward Naples High. I immediately noticed sheriff's deputies outside their vehicles, lights flashing, had stopped all the traffic traveling on Pine Ridge Road. It was like a presidential motorcade. I looked out and saw cars stopped at all the cross streets. Some had been stopped for a while, as people were out of their cars gawking at us while we did the same at them. I worried that, when these folks found out that it was Naples High football causing them to be late to wherever they were going, they would probably not be fans. I wondered if we might have a hard time filling up foursomes in our upcoming golf tournament fundraiser.

We had the slow royal treatment all the way to the school parking lot. We were greeted by a parking lot full of fans and every media outlet in southwest Florida. Our entourage had been slowed down so that the TV stations could carry us live at the top of the hour as we got off the buses. I still cannot believe that anyone would think our arrival back to school would warrant all of that fanfare. It was a wonderful reception, but I couldn't help but think of the military veterans who, through the years, have returned from real war and never got a similar salute.

It struck me that my decision to come to Naples would not be deemed a success by that state championship trophy. We would be a success when we saw the great fathers, husbands, and leaders that the guys in our program would become.

And the truth is, we would not know that for many years.

AFTERWORD

I resigned from coaching football at Naples High just before Thanksgiving week 2019, after 22 years as head coach. The staff changed through the years, but Paul Horne is still there and better than ever. Mike Sawchuk came back after a very successful run as a head coach at one of the big schools in Michigan. Ron Byington was back on staff after leaving to head up the gang unit for the county sheriff. Dan McDonald returned to coach at Naples too; Dan had to first finish a graduate degree and compete in triathlons and marathons to raise awareness and money for children with autism. In 2020 there are also five coaches on staff who played at Naples High.

One of those five is the head coach after me, Rick Martin. During Rick's senior year, I saw in him the stuff that makes a great coach. He began coaching with us his freshman year in college and earned both his bachelor's and master's degrees while he coached with us. Rick is totally committed to using football as a tool to build men, and he bleeds blue and gold. Players and coaches alike cheered when Rick was announced as the head coach. Coach Martin is a vital part of the legend and legacy of Naples High Football.

In my 22 years coaching at Naples High, we won way more than our share of football games, with a record of 216-51. I can't count how many times, after we won a game, an opposing coach would tell me that we should not have won the game. They just did not believe our team was better than their team. I always thought that they were confusing having better players with having a better team.

The bottom line is: God blessed our program. That is not to say that God loved us more and waved a magic wand on our behalf. I do not believe that God loved me or loved our teams more than others. I am not saying I deserved God's blessing, or in any way have earned it; I simply do not have any other explanation for all of the success we have experienced.

I came to Naples claiming II Chronicles 16:9 as my guidance — *"For the eyes of the Lord run to and fro throughout the whole earth, to show Himself strong on behalf of those whose heart is loyal to Him."* And now, 23 years later, that is the only explanation I have for the disproportionate success we have had.

God gives each of us a brain to use and talents to develop. So while there is no doubt that God's hand was evident in my career at Naples, I should also let you know we worked really hard for a very long time to be the best at what we do. Coaching and teaching was not a job at Naples High; it was a lifestyle. And it was a lifestyle for the entire family. I am grateful for coaching-families who understood and embraced that reality. They were and are blessings in my life.

I am convinced that in any endeavor, focusing on the process is key. If a process is great, the outcomes will be great. They may not be as disproportionate as the success we experienced at Naples High, but they will be great nonetheless.

I am often asked how I did "the faith thing" at a public high school. The answer is we were not proselytizing. We were living our lives knowing that God holds us accountable for how we treat our players. Our focus was not on wins and losses, but on relationships and developing great future husbands, fathers, and sons – great future employees, employers, and leaders in their families and community.

"The faith part" is an integral part of the story. When I am asked about why I came to Naples, the truthful answer has to include our faith. When a player or another coach wants to know the secret behind the success, or about the commitment of our coaches and their families, the truthful answer has to include our faith. How could we leave that out? And there is no law in these United States that says we cannot tell our story when we are asked about it.

We wanted to develop habits in our guys and put tools in their toolboxes which could change negative cycles in their lives and families, and create new and positive cycles which could last for generations – or maybe even eternity. We used football as a tool for that.

I won enough games and championships, and coached in enough All-Star games to be in the Florida Athletic Coaches Association Hall of Fame, the Florida High School Athletics

Association Hall of Fame, and to receive the Florida Athletic Coaches Association Lifetime Achievement Award. That is amazing and wonderful and humbling, all at once.

But the truth is, the legacy is not in the wins, championships, rings, or awards.

The legacy is in the lives.

ACKNOWLEDGMENTS

Words cannot express the gratitude I have for God bringing my wife Susan into my life. I could fill volumes with stories of the selfless work Sue has done behind the scenes to support our football program, our coaches and their families, and our players and their families. She has worked tirelessly for decades, with the most beautiful smile and the sweetest spirit. Thank you, Susie.

Katie, Courtney, Kelly, and Cassie, I love you more than I can say and more than you will ever know. Thank you for understanding that coaching for us is a family affair, and that servant-leadership requires time and energy and attention to detail. Thank you for embracing the high standards that our family is bound to. And thank you that our home has always been a zero-drama zone.

My mom, Raymona Kramer, taught me to have an attitude of gratitude from as early as I can remember. She counted her blessings, regardless of the circumstance she was in. No amount of money can buy the resilience that habit brings. My mom is also a wordsmith and spent countless hours proofreading this book.

My wife Sue's mom and dad, Duke and Angel Sistrunk, are two of the kindest and most generous people that God ever put on the earth. They have trusted me, believed in me, and done all they can to support and help me and Susie as we have made coaching and teaching our ministry. Duke went to heaven in 2005, and we miss him every day. Granny Angel continues to amaze everyone who knows her with her thoughtful kindness and boundless energy.

Anne, Sharon, Becky, Lynette, and Brenda are my sisters. My sisters are smart and strong and tough and kind. Thank you all for loving me and believing in me always.

The football coaches and players at Naples High from 1998 to 2001 are the bedrock and the scaffolding that have supported all of the Naples High football coaches and players since. All who have followed you are in your debt.

Sam Dollar, Paul Horne, and I were together for 21 years. Sam moved back to Oklahoma to teach and coach in 2019. As of the printing of this book, Paul is still coaching and teaching at Naples High. They are very different men, but both consistently amazed me with their intelligence and expertise. I am forever grateful for their loyalty and commitment. Mostly, I am grateful for their friendship.

Ernie Modugno is the best high school athletic director I have known. Ernie has stretched me and grown me and taught me numerous valuable lessons. He is also a good friend.

I met Ken Sparks at an FCA event in 1995. I do not know what he saw in me, but I do know that he invited me to his home in

Jefferson City, Tennessee, and I took him up on it. I spent three days with Coach Sparks and his wife Carol. We discussed everything from offensive, defensive, and special teams philosophies to leadership development, growing coaches, and growing healthy marriages and families. We continued that conversation for the next 22 years. Coach Ken Sparks was an incredible mentor, and he encouraged me to write this book. In March of 2017, I was able to show him a nearly completed version as I visited him bedside, a few days before he went to heaven. I wish Coach Sparks had seen the final version. I have not known a more faithful Christian man. Ken Sparks was incredibly tough and loving, and I could not ask for a better mentor or friend.

I met Norm Evans in the winter of 2002. Norm sought me out. He wanted me to get involved in Pro Athletes Outreach (PAO). Norm started every game for the 1972 Dolphins, the only professional football team to go undefeated from start to finish and win the Super Bowl. He played 10 years for the Dolphins and was All-Pro — twice. When Norm Evans is talking, people listen. I did get involved with PAO; Norm and his wife Bobbe have become dear friends to me and Sue. Norm has also mentored me for a long time. Norm's tough questions and accountability are priceless for me. Norm also encouraged me to write this book.

Thank you to April O'Leary and her crew who got me across the finish line on this book. Start to finish, the folks at O'Leary Publishing are the consummate professionals; always available, kind, capable. I need a special shoutout to Boris for his attention to detail in the final editing process.

Back Row: Danielle Thornton, Coach Paul Horne, Coach Bill Kramer, Coach Sam Dollar, Coach Mike Sawchuk, Coach Tony Ortiz, Coach Jamie Lemmond, Coach Ron Byington, Coach Ryan Krzykowski, Coach Marlin Faulkner, Joe McMahan, Sandy Dollar-ATC

Fourth Row: LJ Montinar, Thomas Martucci, Josh Greco, Jules Montinar, Chris Jones, Joe Wise, David Cawfeild, Pat Liebig, JB Glancy, Hank Gasperson, Steve McMullen

Third Row: Jeremy Bond, Torey Brenco, Ricky Martin, Josh Bostwick, Reggie Carter, Steve Alajajian, Andrew Pavel, Jesse Riggins, Cisco Clervoix, Francesco Zampogna, TBD

Second Row: David Lightner, Alex Nickell, Danny Murray, Willie Brice, Jared Cullen, Jake Pollom, Josh Larabell, Francisco Ramirez, Jason Dickerson, Mason Rose, Justin Schoefield

Front Row: Jimmy Lene, Jason Gore, Scott Turner, Reggie Gavin, Jameson Kalvin, Watley Etienne, Ryan Campins, Artiium Arbyummi, Chris Leonard, Justin Kalvin, Billy Figlesthaler, Steve Hartz

Not pictured: Duane Coleman, Joe Cosimano, Bruce Gordon, Cleannord Saintil, Bob Steiss, Steve Weigle

All my girls and their men in 2017

CPSIA information can be obtained
at www.ICGtesting.com
Printed in the USA
LVHW040739270721
693754LV00006B/16